BASIC HUMAN NEEDS

Center for Integrative Studies

College of Social Sciences
University of Houston
Houston, Texas, 77004.

Center Contributors
Guy F. Streatfeild
Laurence I. Tobias

Other Center Members on this Study

Daniel Radell
Sandra Simmons
Susan Kirkland Casella
Angelina Gonzales
Joan Kehlhof
Bernard Hobson

Special Advisor
Harlan Cleveland
Program in International Affairs
Aspen Institute for Humanistic Affairs
Princeton, New Jersey

External Consultants

William Simon
Institute for Urban Studies
University of Houston
Houston, Texas

Shoji Sadao
Fuller and Sadao, Inc.
Long Island City, New York

This report has been sponsored by
United Nations Environment Programme

BASIC HUMAN NEEDS
A Framework for Action

by
John McHale
Magda Cordell McHale
Center for Integrative Studies
University of Houston

Introduction by
Harlan Cleveland
Program in International Affairs
The Aspen Institute for Humanistic Studies

Foreword by
Mostafa Tolba
Executive Director
United Nations Environment Programme

A Report to the U.N. Environment Programme
April 1977

Transaction Books
New Brunswick, New Jersey

Library of Congress Catalog Number: 77-17100
ISBN: 0-87855-272-3 (cloth); 0-87855-670-2 (paper).
Printed in the United States of America.

Library of Congress Cataloging in Publication Data

McHale, John.
Basic human needs.

Includes bibliographical references.
1. Underdeveloped areas—Social indicators.
2. Underdeveloped areas—Economic policy
3. Underdeveloped areas—Social policy. 4. Underdeveloped areas—Environmental areas—Environmental policy. I. McHale, Magda Cordell, joint author. II. United Nations.
Environment Programme. III. Title.
HN980.M26 309.1'172'4 77-17100
ISBN 0-87855-272-3
ISBN 0-87855-670-2 pbk.

Contents

FOREWORD

Mostafa Tolba

I am indeed pleased to write a foreword to this study which has been produced with the support of the United Nations Environment Programme. Eradication of poverty in general and satisfaction of basic human needs in particular, have correctly been placed at the forefront, as an essential element of the implementation of the new international economic order, in recent international discussions on development. While not necessarily agreeing with all the views expressed in this monograph, I feel confident that the present study will help take the ongoing discussion forward and stimulate thought and action for the international cooperation for achievement of satisfaction of basic human needs for all.

There are, of course, several dimensions, among them social, economic, cultural, political and historical, to the problem of persistent mass poverty. Since its inception, the United Nations Environment Programme has maintained a deep concern over this problem, one of the most pressing facing mankind. UNEP's concern over satisfaction of basic human needs stems specifically from basic considerations.

Poverty is often accompanied by degradation of the immediate living environment. Moreover, persistence of mass poverty entails harmful, longterm consequences for the environment in general, and for the natural resource base in particular. The problem of achieving sustainable satisfaction of basic needs therefore has been becoming progressively more intractable. This is evidenced, for example, by desertification resulting from excessive use of firewood as fuel, and soil erosion resulting from intensive land-use as rapidly increasing populations try more and more desperately to live on it.

Paradoxically, however, in terms of availability of essential natural resources, technology, and knowledge, the world has the capacity to achieve sustainable satisfaction of basic human needs for mankind as a whole. And while there are more impediments in the path of realizing this objective, the most important are perhaps lack of political commitment and absence of appropriate institutional mechanisms for cooperation and planning for rapid assessment of the potentialities as well as the risks and dangers. We in UNEP further believe that the objective of basic human needs for all can and should be achieved without transgressing what we refer to as "Outer Limits", i.e. the carrying capacity of this planet earth. Consequently, when UNEP commissioned the present study with the Center of Integrative Studies, our primary preoccupation was to get an analytical and methodological contribution that would help the proper delineation of basic human needs and the accurate assessment of the impact of their non-satisfaction and the effects on the environment of the world's endeavours to satisfy them. We are still very far from achieving what we are aspiring to from such studies which definitely require new and extensive levels of global cooperative efforts. I am sure the authors do not claim that they have even approximated their ultimate goals in this endeavour. However, their contribution should stimulate further research, studies, analyses and assessments that should eventually set this problem in its proper perspective so as to elicit the most effective international cooperation and national action.

I should emphasize that we see achievement of basic human needs as the starting point in the enhancement of the human environment. Obviously, living standards higher than mere achievement of basic needs, and improvement in quality of life in general, should be pursued. This is a major consideration which should be kept in mind when formulating appropriate programmes for environmentally-sound development.

When the global aspect of the problem and its intimate connection with the environment are fully appreciated, it becomes clear that the problem of achieving sustainable satisfaction of basic human needs is only part of the problem of evolving environmentally-sound patterns of development and lifestyles everywhere—in developing and developed countries as well. Poverty cannot be viewed in isolation from such issues as wastefulness in consumption patterns, or high and rising military expenditures. Nor can it be—conceptually or operationally—separated from the general problematique of improving the quality of life of present and future generations. In most developing countries this obviously cannot be achieved without rapid industrial and agricultural development, diversification of production and trade, and influence over growth and distribution of populations. In the post-industrial societies, on the other hand, no lasting improvement in the quality of life can be effected without significant reorientations of life styles and social goals. It is in this context that the environmental issues can provide an essential and unifying perspective to the aims of a new international economic order and contribute to a lasting eradication of mass poverty in this world.

INTRODUCTION
Toward an International Poverty Line

Harlan Cleveland

Basic human needs have "arrived."

During three years of sudden conceptual change, from 1974 to 1977, national development strategies, international negotiations and global organizations have begun to be deeply affected by the simple notion that the purpose of economic development and international cooperation is to meet the human requirements of people, and especially the minimum needs of the neediest. Combined with new attitudes toward economic growth and environmental damage, the appearance of "basic human needs" at center stage begins a new act in the continuing drama of world development.

I

It is hard to remember, in 1977, that we are still less than thirty years into the era of conscious concern with "development."

Before 1949 the pre-industrial areas, mostly not yet independent nations, were "developed" by colonial policies whose central purpose was to assist the industrialization of the metropoles. The early ex-colonies (North America and the South Pacific) and later converts to the credenda of economic growth (Russia, Japan, Eastern and Southern Europe) joined the industrial revolution through investment by, importing labor and ideas from, and exploiting their interdependence with, the nations of northwest Europe which first discovered the multiplier effects of mass production and control of the terms of trade with the sources of fuel and raw materials.

Far-reaching decisions about trade, investment and money were taken in a very few places, by what now seems an astonishingly small number of men (hardly any women). Generating and fulfilling effective demand, not meeting basic human needs, was the criterion of business judgment. The "bottom line," not the "bottom billion," was the central focus of public policy. What later came to be known as the "Kuznets curve," the doctrine that in the early stages of industrial growth the gap between rich and poor was bound to get wider but the distribution of benefits would tend to improve at later stages of growth, was already a widely accepted social attitude before Professor Simon Kuznets made it an economic theorem.

Rivalries among the industrial powers, partly the result of economic infighting, led to many skirmishes, much military spending and two great wars. After the second of these the ideas about nationalism, equality and democracy popularized by the industrial nations (even as they disputed among themselves what they meant) broke open the colonial system, which was already so enervated that most new nations were created by peaceful protest and constitutional change. A generation of leaders educated for "free trade" began to adopt historically unprecedented policies, by which richer countries provided technical assistance, economic aid, and eventually trade preferences to "poor countries" just because they were poor. Most important of all, large numbers of young people were educated in the theory of economic growth and the techniques of development, including the use of modern military weapons and internal police control. New political leaders emerged to take charge of newly national destinies, build their own military establishments, and set their own development strategies.

But the definition of "development" was still economic growth, macromeasured in money equivalents. A rising gross national product and a surplus in the balance of international payments were the accepted stigmata of success, in the industrial world and the would-be industrial world alike; their leaders and experts had done their graduate work in the same economics departments. Such criteria were even frozen into United Nations resolutions setting goals for the first two Development Decades, the 1960s and the 1970s.

Very large and useful works were recorded in this post-colonial generation. Despite the siphoning off of profits to the more affluent parts of the world, despite the popularity of prestige projects (the national airlines, the premature steel mills), despite the importation of sometimes inappropriate technologies, despite the widespread neglect of indigenous food production, despite the skewing of priorities to serve export industries, despite population policies that were too little and too late, this first development generation chalked up some large accomplishments. It put millions of people to useful work, provided thousands of new and needed products, educated millions of young people, helped save millions of infants and lengthen millions of lives.

Measured by the yardsticks then in vogue, the developing countries (most of Africa, Asia and Latin America) were on the move: In the decade of the Sixties the developing countries as a group increased their combined GNP by nearly 5 percent a year, the highest sustained rate of economic growth for any group of countries in history and substantially more rapid than the growth of presently industrialized societies at comparable stages of development.[1]

II

Rising demands for fairness in international economic relations, combined with a rising capacity to insist on them, came to a head in the early 1970s. The UN General Assembly and other world agencies provided forums for the weak to band together to bargain collectively with the strong. The Arab embargo, and the solidarity of the oil-producing countries in making the quadrupled oil price stick, encouraged the Third World to become an effective political unit in world politics—at enormous economic cost to its oil-importing members. Third World demands for a new international economic order became more urgent as commodity prices continued wide and irregular swings, and the international debt of the poorest nations built up to $150 billion by the end of 1976. (The debt service for 86 developing countries has come to exceed the aid they get from the richer nations.)

At first the Third World's demands for more stable prices, preferential access to markets and more say in international financial institutions were resisted by the industrial democracies. (The industrial nations with centrally-planned economies have so far been on the sidelines in the global bargaining. But the Chinese success with a self-reliant development strategy has been an influential lesson in how selectively interdependent a determined nation can manage to be.) But in time the more developed nations saw the damage to their own interests of a bruising rich-poor confrontation, and began to look for ways to achieve by bargaining the more predictable business conditions, the more stable access to oil and raw materials, and the more effective international institutions which their own fragile interdependencies made imperative.

New rules of the international economic game were thus becoming a common interest of the world's "North" and "South"—new rules, a new propensity to follow them, new international institutions to arrange and monitor the planetary bargaining, and new arrangements to govern resources, such as the deep seabed, which have not yet been claimed by any nation.

Active confrontation had been a staple of international politics for a decade: the demands were put forward in the annual General Assembly debates, in a series of UNCTAD meetings (Geneva 1964, New Delhi 1968, Santiago de Chile 1972, Nairobi in 1976), in the Cocoyoc Declaration, in the UN resolution on the Rights and Duties of States, in the statement from the Non-Aligned summit in Colombo and the Manila Declaration by the "Group of 77" early in 1976. The crunch had come at the 6th Special Session of the UN General Assembly in May, 1974; there a resolution on The New International Economic Order was adopted by a "consensus" shadowed by the subsequent objections of a number of industrial countries to the redistributive concepts it contains.[2]

The beginning of accommodation came the next year, when a long speech by U.S. Secretary of State, Henry Kissinger, was read to the 7th Special Session of the UN General Assembly.[3] The United States said, in effect, that it was willing to come into negotiating range; most of the other industrial countries had already decided they would have to do so.

Soon thereafter a sluggish process of bargaining—on oil, commodity stabilization, access to industrial markets, and development aid—commenced among a representative group of 27 nations, meeting in Paris under Venezuelan and Canadian cochairmen. But it turned out that the nations of neither side had really done their homework or readied themselves to bargain about vital interests and crucial relationships. The global recession combined with inflation, "Northern" resentment of OPEC, and political uncertainties in several of the industrial democracies held them back from serious dialogue. In the developing "South," the concentration on effective rhetorical efforts had left little time and effort for the formulation of specific proposals for new rules and institutions that might help the "poor" nations while not being disadvantageous to "rich" nations preoccupied with unemployment, precarious exchange rates and government institutions coping uncertainly with problems for which Keynesian economics and parliamentary politics had not prepared them.

By the Spring of 1977, the old economic order was struggling for breath, and a new order—the post-post-colonial order—was still struggling to be born.

III

Both the confrontation and the dialogue have been wrestling ineffectually with the issues of poverty and fairness, because until very recently two critical factors in world development were not even being seriously discussed among governments. They are the emerging ethic of ecology, and the meeting of basic human needs. Both have a potential for cutting through the fog of debate about national growth rates expressed in money measures, and getting on to an analytical framework that deals in requirements and supplies of things for people.

The need for such a framework is evident when you examine and compare—as John and Magda McHale have recently done in another connection[4] —the national plans of many nations. It is evident that most development planners go about their difficult task with only the vaguest idea of the interaction among climatic change, food production, water availabilities, population growth, the price of oil, alternative fuel sources, substitutability of raw materials, marine resources, investment policies of transnational enterprise, shifting fashions in economic theory, trade restrictions, monetary polities, mutations in technology (including new weapons systems), and the fact that some 50 nations change their political leadership each year.

Some of these factors, such as the weather, are natural forces of which even the best-informed experts still have only a limited understanding. Others are the product of complex decisions pluralistically arrived at by multiple decision-makers in faraway places, decisions expressed in language or formulas which only specialized priesthoods can even decipher.

The rate of growth of the world money supply, for example, is an essential datum in any national planner's guess about the rate of inflation in international commerce and derivatively in the internal economy as well. No international agency publishes an authoritative projection of future monetary growth. A hundred different guesses are available in national economic forecasts and international bank newsletters, which the planner is unlikely to have either the time or the training to take into account in his daily work.

Whether fashioned by Nature or by people, the factors that make development strategies "successful" (however defined) are essentially out of the control, even beyond the ken, of the flesh-and-blood human beings trying to manage the sovereign independence of 160 nation-states in an interdependent world. And this is just as true in the industrialized world, "market" or "centrally planned," as it is in the Third World. Recent imbroglios about the incidence of drought, the purchase of wheat, the future of sugar, the investment of petrodollars, "limits to growth," and estimates of world population are only the most obvious examples of cases where some of the best experts have been dramatically mistaken, even in short-term forecasting. Whether it is or not a fruitful expression to use in foreign-policy debates, the Chinese phrase "great disorder under heaven" applies all too well to the state of human knowledge about needs and resources.

For analysts and planners of development strategies, the newest factor and the hardest to decode is the effect of human actions on the environment, and *vice versa*. For the past decade it has been difficult to write about this subject without being shrill, or to read about it without getting breathless. But now the insights of the biological sciences have provided new clues to the interrelatedness of organisms and popularized the idea of ecology, the study of the way varieties of life relate to each other and to the environmental "support systems" which make life possible. New information systems, made possible by orbiting satellites and fast computers, also make it possible to relate distant complexities to each other. We are beginning in consequence to perceive an interlocking system of limits—not "limits to growth" but limits to thoughtlessness, unfairness and conflict.[5]

Thus an emerging ethic of ecology suggests socially-determined limits (1) to the damage people should do their physical environment (air and water pollution, stripping of the land, thinning of the ozone shield); (2) to the dangers inherent in people-managed processes (nuclear power programs, chemical reactions, traffic accidents, weather modification, contraception and sterilization, genetic engineering); (3) to the rate at which people use up non-renewable resources (fossil fuels, hard minerals); and (4) to practices that affect the renewability of renewable resources (soil erosion, destruction of wildlife, overcropping of farmland, overcutting of forests, overfishing of lakes and oceans).

An ethic is not a policy, much less a system of law and organization. But it is already something for the world community to have decided, in the words of the Declaration of the 1972 Stockholm conference, that:

> A point has been reached in history when we must shape our actions throughout the world with a more prudent care for their environmental consequences. . . . To defend and improve the human environment for present and future generations has become an imperative goal for mankind . . .
>
> To achieve this environmental goal will demand the acceptance of responsibility by citizens and communities and by enterprises and institutions at every level, all sharing equitably in common efforts.[6]

IV

The most serious flaw in the doctrines of the first two Development Decades was the neglect of the requirements side of the equation. That impressive 5% a year growth in GNP during the 1960s was partly soaked up in population increase of 2.5% for the developing countries as a group—the consequence of "modern death rates combined with medieval birth rates."[7] The other half seems to have gone mostly to the more affluent "middle class" countries in the group, and to the upper and middle-income classes inside the poorest countries.

Beginning in 1974, a number of nongovernmental organizations and several international agencies began to question sharply the whole idea of basing development strategy on the achievement of gross increases in production, and ask with growing asperity hard questions about who was getting the benefits. One of the nongovernmental efforts was a 1974-75 collaboration between the Aspen Institute for Humanistic Studies and the Center for Integrative Studies which continues in the present Report.

"A new moral imperative begins to emerge in world politics," said the consensus report from an international working group that assembled at Aspen, Colorado, in the summer of 1975 to chart a "planetary bargain." "If it is physically and technically possible to meet the basic human needs of the world population within a foreseeable period of time, then it is a moral outrage that national governments and the international community are not better mobilized to do just that—even if development strategies and priorities have to be altered, even if the affluent have to change some of their ways, even if the international system has to be reformed . . . . [It] is high time that the world community come together to set agreed floors under individual human needs—rather than comparing national averages which obscure the distribution of benefits from development . . . . [The] time has come to relate international economic arrangements to the meeting of basic human needs.[8]

The judgment that it *is* possible to "meet basic human requirements in terms of resource adequacy and without transgressing the carrying capacity of the planet'' was based on a first effort by John and Magda McHale to develop a quantitative and analytical framework for thinking about the planetary bargain.[9] Their present Report is a direct successor to that pioneering work.

Other analytical pioneers had been trying to define and quantify inequities in development; Hollis Chenery, Irma Adelman and other scholars[10] drew a picture of ''a pattern of wealth distribution [in developing countries] which made the developed countries look positively egalitarian.''[11] A World Bank issue paper written in March 1977 summarizes what has quite suddenly become a widely held opinion:

> .... [E]conomic growth appears to have done very little for the poorer of the Third World's rapidly growing populations. For what they are worth, the data and impressionistic evidence suggest that the poor in some countries, mostly smaller ones, are better off: Taiwan, Singapore, Hong Kong, Sri Lanka and the Caribbean are examples. In Brazil, their real income per head is estimated to have grown by less than 1% in the sixties, while that of the richer half by over 30%. In almost all large, poor countries of Asia (India, Pakistan, Bangladesh, Indonesia and the Philippines), there has probably been stagnation or decline in the living standards of the poorest 20% to 45%. In absolute numbers, there are many more poor, though the proportion of the poor in the total population may have declined.
>
> Unemployment and underemployment were only a small part of the problem. The trouble was not so much an absence of work, as unremunerative work .... It was not growth as such, but the structure of ownership and power, and the policies pursued by governments, which prevented the poor from benefiting from growth .... Critical social services have been neglected on the ground that they are of undefinable value to GNP.[12]

The spreading disgruntlement with this state of affairs, and the urgency of making the connection between development strategy and basic human needs, were reflected in the Third World-oriented Dag Hammarskjold report advocating ''another development . . . geared to the satisfaction of needs.''[13] They are a key element in the mathematical models of development strategies worked out by the Bariloche Foundation in Argentina.[14] They have been continuing emphases in the vigorous and imaginative writings of James Grant and his colleagues in the Overseas Development Council of Washington.[15] They are major themes of the RIO (''Reshaping the International Order'') Report coordinated by the Dutch Nobel Laureate Jan Tinbergen for the Club of Rome, which speaks of ''the need for new development strategies—national and international—defined and designed, not merely to meet the criterion of private or state profitability, but rather to give priority to the expression and satisfaction of fundamental human values. Society as a whole must accept the responsibility for guaranteeing a minimum level of welfare for all its citizens and aim at equality in human relations.... It follows that the problem of development must be redefined as a selective attack on the worst forms of poverty.''[16]

Interacting with the nongovernmental pressure, several influential international organizations have been talking—and to the extent that their more orthodox mandates permit, acting—along parallel lines. The earliest drumbeaters for a ''basic needs'' approach were Maurice Strong and his successor as Executive Director of the United Nations Environment Programme, Mostafa Tolba; President Robert McNamara of the World Bank; and Francis Blanchard, Director General of the International Labour Organization. By now every element of the U.N. system is engaged in, or reaching for, a piece of the ''basic needs'' action.[17]

Robert McNamara bluntly told his Board of Governors in Manila last October that ''Growth in the gross national product, as essential as it is, cannot benefit the poor unless it reaches the poor. It does not reach most of them now by any meaningful measure.''[18] A World Bank staff paper six months later puts it just as strongly:

> ... the economic emphasis has tended to lose sight of the ultimate purpose of the policies.... The demand now is to put man and his needs at the center of development. If this is done, ''basic needs'' becomes an illuminating organizing concept, which throws light on a whole range of other issues.[19]

The International Labour Organization approved at its 1976 World Employment Conference a proposal ''that development planning should include, as an explicit goal, the satisfaction of an absolute level of basic needs.'' ''This proposal goes somewhat further,'' I.L.O.'s Director General explained to the Conference, ''than the intention, already expressed by many governments, to concentrate development measures more directly on the poorest groups of the population. The definition of a set of basic needs, together constituting a minimum standard of living, would at one and the same time assist in the identification of those groups and provide concrete targets against which to measure progress.''[20] The United States voted against the ''basic needs'' theme in the Conference action, but a new U.S. approach was foreshadowed in President Carter's address at the United Nations: '' ... the U.S. will be advancing proposals aimed at meeting the basic human needs of the developing world and helping them to increase their productive capacity.''[21]

V

It was a year ago, in the Spring of 1976, that Mostafa Tolba, Executive Director of the United Nations Environment Programme, commissioned the Center for Integrative Studies (which moved that year from the State University of New

York to the University of Houston), with the assistance of the Aspen Institute, to:

(a) Develop a detailed quanititative, and qualitative, framework of human requirements—including the operational definition of international standards for meeting these requirements.

(b) Assess the material supply levels and cooperative arrangements necessary for the attainment of these standards, at world and local levels.

(c) Explore strategies for the development of international standards as the bases for international planning and developmental assistance.[22]

The rapid emergence of "basic human needs" as a major theme in international politics had created a major analytical gap, and a search for concepts, categories, and quantitative measures of need. But because the center of attention in development economics had been so thoroughly on the supply/production side of the equation, there simply did not exist a ready-made analytical framework for defining, targeting, and measuring human needs.

Even where standard "social indicators" have been widely used, the indicators often indicate what society is trying to do about poverty, rather than defining the needs of the poor. Most of the measuring sticks commonly used in the field of health, for example, measure not the people's health but the capacity of a society to handle illness—that is, the health of the health delivery system. Similarly in education, the measures of educational achievement are often expressed as the number of years the person has spent in a formal course of study, rather than what he may have learned in school or indeed from life experience.

There nevertheless exists, in every industrial country and some pre-industrial societies, a practical "poverty line"—that is, a minimum value of goods and services to which every citizen is entitled. In most societies the quantitative definition of this poverty line would be very complicated; it would have to add together such individual entitlements as food stamps, school lunches, free or low cost health care, compulsory education, a right to work (or to draw unemployment benefits), compensation for accidents, and retirement schemes, and such collective entitlements as mass transit, air and water quality standards, parks and recreation areas, and more or less limited rights to travel, to be informed, to assemble, to speak and to participate in community decisions.

When one sets out to analyze the minimum human needs of a billion people, most of them living in societies which have not been able to afford to legislate such entitlements, the guidance available from earlier writings is rather thin, and mostly quite recent. Some notion of basic human needs has a long history as a moral idea.[23] But it did not come to life as social policy until the excesses of the industrial revolution and the misery justified by "Social Darwinism" produced powerful social reform movements in the 19th Century. Even then, the relief of poverty was viewed more as charity than as entitlement. Only later in the century did the industrializing nations move from charity to rights, the rights being reinforced by child labor laws, minimum wages and maximum hours of work, compulsory education and public health, housing codes, and Social Security, pensions, and disability allowances. These developments did not come easily; they had to be extracted from established authority, step by painful step, through the extension of political franchise and participation, movements of social protests, and trade unionism. By and large, it seems, people do not get what they are entitled to unless they organize to insist on it.

Some of the earliest analytical work on basic needs was done in England by Booth[24] and Rowntree[25] before the end of the 19th Century and was later carried further by Rowntree in a series of studies which estimated the "basket cost" of commodities for minimal maintenance of households of different sizes, ages, and sex composition. Those with insufficient income to meet the basket cost were judged to be below the poverty level. Rowntree calculated that 28% of Britain's 1899 population was below this level; his later survey in 1938 found 18% still below his standard; but by 1950, the poverty ratio had fallen to 2%. With today's much greater technological capacities, the attack on world poverty could achieve a similar result in considerably less than fifty years.

After World War II, much more comprehensive social welfare programs were achieved in the more industrialized countries. In this respect the differences among governments calling themselves communist, socialist, capitalist, social democratic, Christian democratic or democratic republican have been a matter of degree, not doctrine; all have moved toward welfare-conscious governance.

By 1948 the meeting of basic needs had been declared a global entitlement in the United Nations' Universal Declaration of Human Rights, in the negotiation of which Mrs. Eleanor Roosevelt was a prime mover:

> *Article 22*: Everyone, as a member of society, has the right to social security and is entitled to realization, through national effort and international cooperation and in accordance with the organization and resources of each state, of the economic, social and cultural rights indispensable for his dignity and the free development of his personality.
>
> *Article 25*: 1. Everyone has the right to a standard of living adequate for the health and wellbeing of himself and of his family, including food, clothing, housing and medical care and necessary social services, and the right to security in the event of unemployment, sickness, disability, widowhood, old age or other lack of livelihood in circumstances beyond his control.
>
> *Article 26*: 1. Everyone has the right to education. Education shall be free, at least in the elementary and fundamental stages. Elementary education shall be compulsory. Technical and professional education

shall be made generally available and higher education shall be equally accessible to all on the basis of merit.[26]

In 1954 a comprehensive report on ''International Definition and Measurement of Standards and Levels of Living'' was prepared by the United Nations and its Specialized Agencies. This report gives a list which

> ''. . . could be considered as an acceptable international catalogue of the components of the level of living, although the precise connotations of each would to some extent be determined by national attitudes and standards resulting from peculiarities of environmental conditions, cultures, values and economic, political and social organization:
>
> 1. Health, including demographic conditions
> 2. Food and Nutrition
> 3. Education, including literacy
> 4. Conditions of work
> 5. Employment situation
> 6. Aggregate consumption and savings
> 7. Transportation
> 8. Housing, including, household facilities
> 9. Clothing
> 10. Recreation and entertainment
> 11. Social Security
> 12. Human freedoms[27]

Noting the ''immense difference in range and quality of the statistical material now available'', this report does not go beyond discussing definition and measurement. Since 1954, the statistical situation has greatly improved, due in part to some excellent analytical work in the United Nations itself. It is, however, still far from satisfactory in terms of our ability to estimate the material quantities required to sustain specific living standards in different countries.

This groping for relevant definitions, measurements and standards has been going on continuously for more than two decades, for specific areas of need, in many national institutions both governmental and nongovernmental, and in the U.N. Secretariat, WHO, ILO, FAO, UNESCO, UNEP and the World Bank.

An Indian Labor Conference laid down norms in 1957 for the guidance of minimum wage fixing:

> ''1. In calculating the minimum wage, the standard working-class family should be taken to comprise three consumption units for one earner, the earnings of women, children and adolescents being disregarded.
>
> 2. Minimum food requirements should be calculated on the net intake of calories . . . for an average Indian adult of moderate activity.
>
> 3. Clothing requirements should be estimated on the basis of consumption per head of 18 yards per annum which would give for the average worker's family a total of 72 yards.

> 4. In respect of housing, the rent corresponding to the minimum area provided for under the Government's Industrial Housing Scheme should be taken into consideration in fixing the minimum wage.
>
> 5. Fuel, lighting and other miscellaneous items should constitute 20 percent of the total minimum wage."[28]

The International Labor Conference adopted in 1964 a resolution concerning minimum living standards and their adjustment to economic growth and calling for a program of research:

> " . . . to discuss the concept and measurement of minimum human needs; to give examples of estimates that have been made in different countries of minimum requirements for food, clothing, housing and other needs; and to discuss the validity of such methods and the purposes served by the results of such studies."[29]

What was emerging, then, was a doctrine of universal entitlement. Just as, inside some countries in the 19th Century, a national consensus coalesced around the idea that all classes have an equal claim to some minimum requirement for a decent life, so, in this century, an international consensus has been coalescing around the idea that people have a right to *some* minimum standard of needs simply because they are people.

The political thrust that produced formal U.N. action on the New International Economic Order was concerned essentially with fairness among nations, not within nations. But the emphasis placed by nongovernmental organizations on the distribution of benefits inside developing countries has begun to affect the thinking of governments during the past three years. As early as October 1974, a symposium sponsored by two intergovernmental bodies but attended by a number of people without official responsibilities, included in its "Cocoyoc Declaration" a paragraph which treated basic needs as a primary object of the New International Economic Order that had been adopted by the General Assembly of the United Nations just a few weeks before.

> "Our first concern is to redefine the whole purpose of development. This should not be to develop things but to develop man. Human beings have basic needs: food, shelter, clothing, health, education. Any process of growth that does not lead to their fulfillment—or even worse disrupts them—is a travesty of the idea of development."[30]

The Aspen working group, however, made a distinction, crucial for the coming politics of human needs, between a "first floor" and a "second floor":

> The first floor is minimum human needs, the food, health and education to which each person should be entitled by virtue of being born into the

> world we call civilized. Making this entitlement a reality for every one, in a realistically time-phased plan, should be regarded as a joint responsibility of each nation concerned and of the community of nations.
>
> The second floor would be such *other basic needs* as are defined (and redefined over time) by each nation-state for its own people, within the context of the interdependence of all societies. The definition of such basic needs should be a key element in development planning, in investment policy, in social welfare policy; trying to meet them is the purpose of political and economic self-reliance and environmental self-restraint, the criterion of fairness and the basis for international cooperation. But here the concept of ''joint responsibility'' would not apply: the meeting of ''second floor'' needs is essentially the responsibility of each nation-state, through its choice of development strategies and the negotiation of international assistance on its own initiative.[31]

The Aspen group went on to suggest that the setting of standards for minimum (''first floor'') needs would have to be initially approached from the bottom up in each country and region—simply because needs vary so much according to climate, geography, access to resources, cultural and social traditions, stages of life, and time. As an illustration, the working group suggested that a nation's goal might be expressed this way:

> ''By the Year (1985) (1992) (2000) we intend to meet the following standards through national action and international cooperation:
>
> *Food*. At least 2,200 calories for every adult, with appropriate variations for hard physical workers and for children. Dietary standards for protein and fat will also be specified.
>
> *Life*. Not more than 30 infant deaths per 1,000 live births, and a range of 55-65 for life expectancy at birth for those born in (1985) (1992) (2000).
>
> *Education*. 98% literacy for those born after (1970) (1975) (1980).''[32]

VI

Against this background the work of John and Magda McHale stands out as a bold attempt to invent a method of analysis that could make operational the new moral imperative of meeting basic human needs.

It was neither feasible nor desirable for them to deliver to a U.N. agency a calculation of basic needs for any developing country, or even for all developing countries put together. What is needed is for the needy to say: it is a function of choices about national development strategies, about the distribution of benefits within nations, about the desires of communities and families and individuals. What is needed will vary from person to person, from time to time, from culture to culture, from farm to farm, from city to city, from country to country.

Faced with this complexity, in global perspective, the McHales have assembled a mass of raw material for use by those who will propose standards, set targets, and make decisions about the meeting of basic human needs: the national planners and community leaders within each developing nation. This Report is intended as a first stage—a "feasibility study," Dr. Tolba called it—in a process that would soon involve national and regional teams of researchers and planners, and wide consultation with real-life people in needy communities.

The suggested framework departs in six important ways from the orthodox methods of analyzing, expressing, and using data about requirements and resources to meet them.

1. The McHale Report deals, so far as possible, in things rather than in money. Treating needs in this fashion makes it possible to cast physical needs up against availabilities of resources, also expressed in physical measures, in a "balance of things" rather than a fiscal budget or a balance of payments.

2. The Report tackles directly the question, "Whose needs?"

Some needs are individual; but individual needs vary enormously in kind and in quantity, as the infant moves through childhood and adolescence to a growing maturity and eventual old age. Needs analysis therefore reqires special attention to the *life cycle*.

Some needs can only be sensibly considered as pertaining to a cluster of individuals. Needs analysis therefore requires a category this Report calls the *unit household*.

Some needs can be attached only to a much larger unit of society. In the foreseeable future the sovereign nation-state will probably still be the most important actor in the world's political economy. An outside analyst cannot presume to specify the needs of particular nations without touching sensitivities that would inhibit the rational discussion of how basic needs might practically be met. This is why the Report uses for much of its analysis composite nations fashioned from the indices of real countries at similiar stages of economic and social development—the *reference countries*.

3. The Report leaves room for answering the question, "*Where* do the needs have to be met?" Not only needs, but also the resources to meet them, vary greatly from area to area. In a future world food *system* (thus far we only have a world food *problem*) it will be important to correlate food needs so far as possible with nearby means of satisfying them. Thinking of food requirements not in world aggregates but in terms of food zones (pages68-75) helps make them appear manageable, and in time may help manage the complex process of making sure they can be met.

4. The Report related development to the environment, stepping past the fruitless debate about which should take precedence. The intriguing matrix on pages 118-119, showing the interactions between environmental sectors and basic human activities, is only the gateway to a field of analysis that has been

retarded by enthusiasts for growth and enthusiasts for conservation, too busy debating with each other to search together for ways to enhance the natural environment through prudent growth.

5. The Report sees new technologies moving in directions that may help limit the depletion of key resources and reduce the burden on the biosphere of meeting human needs. (Pages 76 to 79 contain an extraordinarily concentrated short course about hopeful signs on the technological horizon.) Treating information as a resource, communication as a global system, miniaturization and "ephemeralisation" as ways to diminish the material and energy inputs per function, and the biological sciences as the source of a "regenerative" potential, the McHales open up possibilities for the next few decades that are not dreamt of in the gloomier contemporary philosophies of depletion, limits, and despondency about the capacity of human beings to cope.

6. The Report points toward a practical, pluralistic, and politically feasible way of analyzing human needs worldwide. In a separate but parallel study, John and Magda McHale have developed in considerable detail the characterisitics of a composite developing nation—complete with geographical location, ethnic groups in its population, resources and traditional trading patterns, social indices and financial problems. This nonexistent but curiously realistic "country," which they call "the Exeland construct," will provide analysts in real countries with a set of analytical approaches and a demonstration of their utility in devising a "basic needs" strategy for an independent nation in an interdependent world.

This new McHale report, in an earlier draft, was subjected to candid and rigorous review by an international group of experts assembled by UNEP for a six-day workshop held in Barbados April 1 to 6, 1977. The present Report has been adjusted at some points to reflect the reactions of these experts, whose names and affiliations will be found in Appendix III.

VII

The analysis of basic human needs raises tantalizing questions about the purposes for which, and the manner in which, the international community interests itself in the distribution of wealth and benefits inside sovereign nation-states. While these questions go beyond the initial purpose of this Report, they will be germane to any consideration of international mechanisms to help meet the minimum needs of the world's neediest.

Part of what is "new" about the New International Economic Order is evidently to be this focus on human needs—which is to say, on the requirements side of the development equation. Such a focus is becoming politically necessary as education and expectations spreads the effective demand for fairness inside the developing nations. It is also becoming politically necessary as people in the industrial countries say more openly that, as candidate Jimmy Carter put it in one of his campaign speeches last year, "The time has come to stop taxing poor people in rich countries for the benefit of rich people in poor countries.''[33]

Even if the newly-recognized moral imperative makes the meeting of minimum (''first floor'') human needs a first charge on world resources and on the energies of international institutions, it is still true that the task of defining people's needs and formulating a strategy to meet them is first of all the responsibility of each nation. But if a nation needs international cooperation to carry out such a strategy—that is, if it is going to make an effective claim on world resources and international institutions—the international community is going to want to know what needs are defined as minimum, and for what internal strategy to meet them the external cooperation is required. A new kind of bargain is implicit in the New International Economic Order: the reform of the international order depends on internal reform in the cooperating nations. And the same applies the other way around.

Nor is it only in the developing nations that internal reforms are part of the bargain. If peoples and leaders in the industrial countries have begun to interest themselves in the distribution of wealth in less developed countries, peoples and leaders in the Third World have noticed that their plight is partly the consequence of waste and overconsumption in the richer nations. They are likely to insist that an internationally sponsored limit to poverty is matched by a limit to the share which the most affluent person takes from a pool of resources that is flexible but finite.[34]

These observations suggest the following chain of reasoning, to relate the meeting of minimum (''first floor'') needs to international economic arrangements:

1. The first reason for exploiting and distributing world resources is to meet the minimum human needs of individual children, women, and men.

2. For any people, at any time and place, the standard of minimum need is defined in the first instance by the community and nation-state in which they reside.

3. Strategies developed by each nation-state to make possible the meeting of its people's minimum human needs are constrained by its own resource potentials and by impacts on the local and global environment.

4. If for any nation the meeting of minimum human needs, so defined and constrained, requires special arrangements for international economic cooperation and international resource transfers, the international community is going to want to scrutinize that nation's definition of the needs it is trying to meet, the measures being taken locally to meet them, and the impact of those measures on the environment.

5. The international community has a primary obligation to mobilize the means of satisfying minimum human needs within nations whose programs for tackling absolute poverty have been internationally reviewed and agreed.

6. Nation-states in which minimum human needs are already met have an

additional obligation to avoid policies which deprive other peoples, or future generations, of the opportunity to fulfill their own minimum needs.

There is no reason why such an international review process needs to be all done in global institutions; indeed, there is every reason to decentralize the process. Groups of countries banding together for "collective self-reliance" may be able to develop common or at least compatible minimum-needs strategies and thus strengthen their claim on the resources of the rest of the world. Such groups may be organized by geographical proximity, by commonality of development strategy, or by ethnic or political congeniality.

Sooner or later the planetary negotiating about human requirements, outer bounds and supply levels will require more effective extranational institutions which—acting for the international community as a whole or for "communities of the concerned"—can maintain useful information in a comparative data bank, conduct objective analyses of needs and the resources to meet them, and arrange for bargaining among the cooperating nations. One condition precedent for positive-sum international bargains about minimum human needs is quite suddenly being fulfilled: a wide consensus that in the international economic order a much higher priority must now be given to meeting minimum human needs. But it remains to develop a practical international system for analyzing them, reviewing them, and fulfilling them.

Absolute poverty is due not to shortfalls of material or technological resources but to shortcomings of social imagination and political management. Minimum human needs can in fact be met worldwide, by a generation of relevant and cooperative effort. This Report is presented as a first step on a rough road to a reachable goal.

NOTES

1. *The Planetary Bargain: Proposals for a New International Economic Order to Meet Human Needs*, a consensus statement by an Aspen Institute International workshop (Princeton, N.J.: Aspen Institute for Humanistic Studies, Program in International Affairs, 1975), p. 16.

2. "Declaration on the Establishment of a New International Economic Order," General Assembly Resolution 3201 (S-VI), May 1, 1974.

3. Henry Kissinger, "Global Consensus and Economic Development," speech delivered by Daniel P. Moynihan, U.S. Representative to the U.N., at the Seventh Special Session of the U.N. General Assembly.

4. John McHale and Magda Cordell McHale, "Long Range National Planning: A Proposal for Comparative Analysis," in *United Nations and the Future*, proceedings of a UNITAR conference on The Future, Moscow, June 10-14, 1974.

5. A fuller discussion of this subject will be found in Harlan Cleveland *The Third Try at World Order* (Palo Alto: Aspen Institute for Humanistic Studies, 1977), Chapter 5, pp. 25-31.

6. "Declaration of the United Nations Conference on the Human Environment,"

Report of the United Nations Conference on Human Environment (United Nations: New York, 1973), p. 3.

7. John Cole, *The Poor of the Earth* (London: The MacMillan Press, 1976), p. 11.

8. *The Planetary Bargain, op. cit.*, p. 16, 17.

9. John McHale and Magda Cordell McHale, *Human Requirements, Supply Levels and Outer Bounds: A Framework for Thinking about the Planetary Bargain* (Princeton, N.J.: Aspen Institute for Humanistic Studies, Program in International Affairs, 1975).

10. Among the most useful of these studies are Irma Adelman and Cynthia Taft Morris, *Economic Growth and Social Equity in Developing Countries* (Stanford: Stanford University Press, 1973); Hollis Chenery, *et al, Redistribution with Growth* (London: Oxford University Press, 1974); and Irma Adelman, "Growth, Income Distribution and Equity-Oriented Development Strategies," *World Development*, February-March 1975, pp. 67-76. But even these pioneering analyses still used mostly money measures to describe the distribution of wealth.

11. Cole, *op. cit.*, p. 10.

12. "Basic Needs: An Issues Paper" (Policy Planning and Program Review Department, World Bank, March 21, 1977).

13. "What Now: Another Development," The 1975 Dag Hammarskjold Report on Development and International Cooperation (Uppsala, Sweden, *Development Dialogue*, 1975, No. 1/2).

14. Amilcar Herrera, *et al, Catastrophe or New Society? A Latin American World Model* (Ottawa: International Development Research Centre, 1976).

15. Among these are *The U.S. and World Development: Agenda for Action*, a report published annually since 1974: the Development Paper Series which includes Mahbub ul Haq's "The Third World and the International Economic Order," (1976); James Grant's "Growth from Below: A People-Oriented Development Strategy," (1973); and a number of significant studies such as *Beyond Dependency: The Developing World Speaks Out*, edited by Guy F. Erb and Valeriana Kallab, (1976).

16. Jan Tinbergen, *et al, Reshaping the International Order*, A report to the Club of Rome (New York: E.P. Dutton and Co., Inc., 1976), p. 63.

17. "Development Objectives and Programmes of the United Nations System to Attain Them (with particular reference to eradication of poverty and satisfaction of basic needs)," Informal Working Paper of the U.N. Administrative Committee on Coordination, March 10, 1977.

18. Robert S. McNamara, *Address to the Board of Governors of the World Bank Group*, Manila, The Philippines (Washington: The World Bank, October 4, 1976), p. 5.

19. "Basic Needs: An Issues Paper," *op. cit.*

20. *Employment, Growth and Basic Needs: A One-World Problem*, Report of the Director General of the International Labour Office to the Tripartite World Conference on Employment, Income Distribution and Social Progress and the International Division of Labour (Geneva: ILO, 1976), p. 31.

21. President Jimmy Carter, *Address at the United Nations*, March 17, 1977.

22. John McHale, Magda Cordell McHale and Harlan Cleveland, "Human Requirements, Supply Levels and Outer Bounds: Phase Two," a Joint Proposal to the United Nations Environment Programme, March, 1976.

23. Elaine H. Pagels, "Policy on Basic Human Needs: An Inquiry into the Ethical

Assumptions,'' a paper prepared for the 1976 Aspen Workshop on The Politics of Human Needs (unpublished).

24. Booth, Charles *Life and Labour of the People*, 17. Vol. set, 1891-1903.

25. Rowntree, B. Seebohm, *Poverty-A Study of Town Life*, (London: 1902); *Human Needs of Labour*, (London: Nelson, 1917); *Poverty and Progress*, (London: Longmans Green, 1941).

26. ''Universal Declaration of Human Rights,'' *Yearbook of the United Nations 1948-49* (United Nations: Lake Success, New York, 1950), pp. 535-537.

27. *Report on International Definition and Measurements of Standards and Levels of Living*. (New York: United Nations, 1954).

28. *Indian Labour Conference*, 15th Session, New Delhi, 1957.

29. Franklin, W.N., ''The Concept and Measurement of Minimum Living Standards,'' *International Labor Review*, Vol. 95, January-June, 1967.

30. ''Patterns and Resource Use, Environment and Development Strategies,'' UNEP/UNCTAD Symposium, Cocoyoc, Mexico, October, 1974.

31. *The Planetary Bargain, op. cit.*, pp. 17-18.

32. *The Planetary Bargain, op. cit.*, p. 19.

33. Address by Governor Jimmy Carter to the Chicago Council on Foreign Relations, March 15, 1976.

34. *The Third Try at World Order, op. cit., p. 28.*

BASIC HUMAN NEEDS: A FRAMEWORK FOR ACTION

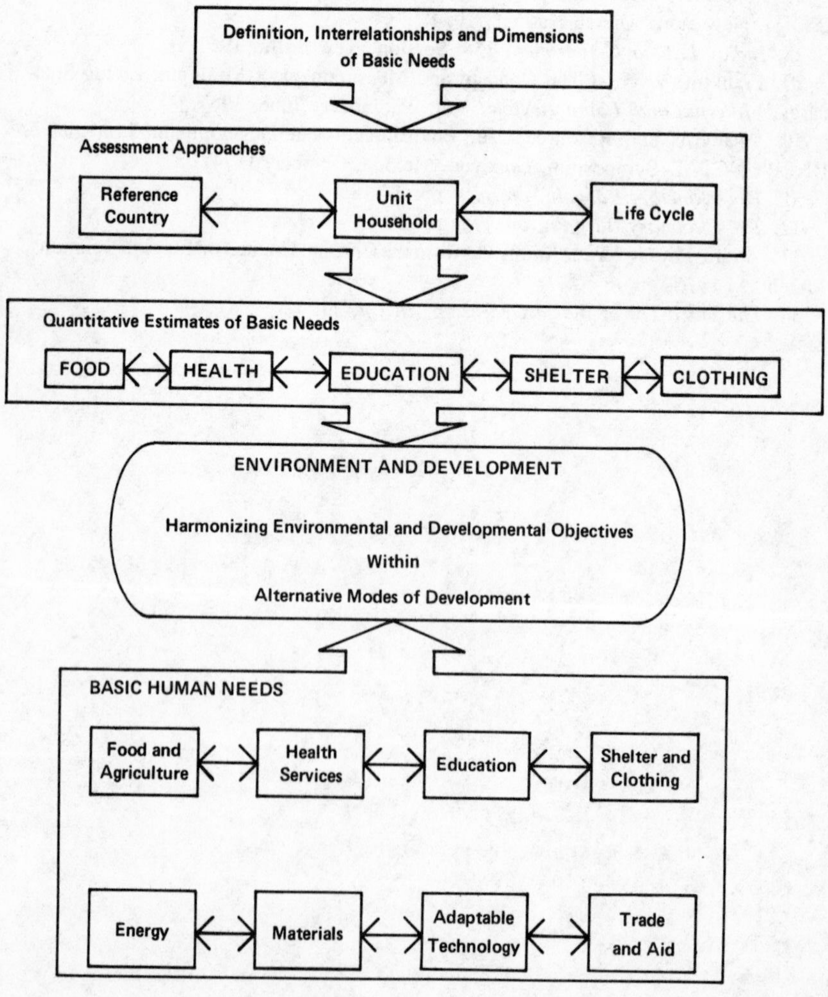

Fig. I

PREFACE

The purpose of this report is to present some quantitative assessments of basic human needs in the areas of food, health, education, shelter and clothing,[1] and to consider how these might be met in ways that are harmonious with sustainable environmental and developmental objectives.

Though normative in character, advocacy of specific solutions is avoided. We recognize that the essential diversity of peoples, countries and regimes naturally precludes any singular and linear approach to the satisfaction of needs. We have sought therefore to suggest varied approaches and to demonstrate, by example, the kinds of information required for more adequate policies, and to present these in a manner which may allow social, environmental and developmental concerns to be viewed in more holistic terms as a guide for appropriate action.

The report itself is not a blueprint for satisfying needs but seeks rather to provide a usable framework of ideas and data for further thinking and action. It is not an end in itself but one step in a much longer time process.

The central questions addressed are:

1. How may we define basic human needs and their interrelationships in the circle of poverty?[2]
2. Who are the neediest in world terms?
3. What are the estimated deficiences in vital need areas?
4. How might needs be met in terms of sound environmental management and appropriate developmental directions?

These questions are pursued by means of parallel approaches which range from analysis of indicators for "reference countries", through examination of unit household and life cycle dimensions, to more specific quantification of deficits and targets in the basic need areas.[3] Problems of self-reliance or dependence in coping with needs are reviewed through assessments of resource availability and technological and institutional constraints within the context of environmental and developmental criteria.

From this framework, the wider concerns of the basic needs project may be expressed as follows:

a) to accomplish this phase of the exploratory work in ways which anticipate problems and suggest solutions so that information, approaches and ideas may be made available for wider policy discussion.

b) to take due cognizance of present constraints on the implementation of basic needs programs and to go beyond these in terms of normative considerations.

c) to suggest ways in which the further development of such programs may be decentralised and explored by the poorer nations and peoples themselves, e.g. through a cooperative network of institutions and individuals working within a common framework of approaches and comparable data, and by demonstration programs in one or more countries.

The assessment of basic needs and their satisfaction is a moving target—in terms of numbers, the variability of needs in different cultures and regions and in the time scale of development.

For present purposes we have chosen to define our priority target largely in terms of those peoples who are below some agreed standard of adequacy in terms of what is needed for basic survival i. e. for those suffering from absolute *deficiency*, or first floor, needs. The target group is therefore those who are below or just on the poverty line, as distinct from those who may be relatively deprived, but are above the minimum on the needs scale.

The definition and estimation of basic need requirements also implies consideration of the extended services and support systems beyond the level of singular need definition. These include energy fuels and materials supply, water and sanitation systems, transportation, communications, education and health facilities, construction, social institutions and additional factors relating to the living and working environment.

It is recognised that many other quantities and qualities may define the meeting of human needs in the larger sense, but without the physical minima, deterioration of the body restricts the mental vision and degrades the spirit. Deprived of basic shelter, on the edge of starvation, and without the rudiments of education no one can make relevant choices or seek personal self-fulfillment. Whilst recognizing the importance of the non-material and qualitative aspects of human requirements, the report emphasises more those demands and needs which can be physically met or delivered.

The setting of agreed floors under acceptable human need standards has long been a major part of public policy in many countries. There is now growing acceptance of the idea that the satisfaction of such needs is a fundamental aspect of governmental responsibility. Development itself was hitherto seen as primarily an economic process of national growth gauged in terms of aggregate productivity and maximal resource exploitation. Today it is viewed as a much more complex integration of social, cultural, economic and environmental factors within which the satisfaction of the needs of the individual citizen for an adequate standard and quality of life is the basic measure.

Sound developmental and environmental planning is a logical corollary to any consideration of the meeting of basic human needs. However, a distinction has arisen between environmental concerns and developmental priorities. Recent environmental anxieties spurred by the more visible problems of the industrialised nations have tended to be focused on the 'pollution of affluence'. It was assumed that developing nations with less industrialisation had fewer such problems, and that the urgencies of their developmental process imposed priorities which overrode environmental considerations. The 'pollution of poverty'—land exhaustion, deforestation, insanitary conditions, urban overcrowding—was due to underdevelopment and could only be ameliorated by more rapid exploitation of resources along traditional lines. Trading hunger and unemployment for factory smoke and loss of aesthetic amenity has, historically, seemed a distinct and immediate gain for those in poor straits.

The swifter incorporation of environmental policies into development may have been skewed by the over-concentration on the physical aspects of the environmental process. By posing a strong distinction between the human and the natural environment, the human tends to be viewed mainly as an agent of deterioration whose activities perturb an otherwise perfectly functioning system. This viewpoint, whilst important in drawing attention to the more deleterious areas of human activity, de-emphasises the fact that many aspects of environmental quality are dependent upon individual and collective perceptions derived in turn from our social and cultural attitudes.

The perception of land use differs markedly from the viewpoint of the rural peasant, the urban worker or the real estate developer. Quality demands for clean water for recreational fishing vary considerably from the survival requirements of irrigation water for marginal farming. Singular emphasis on the amelioration of material environmental impacts has tended to mask the indirect consequences both of poor physical and social environments as limitations on human welfare.

This dichotomy between the human and the natural has also given rise to sets of physically limiting assumptions regarding the growth of population, the availability of resources and the capacity of the biosphere to sustain further human growth. These, in turn, cast doubts on the prospects for more adequate development of the poorer regions. As many of these assumptions erode, we can see more clearly that it is the directions of sustainable growth which are more crucial than its hypothetical limits, and that social and institutional forces are likely to be more constraining on the prospects for development than any set of physical factors alone.

A more satisfactory model of the systemic inter-relationship of environment and development is required in which the full range of human development is coterminous with our definitions of environment. The ecological context would then include individual biophysical interactions and needs, psychosocial and collective activities, and the various levels of technology through which human environmental actions are conducted.

Our present report will hopefully add to the elaboration of such a model in its attempts to identify the directions through which the satisfaction of basic human needs may be met within environmental bounds and in ways which contribute to the development process.

NOTES

1. Employment might also be considered as a basic need but is viewed here more as a means (of livelihood) to satisfy other needs hence it is not dealt with separately.
2. A parallel discussion of such questions, extended to the larger range of human needs, will be found in *Human Requirements, Supply Levels and Outer Bounds*, 1975, prepared by the authors for the Program in International Affairs, Aspen Institute of Humanistic Studies.
3. The schematic diagram of the report layout, Fig. 1, presents these approaches in synoptic terms.

BASIC HUMAN NEEDS

DIMENSIONS OF NEED*

Although we have underlined our focus on those basic necessities for living which constitute a minimal floor below which physical survival itself may be threatened, some discussion of the overall dimensions of human needs is necessary. At the lowest levels of survival, people have desires and aspirations which go beyond mere physiological maintenance. The inter-relationship of needs, wants, desires, and aspirations is critical to human satisfaction.

Since any notion of what constitutes 'absolute' needs, varies from individual to individual and culture to culture, the dimensions of need do not easily lend themselves to quantitative measure. Personal and collective values powerfully affect both the definition of needs and the ways through which they may be satisfied. Shades of individual, social and cultural diversity should always be taken into account in any interpretation of strictly numerical calculations which, although eminently desirable at this stage, can err at the side of misplaced concreteness.

Although we emphasise here the quantifiable side of needs assessment, we would also underline that in many areas of human concern, even where we have become richer in numerical data we remain somewhat poorer in the meanings we can attach to them.

We should not therefore allow the numbers themselves to assume an authority and sacrosanct quality which is unwarranted by their margins of error, their degrees of aggregation and the highly variable character of their standards of measurement. General errors of measurement in socio-economic data are often of the order of 10 to 20 percent, even in those societies where the book-keeping is relatively good. Apart from the reliability level of the data available they are often inadequately distributed and vary considerably in their mode of collection. We often have the wrong data for the right argument—and on many key questions we have no data at all.

---

*The expert review group recommended that this chapter be augmented with a discussion of other non-material aspects of need. As this discussion was already covered in an earlier report an extract from this has been placed in Appendix II.

Any assessment of basic human needs, therefore, is essentially normative in character. We are concerned with what should be and could be, even where the pursuit has a quantitative and seemingly objective cast.

DIFFERENT NEED LEVELS

In earlier work,[1] we have made the distinction between biophysical and psychosocial needs. The biophysical would include most of what we define as basic, in terms of food, health, shelter and clothing. The psychosocial category represents a much wider range of needs encompassing education, employment, communications, mobility, recreation, security and those which go further in determining self-realisation, growth and adequate participation in social and cultural life.

THE NEEDS ENVIRONMENT

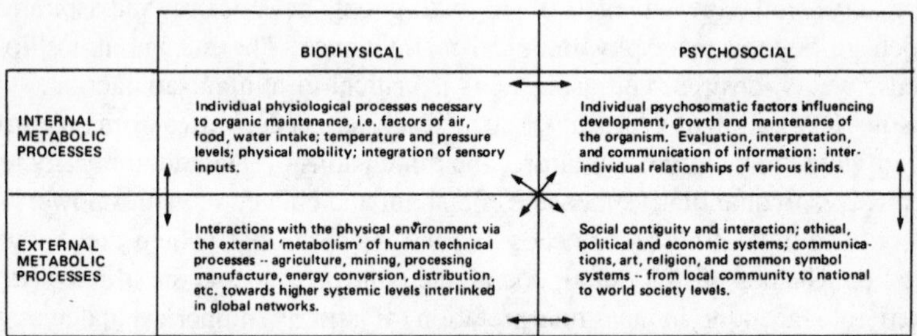

NB. The internal processes refer to individual level systems; the external to socio-technical systems at different magnitudes. All are highly interactive with one another and have various degrees of interdependence.

Source: Center for Integrative Studies.

Fig. 2

We may categorise needs further in terms of three loose and overlapping categories.

a) *Deficiency Needs* are those threshold needs, mainly biophysical, which must be met to maintain survival. They may also be defined as those "first floor" needs to which every person should be entitled by virtue of being born.

Access to basic needs is a two-fold social right. *One*, the right of the individual to have the freedom and opportunity to be responsible for, and be able to meet his or her own needs, and *two*, the right to call upon the support of the society where individual efforts fail due to overriding circumstances.[2] There is also the implied responsibility for the world community that the meeting of such minimal needs should be in some sense a first charge on world resources.

b) *Sufficiency Needs* are those which should be met so as to maintain living standards at some desirable level well beyond marginal survival.

c) *Growth Needs* go beyond the sufficient standard. Their satisfaction allows for individual development above material sufficiency and the enjoyment of non-material ends and aspirations.

Within sufficiency and growth need categories; i.e., beyond the minimum, there should be included the sort of felt needs which, when met, constitute a large part of the quality of living; for example, "A sense of welfare . . . A sense of equity . . . A sense of achievement . . . A sense of participation."[3]

Both sufficiency and growth needs constitute a "second floor" in the needs hierarchy, which are defined by each society for its own peoples within the context of world society. In actual practice, we would consider that even the satisfaction of "first floor" needs should allow for better opportunities, however minimal, for more individual growth and development.

INTERDEPENDENCE OF NEEDS

The dysfunctional linkages between different sorts of deficiencies accentuates the condition of the needy, particularly at absolute poverty levels. Poor nutrition lowers disease resistance. Hunger and ill-health impair productivity which, in turn, lessens the capacity to secure more food, improve general living, and be more resistant to disease. It is a vicious circle of social and economic deprivation.

In the close relationship between health and environmental conditions, problems arising from inadequate housing, poor water supply and sewage systems are marked by the high incidence of diarrheal diseases in the poorer countries. Infants and children are particularly susceptible as is shown by the mortality rates amongst the young. The high rate of child loss encourages reproduction which adds mouths to feed for which there is insufficient food, and bodies to clothe and shelter for which there are insufficient materials.

Any serious consideration of basic needs strategies must take into account these interdependencies and be appropriately comprehensive. Piecemeal attempts to focus exclusively on one need area at a time are unlikely to break the deprivation circle, even though they may fit more easily into bureaucratic divisions. A long and healthy life is not determined by health services alone but by the interactive combination of access to medical facilities, food, clothing, housing and fuel, and by such other factors as meaningful work, education, recreation and security, by the satisfaction of values and by the desire for living itself.

THE DIMENSIONS OF POVERTY

Whilst the terms 'need' and 'poverty' are used interchangeably, we should clarify their application in varying circumstances. When we refer to 'the world's poor', we tend to lump together a considerable range of people in a variety of situations. The range may extend from those who are considered to be lacking access to the opportunities and amenities enjoyed by the majority in their societies, but who still may have relatively adequate food, clothing, shelter and minimal education—to those who may be literally destitute, living in the open in constant threat of hunger and disease, and with little hope of amelioration in their condition. Poverty can be defined, therefore, in terms of relative or absolute deprivation.

Absolute Poverty

We are primarily concerned in this study with the problems of absolute poverty, of those who are more or less close to survival margins in the satisfaction of basic needs. Such poverty is chiefly the problem of the developing countries where there are very large numbers of people at and below subsistence level.

The World Bank, emphasizing income differentials, gives the following figures:

> "Some 900 million of these individuals subsist on incomes of less than $75 a year in an environment of squalor, hunger and hopelessness. They are the absolute poor, living in situations so deprived as to be below any rational definition of human decency. (Absolute poverty is a condition of life so limited by illiteracy, malnutrition, disease, high infant mortality, and low life expectancy as to deny its victims the very potential of the genes with which they are born.) In effect it is life at the margin of existence.
>
> The heaviest concentration of absolute poverty is in Asia, India, Pakistan, Bangladesh and Indonesia are particularly afflicted. One out of every two or three individuals there is enmeshed in it.
>
> In Africa, most countries are plagued with both absolute and relative poverty. Not only are per capita incomes meager on average, but often highly skewed as well.
>
> In Latin America, many countries enjoy higher per capita incomes, with only about one individual in six at Asian or African levels of absolute poverty. But income distribution throughout the region is marked by serious inequality and relative poverty is widespread and severe."[4]

By emphasising the availability of basic needs, rather than abstract measures such as income we may present a more detailed picture of the dimensions of absolute poverty. (See Fig. 3)

Conditions of poverty vary considerably according to rural or urban location. Whilst those in rural settings might be absolutely poor in terms of income, their actual situation may be alleviated by the availability of food from a kitchen plot,

THE WORLD'S POOR, 1976

In Total World Population of 4 Billion	
Undernourished (i.e. Below Suggested Calorie/Protein Levels)	570 Million
Adults Illiterate	800 Million
Children not Enrolled in School	250 Million
With No Access to Effective Medical Care	1,500 Million
With Less than $90.00 Income Per Year	1,300 Million
With Life Expectancy Below 60 Years	1,700 Million
With Inadequate Housing	1,030 Million

Source: Center for Integrative Studies

Fig. 3

by the use of local shelter materials and other minor advantages. The urban poor generally have no such margins to fall back upon.

> "It is estimated, roughly 25 percent of the urban population of the developing countries . . . some 150 million people—live in absolute poverty. These 150 million lack access to safe water and public or private sewage systems and they are also severely undernourished. Some 46 percent of these urban poor live in South Asia, 24 percent in Latin America, 13 percent in North Africa and the Middle East, 10 percent in East Asia, and 8 percent in Sub-Saharan Africa."[5]

The marginal employment picture of the urban poor makes them difficult to assess by income distribution. Many are outside of the market economy as unpaid family workers or are 'self employed' in the variety of marginal occupations afforded by the urban setting—street vending, unskilled casual workers, small scale tailors and odd-job workers. In most cases, their low education levels effectively bar them from more regular and higher income employment. They spend up to 80 percent of whatever income they can make on food but still suffer from serious malnutrition.

Their access to basic needs services in almost every area is usually very limited or non-existent, with regard to medical and hospital care, education and transportation.

In the rural areas of the developing countries three-quarters of the population are estimated to live in relative or absolute poverty. Such areas, as with the cities, are characterised by highly contrasting living conditions. Prosperous land owners live close to small owner-cultivators, poor tenant farmers and the increasing number of landless laborers.

> "There are over 80 million small holdings of less than two hectares, many of them comprising small fragments of land, most of which generate incomes below the absolute poverty level. The tenants, sharecroppers and squatters who represent another 30 million or so families are often less well off."[6]

These conditions create immense problems for those countries where the prime task of development is to concentrate on increased rural production. Such production and its corollary of better environmental management seems unlikely to be forthcoming unless the basic needs of the poorest are met through appropriate reforms, reorganisation and incentives. Even with the drift to the cities the rural populations of the developing countries are still increasing about 2 percent per year. Better human services and life enhancement of the rural poor would not only increase productivity but stem the impact of migration on the urban concentrations.

INCOME DISTRIBUTIONS AND DISPARITIES

Although we place less emphasis on income distribution in this study than on the measurement of material need levels, adequate income as the means through which needs may be obtained is obviously a significant factor. It is important to note that many of those in need may fall outside of the income measure, i.e. the very young and the old, women in family occupations and those who have no measurable income.

Of equal importance is the persistence of large degrees of income disparity within countries indicating gross inequity in access to needs satisfaction. (Fig. 4)

The analysis of income distribution has been particularly useful in showing the extent to which previous development policies and external aid programs have failed to benefit those most in need. Both development programs and aid, generally, still tend to be designed and administered in ways that are of apparent advantage to countries rather than to the people within countries.

> "It is now clear that more than a decade of rapid growth in underdeveloped countries has been of little or no benefit to perhaps a third of their population. Although the average per capita income of the Third World has increased by 50 percent since 1960, this growth has been very unequally distributed among countries, regions within countries, and socio-economic groups."[7]

INCOME DISTRIBUTION PROFILE:
For Selected Countries in Reference Groups.

% Population	Reference Country Groups: % Income Recd. A	B	C	D	E
The Upper 5% Receives	18	19	26	31	28
The Lower 50% Receives	25	26	19	16	20
The Upper 50% Receives	75	74	81	83	80
The Lower 70% Receives	45	44	35	32	35
The Upper 30% Receives	55	56	65	68	64

Data: Adapted from Shail, Jain, Size Distribution of Income - A Compilation of Data (World Bank Publication), Washington, D. C.; International Bank for Reconstruction and Development, 1975.

Source : Center for Integrative Studies.

Fig. 4

The concentration of wealth in the hands of the higher income recipients who are generally a small minority, is a feature of both developed and developing countries.

In the developed countries those with lower incomes may also have margins of security and income augmentation in the form of social security, medical services, subsidised housing, social welfare and other programs which are not so widely available in the poorer countries.

The paucity and unreliability of income data have led many analysts to allocate measurements of Gross National Product per caput for comparing 'income' distributions between countries. In terms of estimating basic need levels and standards of living of people this is faulty in many ways. The most obvious, is that,

> "The great majority of the world's people do not partake of the statistical incomes ascribed to them and the quality of life of the masses can be deteriorating even as gross national product rises."[8]

The problem with such measurements is that they do not usually take into account differences in purchasing power or that the satisfaction of needs from monetary income varies considerably from country to country.

The development of social security and other welfare services are examples of ways in which the meeting of an individual's needs is detached from his or her income or ''earnings''. Indeed, access to the services of society, in the broader sense, has itself become a critical indicator of social equity and participation. At present, such wider access is still income and status dependent. The more privileged by income or education people are the more they use the public facilities such as transportation, telecommunications and information services. They not only have more physical and social mobility but more psychic mobility. They literally live in a larger society in both material and conceptual terms.

One of the reasons that attention is given to the problems of income distribution with developmental growth is that historically, it was assumed that an increase in general social welfare and the wider provision of basic needs could not be achieved in early development. Emphasis has traditionally been placed on high aggregate growth even where this was accompanied by very uneven distribution of the benefits of that growth. The same sort of argument applies to the fitting of environmental concerns within the development process. In both senses, investment directed toward improving the situation of poorer groups in the society (particularly where they may be in the majority and in the rural sector), and investment in productive environmental management, are more likely to make for gains in development—by augmenting total resources and by increasing productivity through social incentives.

Relative Poverty

Whilst not as urgent a problem in world terms both by its nature and by the capacity of nations to deal effectively with it themselves, relative poverty is still an important area for wider needs discussion, albeit beyond severe deficiency need.

In the industrialised countries of the developed world, the relatively poor are numerically in the minority e.g., in Canada, the range is given as between 20 to 30 percent of the population; and in the U.S., about 12 percent. Most of these groups would, however, be counted as fairly prosperous compared to their counterparts in the developing world both in terms of income and in the amount of welfare support they receive—although even in many developed countries there are still pockets of hard-core poverty where levels of deprivation come close to absolute levels.

> ''People are 'poor' because they are deprived of the opportunities, comforts and self respect regarded as normal in the community to which they belong. It is, therefore, the continually moving average standards of that community that are the starting points for an assessment of its poverty, and the poor are those who fall sufficiently far below these average standards. Their deprivation can be measured and their numbers

counted by comparison with average personal income . . . or with a standard of living currently sanctioned by government . . . or with average life chances."[9]

Many may contend that the sort of 'felt' needs that a person experiences when he compares his lot with the experiences and opportunities enjoyed by others do not represent any real measure of poverty and detract from the central question of basic needs by widening it to include wants and desires which go far above those essential to some modest living standard. They may also feel that reducing felt needs below such 'artificially' induced standards is the only way to secure adequacy for all. This denies the fact that even at minimal levels of living, our needs are socially and culturally conditioned. We do not hunger for food but for those specified foods which are culturally acceptable; needs for social communication and self-realisation are almost as basic as water and air.

Lest this issue appear to be marginal, we should note that even in advocating the urgency of meeting the basic needs of the absolute poor we do so not only that they may survive but also that they may have the opportunity to widen their needs and wants further in the process of development and have access to that larger range of desires, aspirations and choices which constitute the quality of life.

> "The relationships between changes in needs, satisfactions, and happiness give rise to various complications . . . First, as a matter of positive fact, given the generally accepted interpretation of the word 'happiness', it may be well that people are happier when they experience an increase in certain needs, even if these cannot be entirely satisfied. Secondly, as a matter of value judgement, one might well hold that, irrespective of whether an increase in needs made people 'happier' or not, it raised human welfare rather than reduced it. Thirdly, it is impossible to draw a sharp dividing line between those of our needs that are innate or natural and those which have been developed as a result of many factors including our whole social environment . . . what is so moral about natural needs and so immoral, or undesirable about artificial needs."[10]

We need to concentrate on fulfilling the minimum needs of those in dire want, but it is important to bear in mind that such minima should not only take into account those factors that provide for the barest physiological needs for survival. They must also include provision for those psychosocial needs which make us human.

NOTES

1. *Op. Cit.* Human Requirements, Supply Levels and Outer Bounds, 1975.
2. Such rights were specifically recognised in Article 25, part 1, of the 1948 U.N. Universal Declaration of Human Rights, "Everyone has the right to a standard of living

adequate for the health and well-being of himself and of his family, including food, clothing, housing and medical care and necessary social services, and the right of security in the event of unemployment, sickness, disability, widowhood, old age, or other lack of livelihood in circumstances beyond his control''.

3. Cleveland, Harlan, *The Future Executive*, New York, Harper and Row, 1972.

4. McNamara, Robert S., *Address to the Board of Governors*, World Bank, September, 1975.

5. *Task Force on Urban Poverty*, World Bank, March, 1976.

6. *Rural Development*, World Bank, February, 1975, p. 5.

7. Chenery, Hollis and others, *Redistribution with Growth*, Oxford University Press, 1974, N.B. See also Annex note on limitations of income distribution data.

8. Penalosa, Enrique, ''The Need for a New Development Model,'' *Finance and Development*, Vol. 13, No. 1, March, 1976.

9. Social Science Research Council, *Research on Poverty*, London, 1968, p. 5.

10. Beckerman, Wilfred, ''*In Defense of Economic Growth*'', London, Jonathan Cape, 1974, pp. 89, 91, 92.

ASSESSMENT APPROACHES

Given the variability of needs and of means to their satisfaction at the individual and society levels we suggest three main lines of approach towards assessing priority areas.

These may be considered as different analytical levels of 'coarseness' according to data available. Moving successively from the national society to the smaller social group then to the individual level, they also underline the importance of considering the satisfaction of needs at these different levels. Though larger models at global and regional levels might be more administratively convenient, the larger the scale the more diffuse the needs hence the due emphasis given here to smaller group and individual needs perception and measurement.

The first emerges from locating the obligation of meeting needs on a larger scale. Responsibility lies with nations themselves and we may usefully compare how nations do in terms of their indicators of needs satisfaction and how they may be classified in terms of need priorities. We have approached this by the *reference country* mode.

This is used within the report primarily as a means to assess the dimensions of needs and how they are met in various groups of countries. Grouping by similarities also highlights some of the differences between countries in this regard. It should be noted that this approach is offered as example not as a method for all purposes—even for this purpose many other comparative groupings might also be used.

The second is to focus more closely on individual needs. Because individuals vary considerably and their needs are usually satisfied within a social context, we suggest the *unit household* concept as a useful approach which can be made operationally specific to different local situations.

The unit household mode should also be considered as an applicable unit of analysis which may be extended to the unit community to extended kinship networks and other groups or settings more applicable in different social and cultural settings.

The third approach deals with the changing pattern of needs over time at the individual level both in terms of the individual life span and shifting population cohorts. This we term the *life cycle* approach.

It may serve to assess different perceptions and need demands between the sexes, between young and old etc. and also to focus attention, for example, on the irreversible need deficiencies which may occur in deprivation of the very young.

Rather than being fully detailed 'models', the three approaches are essentially conceptual frameworks through which various dimensions of need can be assessed. Ideally, they should be considered as an '*example set*' of starting points for those concerned with the planning and development of basic needs strategies.

THE REFERENCE COUNTRY

In classifying nations in comparative development terms, or according to levels of living, analysts have separated the world into two divisions of developed and developing and have latterly introduced third and fourth world categories. But within these characteristics it is recognised that there is considerable variance and gradation.

Focussing, therefore, on levels of need satisfaction we have developed a set of *Reference Country* profiles based on the composite characteristics of groups of countries. Whilst any such composite method may conceal more than it reveals, these profiles may be useful, *one*, in identifying specific aspects of need for present purposes, *two*, in affording a rudimentary set of indicator profiles against which each country might be able to compare its own characteristics.

The set of average reference countries was developed in the following manner. (Fig. 5)

The countries listed below (Fig. 6) are those that were selected as representing different levels of satisfaction of requirement. They are grouped into five sets, A, B, C, D and E.

No 'qualitative' measures were used in assigning countries to groups other than indicator ranking and regional and climatic criteria. Clearly not all countries in each group are strictly comparable. Their specific allocation with other countries may even be questioned in terms of internal cultural, ethnic, political and institutional differences which do not emerge from the indicator range. Singular characteristics, such as whether they are landlocked or island nations, are not covered.

To arrive at the average reference country profile, available indicators are totalled and averaged though with minor adjustments where data were lacking or given for different years. Similar profiles were run through for U.S.S.R., U.S.A., China and India.

THE REFERENCE COUNTRY CONSTRUCT

Five average reference countries were constructed so as to provide a convenient range of different standards of living within which need priorities could be assessed.

(i) Criteria for selection were designed
   (a) to give a relative grouping of population so that the combined population totals in each set would be roughly comparable.
   (b) for regional balance, countries in each group were assigned from different regions and climate zones. This was difficult to accommodate for all groups, most of the richer countries tend to be located in tropical and semi-tropical regions.
   (c) to include representative centrally planned, mixed and market economies.

(ii) Those at the extreme ends of size, population, energy and materials use were set aside so as not to skew the average reference construct within which they might be placed. Hence—U.S.S.R., China, U.S.A. and India are given as comparable reference countries in themselves.

(iii) Five sets of seven countries emerged from this screening process. The characteristics of each set was then averaged to give the Average Reference Countries of A, B, C, D and E.

Fig. 5

LIST OF COUNTRIES USED FOR AVERAGE REFERENCE CONSTRUCT

A	B	C	D	E
Sweden	Romania	Turkey	Bolivia	Afghanistan
U.K.	Argentina	Egypt	Colombia	Bangladesh
Netherlands	Greece	Brazil	Burma	Haiti
Japan	Spain	Sri Lanka	Indonesia	Ethiopia
Austria	Israel	Iraq	Algeria	Upper Volta
France	Mexico	Cuba	Nigeria	Zaire
Australia	Singapore	Guatemala	Zambia	Tanzania

N.B. A complete list of all countries grouped into the ABCDE categories will be found in the Annex.

Fig. 6

About 125 indicators were assembled for each country, ranging through population characteristics, basic need areas, resource base and support systems, as follows:

(i)	(ii)
Population	Employment
Income/Expenditures	Resource Base:
Food/Nutrition	Agricultural
Health	Industrial
Education	Support Systems:
Shelter	Transportation
	Communication

(*N.B*. for reference convenience, set (i) follows at the end of this section; set (ii) is located in the Appendix.)

Our indicator range for the Average Reference Countries is in no way a complete picture but rather a provisional guide for further work. Its present purpose is to provide an under-pinning for the more detailed quantitative need assessments which we deal with later in the report.

The indicators are open to question in terms of their reliability for comparative purposes, and it is important to examine whether they actually do measure specific needs or indicate the quality of suggested standards. For example, the health indicators do not give a measure of health or even much in the way of health maintenance or disease prevention but indicate facilities largely available for ill health; education indicators refer only to formal instruction and give no comparable measures of quality.

Comparative World Distribution

The number of countries and territories in the world, which can be assigned to each reference group are:

A 20 ... (including USA, USSR)
B 17
C 52 ... (including China)
D 27
E 36 ... (including India)

The number and percentage of the world's population in each reference group are:

(Population in Millions)

A	871.4	(21.7%)	(including USA, USSR)
B	324.7	(8.1%)	
C	1,387.2	(34.6%)	(including China)
D	504.8	(12.6%)	
E	922.1	(23.0%)	(including India)

A world map of this distribution has also been prepared to give an overview of where these countries are located in various regions. This distribution may be usefully compared with the various resources' and facilities' flows at the world level. (Fig. 7 at the end of this section).

It may be noted from this mapped distribution that many of the poorer countries, by reference country grouping, lie in the tropical and semitropical regions of the South. This does suggest, minimally, a strong difference in environmental and developmental conditions from those which obtained for the present developed countries of the North in their initial phases of development.

Such climatic variables are often discounted but become critically important

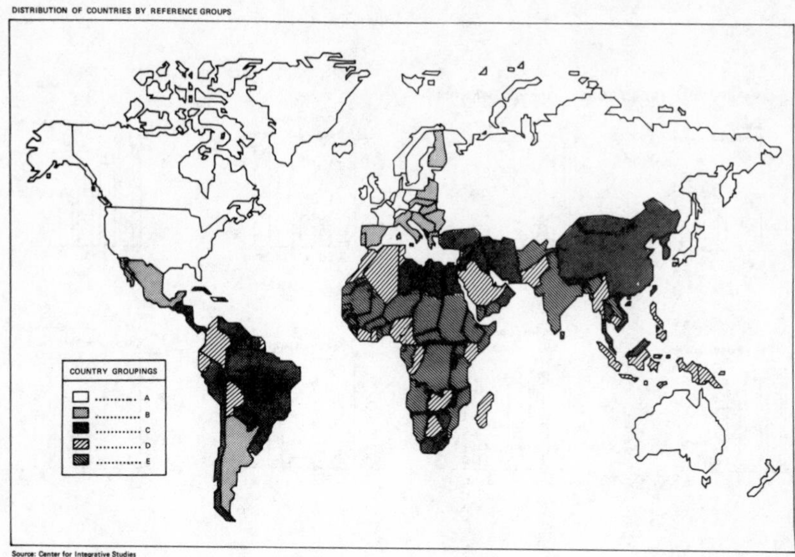

Fig. 7

in considering the more integrative linkages of environmental management and developmental planning.

> "It is in no way claimed that climate has a mechanical one-to-one relationship to economic development or that climate with its effects is the only ruling constraint on economic development or that if the effects of climate are removed as a ruling constraint in today's poor countries, development will be unbounded. What is claimed rather is that in today's poor countries climatic factors will usually be found to have an important hampering effect on economic development through their impact on agriculture directly or through the diseases and pests afflicting animals and plants, on mineral discovery, and on man himself through disease, that these effects used to be better understood and that a high priority needs to be given to investment in research to find ways to minimize the adverse impacts of climate and to find ways to turn the particular manifestations of the local climate to advantage."[1]

In terms of establishing need priorities it is clear that the lowest levels of absolute poverty and the largest number of poor people are grouped in the D and E countries—with the greatest incidence of need occurring in the E countries.

This provides us with a series of 'seriously affected' nations, a defined target population in need, and a specific set of environmental and developmental conditions in which the needs occur.

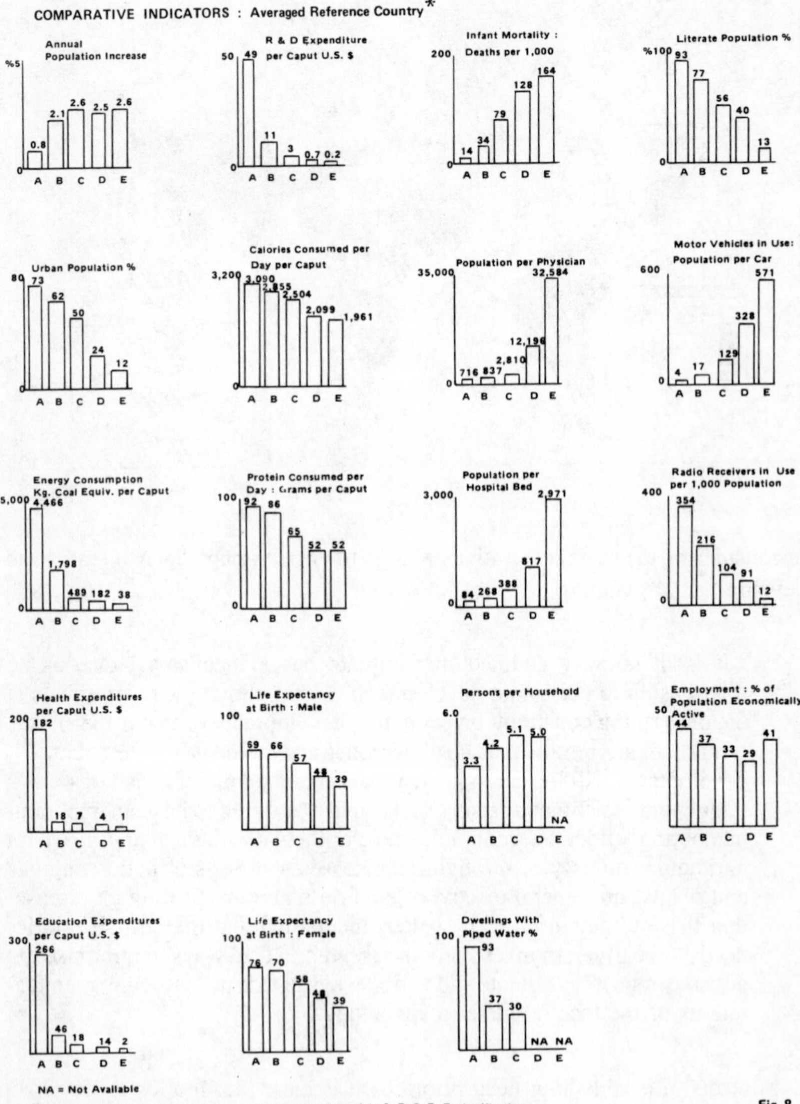

NA = Not Available

* The average of the seven reference countries in the appropriate A, B, C, D, E, classifications.

Fig. 8

Data : Indicator List , Fig. 9.

Source : Center for Integrative Studies.

REFERENCE COUNTRY INDICATORS

POPULATION INDICATORS	AVERAGED REFERENCE COUNTRY								
	A	B	C	D	E	USA	USSR	China	India
Population : millions	38	23	33	40	25	215.3	257	836.8	620.7
Annual rate of increase : %	0.8	2.1	2.6	2.5	2.6	0.8	0.9	1.7	2.0
Crude birth rate : per thousand	16	30	37	42	47	15	18	27	35
Crude death rate : per thousand	9	8	11	18	21	9	9	10	15
Population under 15 : %	24	35	42	44	45	27	28	33	40
Population over 64 : %	11	7	4	3	3	10	9	6	3
Urban population : %	73	62	50	24	12	74	60	23	20
Density : pop. per sq. km.	31	27	19	32	29	22	11	85	175
Area : million sq. km.	1.3	0.8	1.6	1.2	0.8	9.4	22.4	9.6	3.3
Energy consumption : kg coal equivalent per caput	4,466	1,798	489	182	38	11,960	4,927	594	188

INCOME AND EXPENDITURES INDICATORS (Per Year)	AVERAGED REFERENCE COUNTRY								
	A	B	C	D	E	USA	USSR	China	India
GNP per caput : U.S. $	4,190	1,691	517	299	104	6,200	2,030	660	120
Health— Public expenditure per caput : U.S. $	182	18	7	4	1	171	82	2	1
Education— Public expenditure per caput : U.S. $	266	46	18	14	2	348	172	9	2
Education — Public expenditure per pupil first level : U.S. $	306	92	70	25	20	...	...	...	6.5
R & D Expenditure Total : Million U.S. $	1,911	148	35	16	3	30,030	18,934	...	257
R & D Expenditure Per caput : U.S. $	49	11	3	0.7	0.2	144	76	...	0.5
Military— Public expenditure per caput : U.S. $	129	204	29	7	2	373	268	15	4

Fig. 9

FOOD (NUTRITION) INDICATORS	AVERAGED REFERENCE COUNTRY A	B	C	D	E	USA	USSR	China	India
Calories consumed per day per caput	3,090	2,855	2,504	2,099	1,961	3,330	3,280	2,170	2,070
Percentage of calorie requirements met	119	115	106	91	85	126	131	91	94
Protein consumed per day : grammes per caput	92	86	65	52	52	106	101	60	52
Calories from cereal, starchy foods and sugar products as % of total calories consumed	47	59	71	79	80	40	66	80	77
Animal protein consumed per caput as % of total protein	61	43	26	21	15	72	44	16	11

HEALTH INDICATORS	AVERAGED REFERENCE COUNTRY A	B	C	D	E	USA	USSR	China	India
Life expectancy at birth : male	69	66	57	48	39	67.4	65	50.0	41.9
Life expectancy at birth : female	76	70	58	48	39	75.1	74	50.0	40.6
Infant mortality : per thousand	14	34	79	128	164	17	28	...	139
Population per physician	716	837	2,810	12,196	32,584	621	390	...	4,795
Physicians per thousand inhabitants in urban areas	15	26	9	9	2	...	...	...	7.5
Physicians per thousand inhabitants in rural areas	6	7	0.5	0.3	0.1	...	...	...	0.8
Population per nurse and midwifery personnel	264	638	1,747	2,957	7,462	187	174	...	8,165
Population per hospital bed	84	268	388	817	2,971	138	89	...	1,571
All hospitals : Admissions per ten thousand	1,600	1,080	720	419	...	1,611	...	...	...
Mental hospitals : Admissions per ten thousand	48	23	12	2	1	31	...	...	...

Fig. 9 cont.

EDUCATION INDICATORS	AVERAGED REFERENCE COUNTRY								
	A	B	C	D	E	USA	USSR	China	India
Literate population : %	94	77	56	40	13	98	99	37	34
Pre-Primary									
Number of schools : thousands	5	8	0.2	...	...	...	89	...	...
Number of teachers : thousands	24	15	3	...	...	...	636	...	...
Number of students : millions	0.7	0.4	0.1	...	...	3	9	...	...
Student : teacher ratio	31	30	34	...	...	...	14	...	...
Students as % of population under 5	24	19	3	...	...	17	43	...	...
Primary									
Number of schools : thousands	20	19	34	19	7	79	163	...	...
Number of teachers : thousands	147	117	138	114	37	1,274	2,404	...	...
Number of students : millions	4	3	4	4	1	31	39	...	59
Student : teacher ratio	25	26	30	34	38	25	16	...	...
Students' net enrollment ratio as % of primary school age population, males	96	97	68	57	...	...	...	...	48
Students' net enrollment ratio as % of primary school age population, females	97	96	58	56	...	...	...	...	37
Secondary									
Number of teachers : thousands	188	63	93	40	11	1,055	...	...	387
Number of students : millions	3	0.9	1.5	0.7	0.4	20	10	...	8
Student : teacher ratio	16	14	16	17	23	19	...	...	20
Student's gross enrollment ratio as % of secondary school age population, males	85	52	36	24	6	96	67	...	15
Students' gross enrollment ratio as % of secondary school age population, females	81	50	30	22	2	...	...	...	7

Fig. 9 cont.

EDUCATION INDICATORS (Con't)

Higher	A	B	C	D	E	USA	USSR	CHINA	INDIA
Number of teachers : thousands	56	11	20	6	2	748	201	...	...
Number of students : thousands	576	186	179	67	22	8,949	4,630	...	2,009
Student : teacher ratio : thousands	10	17	9	11	14	12	23	...	...
Students' gross enrollment ratio, as % of those 20 – 24 . male	18	12	6	3	0.4	51	22	...	4
Students' gross enrollment ratio, as % of those 20 – 24 : female	13	9	3	1	0.1	45	23	...	2
Daily general interest newspapers per thousand people	430	125	33	23	5	297	347	...	16
Non-daily general interest newspapers: per thousand people	312	77	37	13	4	...	247	...	12
Books and pamphlets produced: per million people	480	303	95	21	4	389	312	...	23
Volumes in national and public libraries : per thousand people	506	580	85	13	27	...	5,199	...	...

SHELTER INDICATORS	AVERAGED REFERENCE COUNTRY								
	A	B	C	D	E	USA	USSR	China	India
Persons per household	3.3	4.2	5.1	5.0	...	3.2	3.7	...	5.6
Rooms per dwelling	3.9	2.9	3.9	3.1	...	5.1	3.0	...	2.0
Dwellings with one room : %	8	23	8	22	...	2	...	...	48
Persons per room	0.9	2.2	1.4	1.8	...	0.6	1.3	...	2.8
Dwellings with piped water : %	93	37	30	...	...	98	...	...	...
Dwellings with toilet : %	87	74	64	...	...	96	...	...	...
Dwellings with electric light : %	99	70	45	...	...	...	...	...	...

Fig. 9 cont.

INDICATOR SHELTER	ADDITIONAL INDICATORS FOR POORER COUNTRIES								
	A	B	C	D	E	USA	USSR	China	India
Urban population served by sewage system : %	...	...	...	49	63	...	...	...	80
Rural population with adequate sewage disposal : %	...	...	...	10	4	...	...	...	1
Total population served by sewage system or adequate disposal : %	...	...	...	20	9	...	...	...	18
Urban population served by house connections or public standposts for water : %	...	...	...	59	27	...	...	...	56
Urban population with reasonable access to community water supply : %	...	...	...	12	30	...	...	...	6
Total population served by, or with reasonable access to community water supply : %	...	...	...	29	30	...	...	...	16

Data: UNESCO Statistical Yearbook, 1974. U.N. Statistical Yearbooks, 1973 & 1974. Yearbook of Labour Statistics, ILO Geneva, 1974. FAO Production Yearbook, 1974. Global Review of Human Settlements, Statistical Annex, U.N., ECOSOC, 1976. FAO Monthly Bulletin of Agricultural Economics and Statistics, 1975 & 1976. 1976 World Population Data Sheet: The Population Reference Bureau. World Health Statistics Annual 1972, WHO, 1976. Sivard, Ruth, World Military and Social Expenditures 1976. 1975 World Bank Atlas. U.N. World Food Conference, Assessment of the World Food Situation, Present and Future, 1974. (E/Conf 65/3). Agricultural Commodity Projections 1970-1980, Vol. 2, FAO, 1971.

Source: Center for Integrative Studies

Fig. 9 cont.

THE UNIT HOUSEHOLD

In putting forward the Unit Household approach, it is important to emphasise that this is a conceptual scheme from which to work and does not represent any fixed assumption of what might meet the basic needs of a specific household in any one country.

Some characteristics of the Unit Household may be outlined as follows:

(i) A household of five persons was chosen as typical of a medium size family unit.

(ii) The various items required to satisfy the basic needs for such a unit were estimated, from a variety of sources, so as to suggest the means by which a modest level of living might be afforded. No completeness of definition is asserted with regard to the items included. They might be added to, or subtracted, according to socio-cultural preference and assessment of local needs.

(iii) The 'building' or shelter for the household could not be costed in, due to the variables of regional need, and climatic, cultural and other factors. We may presume that basic shelter in the poorer countries would be from local materials with relatively low physical and monetary costs.

(iv) Internal material requirements of energy consumption were entered where they could be estimated—but, as we discuss below, they should take into account various adaptive technological approaches. These might combine, for example, different aspects of energy use with autonomous energy generation and the use of waste heat for different purposes.

Our main concern with the Unit Household is to focus on the internal and external household economy as a measure for estimating basic needs and gauging how much might be required in terms of energy, facilities and products to meet such needs.

Ideally, the use of such household assessment measures should cover not only physical aspects but also the less quantifiable amenities and socio-cultural purposes which are served.

The check list for such a 'unit measure' could prove extremely long. To simplify matters we have approached such a listing in functional terms by starting with human needs and working outwardly to the structural, and site and services aspects.

Human Need Functions to be Served

Physical Needs/Functions
Eating, sleeping, bathing, excretion.
Activities such as cooking, laundering, cleaning, waste disposal.
Storage for food/utensils, clothes, personal household and work equipment, books, etc.

Psychosocial Needs/Functions
Sexual relations, privacy, sociability, conversation, reading, religious practices, personal and child care, creative pursuits, communications, play, recreation and entertainment—overall aesthetic amenity of dwelling and surroundings.

Environmental Control
Management of heat and cold, protection from extremes of sun, wind, rain, dust and other external impingements such as insects, vermin, rodents, etc.; energy for lighting, cooling, heating and ventilation aspects.

Internal Structures and Surfaces
Furnishings and equipment for physical and social needs. Surfaces of floor, walls, ceiling to aid internal environmental control.

External Structures and Surfaces
To control externally impinging environmental factors—walls, roofing, screened windows/doors, porches and balconies. Drainage, waste dis-

posal, sewage, energy fuel storage, work/play equipment storage.
Play and recreation areas.
Adjacent kitchen garden and livestock area where appropriate.
Walls, fences, etc., where required for physical security and for cultural purposes.

External Service Aspects
Ease of access to roads, shops, markets, transportation, work place; to neighbors and community; to health, education, communications and other services.

UNIT HOUSEHOLD : PHYSICAL FACTORS

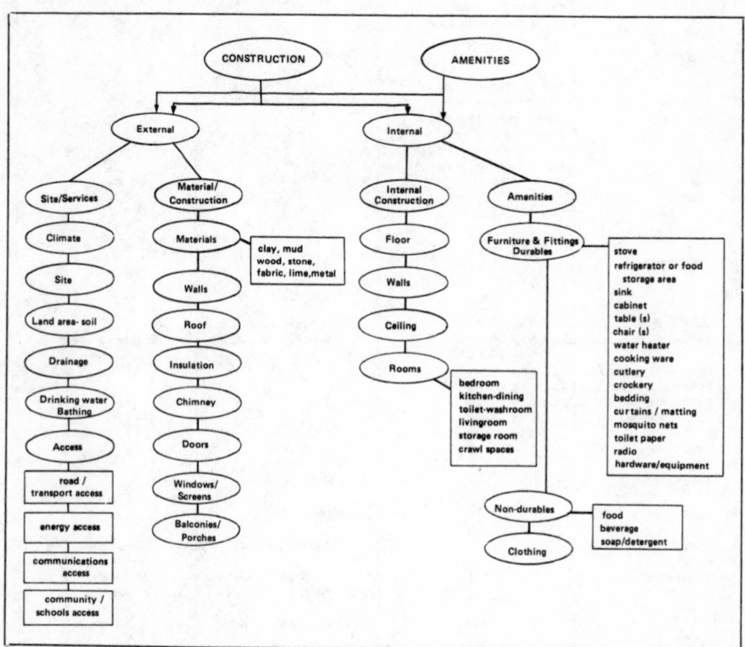

Source : Center for Integrative Studies.

Fig. 10

Some of the physical factors relating to material construction etc., are summarised in Fig. 10.

The table of Household Consumption Indicators, (Fig. 11), is provisional and again highly variable according to socio-cultural preferences. Although some quantities have been assigned, these are very rough approximations rather than definitive estimates.

In planning human needs strategies, the unit household approach may, in appropriate situations, be extended to a unit community measure. Needs for extended services such as energy, light, water supply, sewage, access to health,

UNIT HOUSEHOLD : CONSUMPTION INDICATORS (For Five Person Unit Per Year) ;

WITHIN DWELLING UNIT	ENERGY and MATERIALS	ADDITIONAL PERSONAL CONSUMPTION	ENERGY and MATERIALS
Living Space	50 square metres		
2 Bedrooms 1 Kitchen 1 Livingroom 1 Toilet, washroom and storage			
Utilities		Clothes	
Water	45 cubic metres	Clothing	18 kg. Material
Energy Use (Electricity/Gas)	75 metric tons coal equivalent		e.g. 6 kg. Wool 6 kg. Cotton 6 kg. Rayon
Sewage	Energy, water use, etc. depends on system (e.g., local septic tank, urban sewage, etc.)	Footwear	2 kg. Leather
Furniture and Fittings		Transport	
Stove Refrigerator Sink Cabinet Table Chair Bed Chest Bath/Shower Basin W.C. Water Heater	Material, amounts of metal etc. could be assigned but for aggregate use figures see per capita metals, minerals use. NB, These items have different use life-times and re-use/re-cycle rates.	Personal Transport Public Transport	
Durables		Communication	
Cooking Ware	4 kg. metal	Newspapers	52
Cutlery	3 kg. iron 1 kg. aluminum	Mail	120 (items sent and received)
Crockery/Glass Ware	Local Materials		
Bedding	20 kg. Material		
Curtain/Matting	e.g. 7 kg. Wool		
Towel/Brush/Sponge	7 kg. Rayon 6 kg. Cotton		
Television Radio Telephone			
Non-Durables		Services	
Food		Health	0.5 hospital bed; 0.02 medical personnel
Beverage			
Soap/Detergent		Education/Recreation	$ US 200 Per Year
		Police/Fire/Etc.	0.01 personnel
		Social Welfare Library/Museum/Etc.	

Source : Center for Integrative Studies.

Fig. 11

education and communications facilities may be better served at this level. Providing such services and utilising every advantage of indigeneous materials and self-help could then be a part of local 'eco-development'.

THE LIFE CYCLE

Assessing basic needs according to life cycle infers recognition of changing requirements during the individual life span and the variance in collective demands for services depending on the numbers of persons at different ages in the population.

MATRIX FOR LIFE CYCLE FACTORS

LIFE CYCLE FACTORS	PSYCHOPHYSICAL NEEDS Food Health Education Shelter Clothing	PSYCHOSOCIAL NEEDS Employment Affection Security Self Realisation Social Participation Social Rights Cognitive/Aesthetic Recreation Communications	Mobility	ENVIRONMENTAL FACTORS	SOCIAL AND CULTURAL VALUES	INSTITUTIONAL MEANS AND FACILITIES	ENERGY REQUIREMENTS	MATERIAL REQUIREMENTS	TECHNOLOGICAL SYSTEMS	STRUCTURES AND PRODUCTS
-1 to 0 Conception, Pre-natal, Birth										
0 to 5 Infancy										
6 to 12 Childhood Puberty										
12 to 18 Adolescence										
18 to 30 Young Adult										
30 to 42 Middle Age										
42 to 60 Late Middle Age Menopause										
60 to 100 Old Age Death										

Source: Center for Integrative Studies

Fig. 12

Changes in the proportions of age groups is a particularly important consideration in planning. A high birth rate, for example, not only connotes immediate needs in terms of food, child care and so on, but the rising numbers in that age cohort will eventually necessitate more schools, housing, jobs, health and other services. In periods of rapid change, needs and expectations will also differ markedly for different age groups, so that institutional arrangements to meet the needs of one generation may be wholly inadequate to handle those of another.

These factors may range from the effects of nutrition on prenatal and infant growth to the role of environmental factors in conditioning and facilitating need satisfactions to the differential energy, materials and product needs at varying stages in the life cycle. (Fig. 12)

The role of physical and social environmental factors is particularly critical in the early years of development and has a significant though largely unrecorded effect on growth retardation and susceptibility to disease in later life. Statistics from the poorer countries do show that high rates of infant deaths and those before five years are a major contribution to their mortality figures. All of which shows that environmental quality in the earliest years should be a focal part of basic needs planning.

In the developing world:

> "Measles and poliomyelitis are generally more severe in adults than children . . . on the other hand, children can be more quickly and severely debilitated by diarrhoaeic diseases than adults. Further, a relatively young population, compared to a relatively old population, will have a greater proportion of susceptibles because an individual's immunity to non-vectored (organism transferred) infectious diseases is a function of age. As a consequence, the underdeveloped world probably faces an increasing, rather than decreasing, risk of epidemics during the next few decades unless preventive health measures are increased accordingly. This results, first, from the declining environmental quality in both rural and urban areas resulting from population growth and rural-urban migration. Second, it happens because these areas with their high birth rates are developing a concentration of children with low levels of immunity otherwise unknown in the history of man."[2]

The allocation of social and economic resources to meet needs and effect changes may also be facilitated by life cycle and age cohort considerations. This introduces the importance of projective planning. If some desirable changes were projected as to be required optimally in twenty years time, then one might find the most effective resource allocations would be on the earliest stages of the life cycle, rather than the later.

Turning to our country groupings, it is in the C, D and E groups that the number of children under five is rising dramatically compared with that in the more affluent countries. Similarly, the numbers of those under fifteen years now and in the next twenty years represent considerable demand on educational and employment facilities, in countries where these are already under strain.

An important aspect of basic needs strategies, therefore, will be projecting and planning for the changing profile of needs and demands over the life cycle ranges in the population. Fig. 13 gives a synoptic view of the 'time relationships between a birth and future service requirements'. Such a diagram could be applied and projected for any age cohort group.

To illustrate the variable nature of the relationship between age cohort proportions and needs under different population growth rates we have approximated the same service/need relationships for Bangladesh and France, from reference country group E and A respectively. (Figs. 14, 15).

TIME RELATIONSHIPS BETWEEN A BIRTH AND FUTURE SERVICE REQUIREMENTS

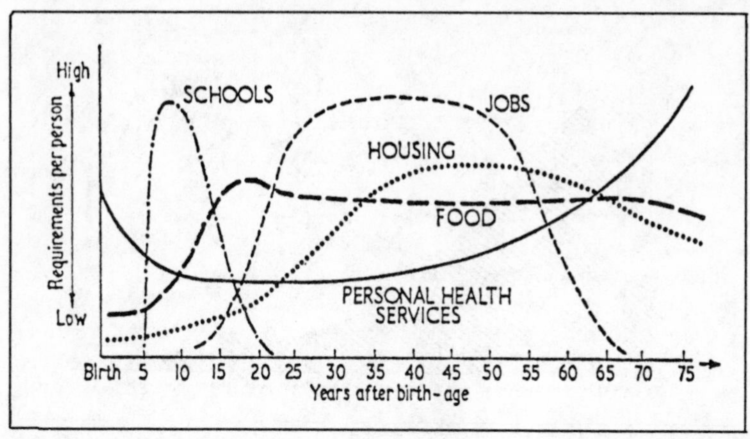

Source: U.S. National Academy of Sciences, Rapid Population Growth, 1971. Fig. 13

AGE COHORTS AND SERVICE REQUIREMENTS – France: 1975(53 million)

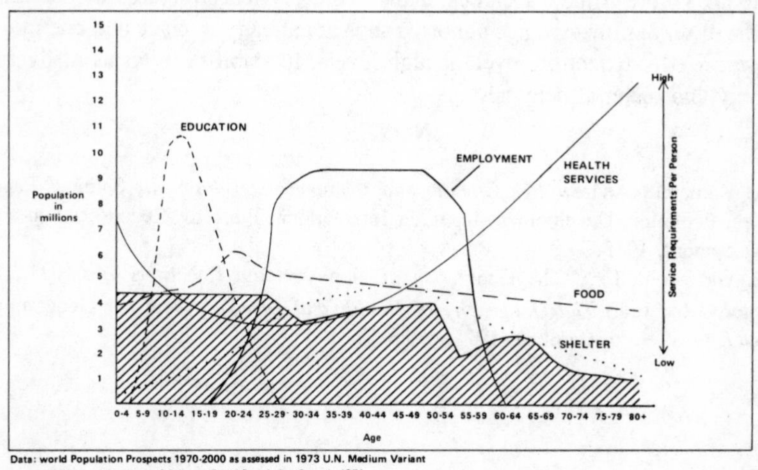

Data: world Population Prospects 1970-2000 as assessed in 1973 U.N. Medium Variant
U.S. National Academy of Sciences Rapid Population Growth, 1971
Source: Center for Integrative Studies

Fig. 14

This type of projection could show that the demand for energy, materials and products does not necessarily rise in due ratio to population growth. What matters is the age cohort distribution in population. A projected large cohort from 0 to 5 years, because of high birth rate, would certainly mean more food, shelter and clothing demand with *their* accompanying energy and materials

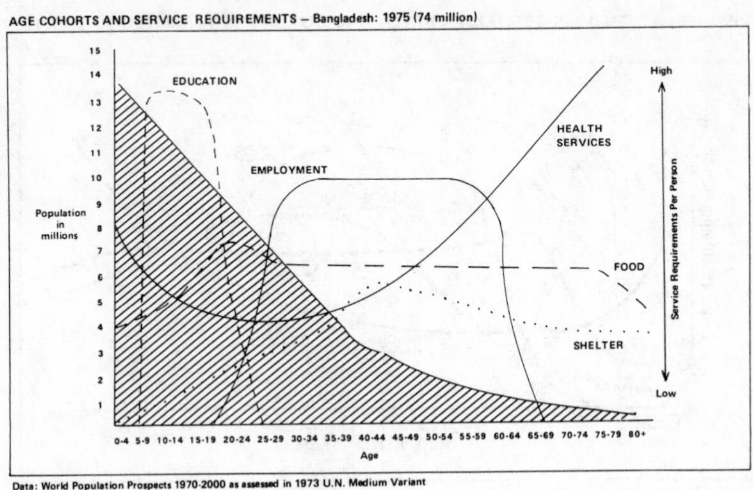

Data: World Population Prospects 1970-2000 as assessed in 1973 U.N. Medium Variant
U.S. National Academy of Sciences Rapid Population Growth, 1971
Source: Center for Integrative Studies

Fig. 15

requirements but the demand for the products required by adults would be not so great. Conversely in situations of relative population stability typical of many of today's more affluent societies, many of the physical structures and facilities that will serve projected age cohort groups are already in place and one might expect need satisfaction, even at high levels, to stabilise in terms of overall energy and material demand.

NOTES

1. Kamarck, Andrew M., *Climate and Economic Development*, Seminar Paper Series, Economic Development Institute, International Bank for Reconstruction and Development, 1975.

2. Girt, John L., "The Geography of Non-Vectored Infectious Diseases", in Hunter, J.M. (ed.) *The Geography of Health and Disease*. Dept. of Geography, University of North Carolina, 1974, p. 86.

QUANTITATIVE NEED ESTIMATES

Discussion of need in this section of the report is limited to establishing basic need levels, deficits, and targets. Exploration of how needs might be met is reserved for larger discussion in the later section on 'Meeting Basic Needs'.

Estimates are prefaced here with a brief review of population trends to establish the relative balance of population in need.

POPULATION

Our main concern here is to establish population trends for estimating present and projected needs. The control of population and access to appropriate means for family planning is, of course, a need in itself but one which is served in a major way by access to other basic needs. The core variables of population change are closely interrelated to the basic need areas. (Fig. 16)

Though our purpose here is not to enter into the population debate, it should be underlined that where we refer to explosive, abnormal, optimal or zero growth rates, these should be related specifically to some desired norm.

a) The question is often one of a particular distribution of population and of relative size. Some small countries may have high rates of growth which are a burden locally but do not add as significantly to overall world numbers as a large country with a relatively low growth rate. Some countries may need to reduce population because of increasing pressure on space and resources, others may have insufficient people to use their living space and resources economically.

b) Another misplaced emphasis associates population density and environmental stress with high population growth overall. The accompanying Fig. 17 shows some relative densities. We may note the highly concentrated populations in some of the developed countries and compare this with the developing countries which have higher growth rates, and much lower overall density.

c) Attribution of the 'population explosion' in the developing countries

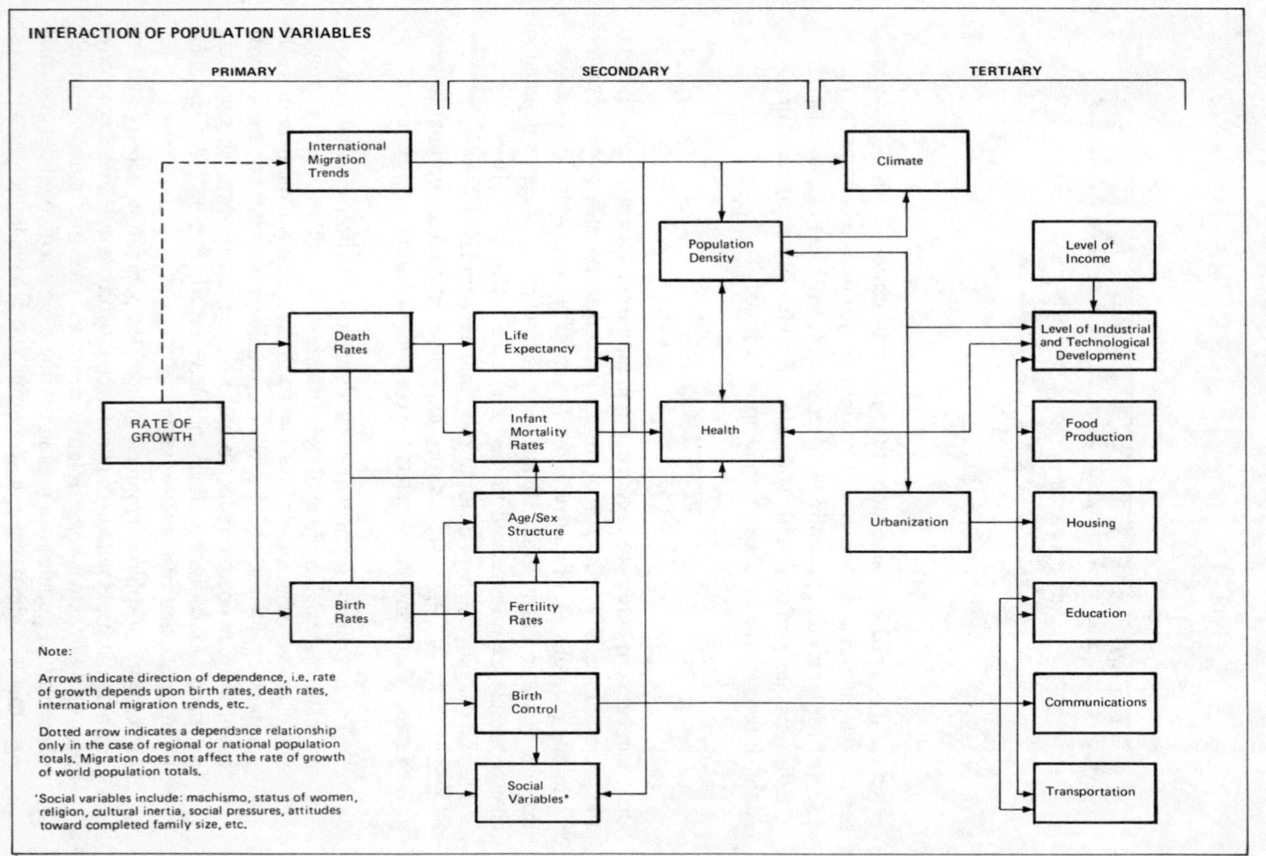

Source: Center for Integrative Studies

Fig. 16

POPULATION DENSITIES IN SELECTED DEVELOPED AND LESS DEVELOPED COUNTRIES

	Population 1976	Density on total areas	Density on agricultural land 1
	Millions		Persons/Hectare
LESS DEVELOPED COUNTRIES			
Sri Lanka	14	2.1	7.0
India	621	1.9	3.8
Pakistan	73	0.9	3.8
Philippines	44	1.5	3.9
Indonesia	135	0.7	7.5
Thailand	43	0.8	3.1
Ghana	10	0.4	3.9
United Arab Republic	38	0.4	13.3
Mexico	62	0.3	2.3
Malagassy Rep.	8	0.1	2.8
Tanzania	16	0.2	1.0
Brazil	110	0.1	3.2
Colombia	23	0.2	4.6
DEVELOPED COUNTRIES			
Japan	112	3.0	21.1
West Germany	62	2.5	7.6
United Kingdom	56	2.3	7.8
France	53	1.0	2.8
United States	215	0.2	1.1
Soviet Union	257	0.1	1.1

1. Agricultural land consisting of arable land and land under permanent crops.

Data: 1976 World Population Data Sheet of the Population Reference Bureau, Inc. 1974 FAO Production Yearbook, Vol. 28.1

Source: Center for Integrative Studies

Fig. 17

to 'death control' and improved health measures may also be somewhat specious. As a recently detailed analysis comments:

"It would seem that the global decline of death rates has been attributed to mass campaigns against malaria which are as yet inconclusive, to drugs which are largely inaccessible, to doctors who are unavailable and to sanitation programs which do not exist."[1]

Actually, the reverse has been shown to be the case. Where infant mortality is reduced, more 'life' security has been given by better ser-

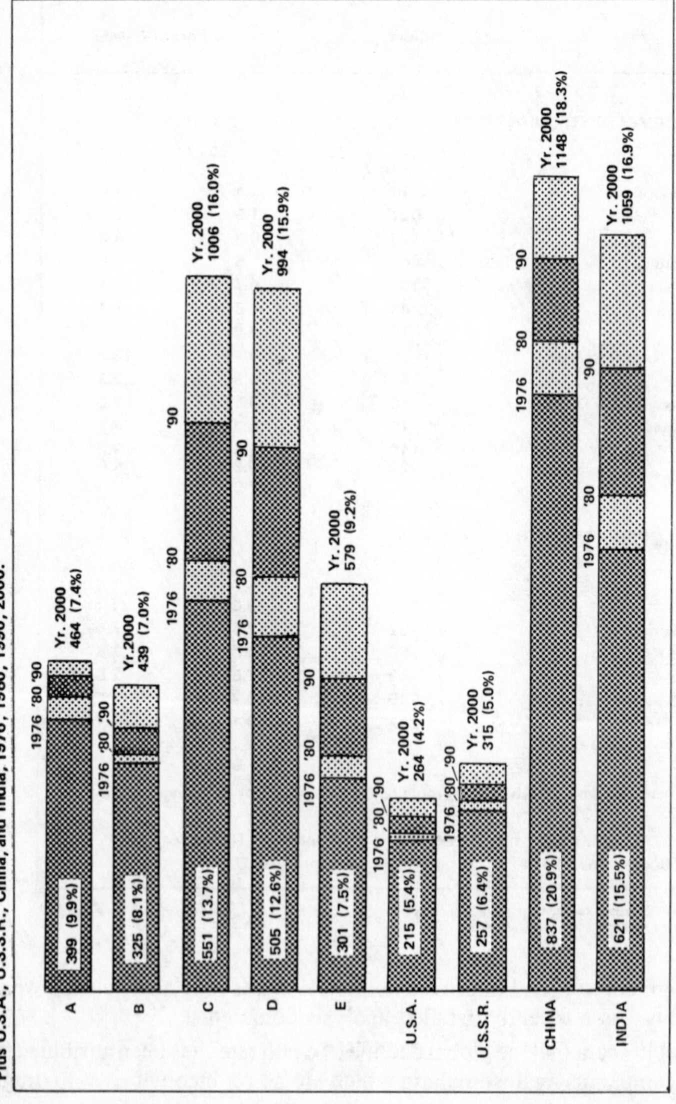

Data: (for 1976 population) World Population Data Sheet of the Population Reference Bureau

World Population Prospects, 1970-2000 as assessed in 1973; U.N. ECOSOC 1975 (Medium Variant)

Source: Center for Integrative Studies

Fig. 18

vices, and basic needs are being met beyond the margins of subsistence; Under these circumstances there are more incentives to reduce family size.

d) Over-emphasis on the population per se may obscure other problems. In many countries even if population growth were suddenly to cease tomorrow, the lot of poorer people would not necessarily change appreciably—for the real problems may be grossly inequable income distribution, land tenure practices or other social and institutional inequalities which restrict access to basic needs security.

The following table (Fig. 18) gives the comparative population growth projections for all countries in the world, classified in our A, B, C, D, and E categories, with their percentages of the world population.

It may be seen that the population size and growth rate of the more affluent countries with higher living standards are relatively the lowest and most stable. Though the growth rates of the less affluent look abnormally high by comparison, shown in this way, the aggregation conceals many successful reductions in undue growth. China is one of the most striking examples where the decline in birth rate was accompanied not only by strong efforts to reduce fertility but also, and importantly, by equally strong efforts to meet the basic needs of the majority of its people. Successful slowing of growth has also been attained by a number of developing countries, for example, in Asia: both Koreas, Singapore, Sri Lanka, Taiwan and the Phillipines; and in Latin America: Costa Rica, Cuba, Puerto Rico, Chile and Uruguay.

WORLD POPULATION PROJECTION

Year	1970		1980		1990		2000		2010		2020
Nos. in millions	3,632		4,434		5,140		5,937		6,689		7,461
% Growth Rate		1.8		1.7		1.5-1.4		1.2		1.1	

Source: "The Timetable Project", Center for Integrative Studies, 1972.

Fig. 19

In terms of projected world totals, though these show an approximate doubling by the year 2000 there is a perceptible slowing of overall growth rates in the next twenty-five years. (Fig. 19)

In 1975, the U.N. Population Division assessing world population prospects stated that, "... for the first time in the experience of the United Nations estimated population trends had to be revised downwards". (Fig. 20)

Notwithstanding this projected decline in population growth rates later in the century, the developing world will still have many more people to take care of i.e. 3,193 million, or 73 percent of the world population by 1980, and by the year 2000, 4,894 million or 78 percent.

POPULATION PROJECTIONS BY REGIONS

(Medium Variant Projections of U.N. Population Division)

	Region	Population (thousands)				Annual Rates of Growth (Percentage)			
		1975	1980	1990	2000	70-75	75-80	85-90	95-2000
World	World Total	3,967,005	4,373,210	5,279,041	6,253,135	1.89	1.95	1.84	1.64
Africa	Eastern Africa	114,498	131,992	177,581	239,861	2.74	2.84	3.00	2.98
	Middle Africa	45,310	51,201	66,735	87,732	2.27	2.44	2.68	2.74
	Northern Africa	98,185	113,055	149,748	191,824	2.74	2.82	2.78	2.35
	Southern Africa	27,678	31,950	42,321	55,669	2.68	2.87	2.77	2.72
	Western Africa	115,469	132,488	177,329	238,034	2.58	2.75	2.95	2.92
America	Caribbean	27,116	30,016	36,847	44,504	1.93	2.03	2.04	1.81
	Middle America	78,652	92,631	128,160	172,670	3.21	3.27	3.21	2.91
	Temperate South America	38,747	41,564	47,152	52,078	1.43	1.40	1.20	0.93
	Tropical South America	179,578	207,421	273,426	350,676	2.90	2.88	2.71	2.41
	Northern America	236,841	248,833	275,136	296,199	0.90	0.99	0.95	0.69
Asia	China	838,803	907,609	1,031,142	1,147,987	1.66	1.58	1.16	1.04
	Japan	111,120	117,546	126,213	132,929	1.26	1.12	0.61	0.51
	Other East Asia	55,742	61,853	75,363	88,153	2.15	2.08	1.91	1.47
	Eastern South Asia	323,836	370,855	478,712	591,622	2.70	2.71	2.46	1.99
	Middle South Asia	837,799	953,997	1,221,669	1,501,213	2.44	2.60	2.40	1.93
	Western South Asia	88,158	101,992	135,877	174,432	2.83	2.92	2.81	2.36
Europe	Eastern Europe	106,297	109,717	115,780	121,749	0.64	0.63	0.51	0.52
	Northern Europe	81,975	83,740	87,424	91,320	0.41	0.43	0.44	0.44
	Southern Europe	132,354	137,106	146,669	155,685	0.72	0.71	0.66	0.57
	Western Europe	152,503	156,049	163,906	171,058	0.58	0.46	0.50	0.40
U.S.S.R.	U.S.S.R.	255,038	268,115	293,742	315,027	0.99	1.00	0.85	0.67
Oceania	Australia - New Zealand	16,840	18,403	21,549	24,512	1.83	1.78	1.49	1.24
	Melanesia	3,126	3,555	4,630	5,847	2.41	2.57	2.64	2.17
	Micronesia - Polynesia	1,341	1,524	1,930	2,356	2.55	2.55	2.28	1.86

Source : World Population Prospects, 1970 - 2000, as assessed in 1973, Population Division, Dept. of Economic and Social Affairs of the United Nations, 1975.

Fig. 20

In the next twenty-five years:

Africa—will increase by 412 million or 102 percent. In the year 2000, the largest single nation will be Nigeria with 135 million: the next largest, Egypt with 65 million.

Asia—will increase by 1,381 million or 61 percent. In the year 2000, the largest single nation will be China with 1,148 million: the next largest, India with 1,059 million.

Latin America—will increase by 296 million or 96 percent. In the year 2000, the largest single nation will be Brazil with 212.5 million: the next largest, Mexico with 132 million.

Europe—will increase by 66 million or 14 percent. In the year 2000, the largest single nation will be West Germany with 66 million: the next largest, U.K. with 63 million.

INCREASE IN POPULATION UNDER 5 YEARS OLD FROM 1975

Increase in Millions

Total Reference Country Group*	By 1980	By 1990	By 2000
A	4.8	8.8	7.8
B	2.8	7.7	12.0
C	13.8	25.6	41.4
D	12.8	36.8	52.1
E	20.3	51.6	65.2
Total	54.5	130.5	647.4

Increase as Per Cent

Total Reference Country Group*	1975–80	1980-1990	1990-2000
A	6.8	5.3	– 1.3
B	8.7	14.0	10.8
C	7.4	5.9	7.4
D	14.2	23.3	12.1
E	13.4	18.3	6.7

N. B. Where minus numbers are given, e.g. -1.3, the population of this age group is less than 1990 i.e. has decreased by 2000.

* All Countries in the world assigned to A,B,C,D,E, classificastions not the average of the 7 reference country set.

Data: World Population Prospects 1970-2000 As Assessed in 1973, UN ECOSOC, 1975 Medium Variant.

Source: Center for Integrative Studies

Fig. 21

INCREASE IN POPULATION UNDER 15 YEARS OLD FROM 1975

Increase in Millions

Total Reference Country Group*	By 1980	By 1990	By 2000
A	– 1.3	16.9	18.7
B	5.4	17.5	33.6
C	43.9	112.0	153.7
D	34.8	104.4	163.2
E	48.3	154.3	226.0
Total	131.1	405.1	595.2

Increase as Per Cent

Total Reference Country Group*	1975–80	1980-1990	1990-2000
A	– 0.6	8.5	0.8
B	5.9	11.8	14.7
C	8.7	12.4	6.8
D	15.5	26.8	17.9
E	12.4	24.2	13.2

N. B. Where minus numbers are given, e.g. -0.6, the population of this age group is less than 1975 i.e. has decreased by 1980.

* All Countries in the world assigned to A,B,C,D,E classifications, not the average of the 7 reference country set.

Data: World Population Prospects 1970-2000 As Assessed in 1973, UN ECOSOC, 1975, Medium Variant.

Source: Center for Integrative Studies.

Fig. 22

U.S.S.R.—will increase by 60 million or 24 percent.
North America—will increase by 59 million or 25 percent.

One of the critical factors in estimating basic needs in changing population growth situations is the large numbers of younger people being added to the population and requiring additional health care, educational and housing services. The relative increase of those under 5 and those under 15 years of age is shown in Figs. 21, 22, for all countries in the world assigned to the A, B, C, D, and E classification. This age differential will be critical in gauging the relative

PROJECTED WORLD POPULATION INCREASE (%)

Total Reference Country Group*	1976-80	1980-90	1990-2000
A	3.8	8.4	6.4
B	4.5	13.9	13.6
C	9.9	20.1	17.6
D	15.4	32.6	28.6
E	11.8	28.0	22.1

* All countries in the world assigned to A,B,C,D,E classifications, not the average of the 7 reference country set.

N.B. The E Countries' relatively slower population growth compared to the D Countries is largely accounted for by India's slower projected rate of growth.
The forecast of population increase for E Countries without India is :

	1976-80	1980-90	1990-2000
E's without India	11.7	31.8	30.3

Data : 1976 World Population Data Sheet, Population Reference Bureau; Medium Variant, World Population Prospects, 1970 – 2000, As Assessed in 1973, UN ECOSOC, 1975.

Source : Center for Integrative Studies.

Fig. 23

needs of these different countries. The poorer will have a larger increase in the young and the employment age range, the richer relative more in the older age ranges.

The generalised picture (Fig. 23) in relation to basic needs is that, *Population Growth will be highest* in those countries:

a) least developed in material socio-economic terms.
b) having a high population to usable resource ratio.
c) with low nutrition, health and life expectancy.
d) with low individual social expectations and security.

Population Growth will be lowest, and most stable, in those countries:

a) economically and technologically developed.
b) with a low population to developed resource ratio and productive capacity.
c) with high nutrition, health and life expectancy.
d) with high individual social expectations and security.

The capacity of the poorer countries to meet their basic needs and raise living levels will, therefore, be hampered by their accompanying increase in numbers. This is a double-bind situation since there is little motivation to reduce family numbers when basic survival appears to depend on the number of persons who can work together to achieve subsistence.

The question of population numbers and basic needs is therefore one of close dynamic feedback, in which strategies for the satisfaction of basic needs should include, and further, population growth policies.

LIFE CYCLE ALTERNATIVES

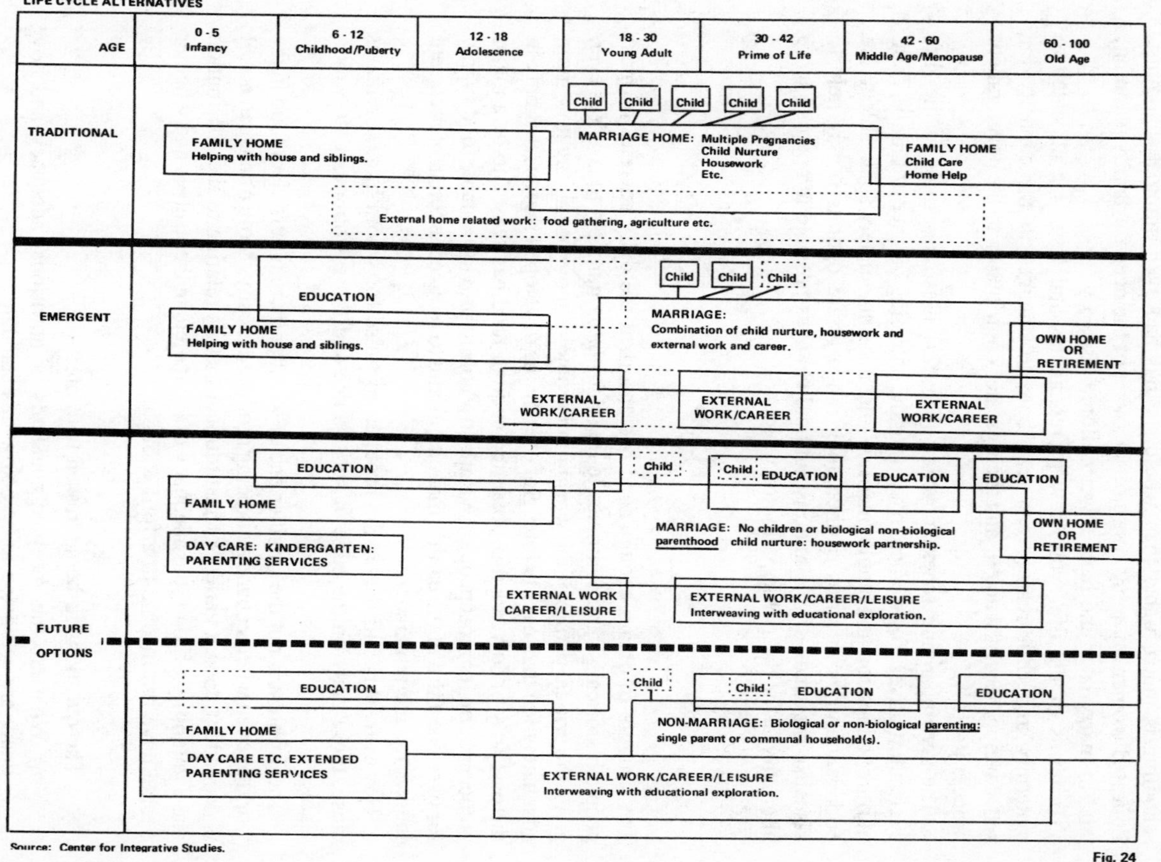

Source: Center for Integrative Studies.

Fig. 24

Education is a key factor in both population and basic needs policies. There is an obvious correlation between population growth and female education. In almost all cases, the average size of a family where the woman has no formal schooling is much higher than where she has had even minimal schooling. Educated women are more consciously aware of the need for family planning, tend to marry later and have fewer children.

In terms of the life cycle, fewer pregnancies and less time allocated to maternity and child-rearing can lead both to changes in the capacity for self-development of women, and their greater contribution to the development process itself.

The accompanying schematic chart (Fig. 24) illustrates some of the 'life cycle alternatives' for women in terms of the changing balance of family, child nurture, education and employment. Whilst not immediately applicable to the poorer countries in terms of their long range future options it may help to visualise the kinds of role and institutional changes possible in opening more alternatives for the participation of women.

FOOD

The struggle to obtain enough food has absorbed the daily energies of most people historically, and continues to do so for large numbers today. Yet even given the critical nature of the world food problem, more people are now more adequately fed than ever before. But even in the developed regions it is only in the past fifty or so years that obtaining enough food has ceased to be a major preoccupation for most people. We are now able to provide a stable food supply for over one-third of the earth's inhabitants and to reduce the threat of recurrent famine for the remainder.

However, this still leaves the problem of those for whom hunger remains close, those daily on the edge of subsistence and those who are at starvation levels.

The problem is not the singular one of whether there is sufficient food in the world or even whether enough is being produced locally. More often than not, it is dependent upon a variety of institutional factors relating to the distribution and availability of food, the adequacy of local diets in themselves and whether people have the income to afford enough.

The questions to be addressed here are:

a) What are the accepted standards of nutritional adequacy and how many are estimated to be below this standard?

b) Given that, in aggregate terms, adequate food can and is being produced at the world level, what are the comparative indicators of food need?

The standards of nutritional adequacy vary over time as more is learnt about what constitutes an individual's food requirements.

> "Nutrition is still a young science; and these requirements, more properly called 'recommended allowances' are not nearly so precise as we would like them to be . . . The blunt truth is that we still do not know the nutritional requirements for various populations under various environmental conditions. The organisations charged with preparing estimates, therefore, have consciously erred on the side of control."[2]

In assessing daily food requirements there has been a recent change in emphasis from protein to overall calorie levels as the major indicator of food energy—on the assumption that if calorie levels are adequate then there will be sufficient protein. The 'average' level of calorie adequacy set by FAO/WHO for an adult is 3,000 calories per head per day. To allow for the age-mix composition for a total regional population, we have set our average working level here at 2,370 calories per day, with calorie conversion to quantities of food at the following rates. A thousand calories are produced by:

0.29 kg. of all cereals
1.11 kg. of starchy roots
0.79 kg. of meat and fish
1.18 kg. of eggs and milk

N.B. No account has been taken here of wastage or of different qualities of the various foods.

Numbers of People at Insufficient Food Energy Levels

FAO gave the percentages or country populations that are below the lower limit for 1970 for the major world regions (excluding centrally planned economies) as follows:

Developed regions	3%
Latin America	13%
Far East	30%
Near East	18%
Africa	25%

If we are to accept that these are the proportions of the world's population that are in need of food then it can be calculated that the numbers and percentages for all countries in the world classified into our comparative reference groups are as follows (Fig. 25):

NUMBERS, IN MILLIONS, AND PERCENTAGE OF PEOPLE WITH INSUFFICIENT PROTEIN/ENERGY (1976)

	A	B	C	D	E
NUMBERS (in millions)	26.1	20.0	119.6	135.6	267.9
PERCENTAGE	3	6	9	27	29

Source : Center for Integrative Studies

Fig. 25

One should note that the small percentages suffering food needs in the more affluent countries could certainly be taken care of within the resources of those countries. The obvious target populations of the most needy are in the D and E country groups, and within those there are considerable variations in food production, marketing procedures and dietary composition.

World Food Production Levels

Concerns over world food levels have been exacerbated by crop failures during 1972 in certain countries. The failures were due to many physical factors such as bad weather but these were amplified by accompanying fuel shortages and inflationary prices for supplies of fertiliser and the like. Overall, this has focussed attention on the urgent need for a food reserve against such contingencies and for ways to increase and stabilise local production.

In terms of actual world food supply this crisis was not evidence for neo-Malthusian alarm. As the U.N. World Food Conference noted in 1974:

> "The fact that for so long a period food production in the developing countries as a whole has kept ahead of a rate of population growth that is unprecedented in world history is a tremendous achievement. Furthermore, food production in these countries in 1972 was 20 percent greater than in 1966, the previous year of widespread bad weather so that even between the troughs of the longer term trend, production has outpaced population growth. In many individual countries, however, developments have been much less favorable."[3]

World production across the ranges of various foodstuffs is given in Fig. 26. The aggregated figures show that according to recorded statistics, even in the poorer countries, more than sufficient cereals and root crops are being produced to satisfy nutritional requirements.

> "Present world grain production could more than adequately feed every person on earth. Even during the 'scarcity' years of 1972-73, there was 9

WORLD FOOD PRODUCTION SUMMARY (Million Metric Tons)

	Total Cereals	Root Crops	Sugar	Total Pulses	Total Nuts	Vegetables & Melons	Fruits	Total Meat	Hen Eggs	Total Milk	Vegetable Oils	Fish[1]
World	1,358.8	566.5	81.9	46.8	3.6	294.7	255.6	117.7	23.3	427.2	41.5	50.8
Developed Market Economies	480.2	72.3	24.4	3.4	1.6	94.1	101.9	55.9	11.3	207.5	12.5	20.1
North America	285.2	17.1	6.2	1.1	0.4	27.1	25.5	25.1	4.1	60.3	9.8	2.5
Western Europe	146.9	48.4	12.8	1.8	1.1	49.0	62.7	24.2	5.0	125.4	2.3	7.8
Oceania	18.1	0.9	2.9	0.2	—	1.3	2.2	3.5	0.2	12.8	0.1	0.1
Other	30.0	6.0	2.5	0.3	0.1	16.8	11.5	3.1	2.0	8.9	0.3	9.7
Developing Market Economies	419.6	175.2	40.6	24.2	1.7	101.7	123.7	21.7	3.5	83.1	20.0	14.4
Africa	41.9	74.2	2.8	4.7	0.6	9.9	22.9	3.3	0.5	6.3	3.7	2.0
Latin America	80.2	45.9	24.1	5.0	0.1	13.4	52.7	11.3	1.8	29.0	4.5	0.7
Near East	53.2	5.7	2.5	1.7	0.7	25.6	14.8	2.7	0.4	13.3	1.5	—
Asia & Far East	244.3	47.7	11.0	12.8	0.3	52.4	32.2	4.3	0.9	34.4	10.0	11.7
Other	—	1.6	0.3	—	—	0.3	1.1	0.1	—	0.1	0.3	—
Centrally Planned Economies	459.0	318.9	16.9	19.2	0.3	98.9	30.0	40.1	8.4	136.7	9.0	16.3
Asia	250.6	158.4	4.3	12.3	—	58.6	7.9	16.2	3.8	5.6	4.7	7.6
USSR & Eastern Europe	208.4	160.5	12.6	6.9	0.3	40.3	22.2	23.9	4.6	131.1	4.3	8.7

1. 1973. From U.N. Stat. Book, 1974. Estimated proportion of fish catch used for food.

Data: Monthly Bulletin of Agricultural Economics and Statistics, April 1976.

Source: Center for Integrative Studies

Fig. 26

percent more grain per person than in 'ample' years like 1960. Inadequate production is clearly not the problem.''[4]

The eggs and milk shortfall is about 23 percent; and meat and fish production is only about 27 percent of what is required for more balanced adequacy. Also figures are aggregated across all the poorest countries which disguises pockets of acute malnutrition.

In general, therefore, the appearance of sufficiency in the major food sources has to be seen against varying situations of maldistribution and of dietary imbalance—with insufficiency in the protein sources of meat, fish, and dairy products. There is also considerable discrepancy in the available data especially where vegetables, roots and berries are concerned.

The forecast volume of food demand is estimated to be 18 percent higher in 1985 than 1970, e.g.,

Africa 3.8% of which 2.9% will be accounted for by population growth
Near East 4.0% of which 2.9% will be accounted for by population growth

CLASSIFICATION OF COUNTRIES BY FOOD ZONES

Group A	Animal foods : Australia, Austria, Canada, Denmark, Finland, Iceland, Ireland, Netherlands, New Zealand, Norway, Panama, Puerto Rico, Sweden, United States, Uruguay.
Group B :	Animal foods/wheat : Albania, Argentina, Belgium, Luxembourg, Bolivia, Bulgaria, Chile, Costa Rica, Cuba, Czechoslovakia, France, German Democratic Republic, Federal Republic of Germany, Greece, Hungary, Israel ; Italy, Jamaica, Malta, Peru, Poland, Portugal, Romania, Spain, Switzerland, Trinidad, and Tobago, U.S.S.R., United Kingdom, Venezuela, Yugoslavia.
Group C :	Animal foods/ cereals other than wheat: Colombia, Dominican Republic, El Salvador, Guyana, Hong Kong, Japan, Mongolia, Philippines, Singapore, Somalia, South Africa, Sudan, Surinam, Tanzania, People's Democratic Republic of Yemen.
Group D :	Wheat : Afghanistan, Algeria, Cyprus, Egypt, Iran, Iraq, Jordan, Lebanon, Libyan Arab Republic, Morocco, Pakistan, Syrian Arab Republic, Tunisia, Turkey.
Group E :	Rice : Bangladesh, Burma, Indonesia, Khmer Republic, Laos, Liberia, Madagascar, Malaysia (West), Sabah, Sarawak, Sierra Leone, Sri Lanka, Thailand, Democratic Republic of Viet-Nam, Republic of Viet-Nam.
Group F :	Mixed Cereals : Burundi, China, Ethiopa, Guinea, India, Democratic People's Republic of Korea, Republic of Korea, Mauritius, Mozambique, Nepal, Saudi Arabia.
Group G :	Millet : Chad, Mali, Mauritania, Niger, Upper Volta, Yemen Arab Republic.
Group H :	Maize : Kenya, Malawi, Mexico, Rhodesia, Zambia.
Group I :	Animal foods/roots/cereals/pulses : Angola, Brazil, Cameroon, Central African Republic, People's Republic of Congo, Dahomey, Ecuador, Gabon, Gambia, Ghana, Guatemala, Haiti, Honduras, Ivory Coast, Nicaragua, Nigeria, Rwanda, Senegal, Togo, Uganda, Zaire.

Source : The State of Food and Agriculture, 1974, FAO. **Fig. 27**

Far East 3.4% of which 2.6% will be accounted for by population growth

Latin American 3.6% of which 2.8% will be accounted for by population growth

Developed Market Economies 1.4% of which 0.9% will be accounted for by population growth

Eastern Europe and USSR 1.7% of which 0.9% will be accounted for by population growth

World 2.4% of which 2.0% will be accounted for by population growth[5]

Supply extrapolations through this period based on 1961/3–1973 production rates are given as:

Developing Countries	2.6% p.a. production growth rate
Developed Market Economies	7.4% p.a. production growth rate
E. Europe and USSR	3.5% p.a. production growth rate

This suggests a degree of cereal dependence of the developing world for the next period—which may be more apparent than real in view of more recent recoveries in production in some of these countries.

Specific Deficits in Needy Countries

We can gain a closer approximation of food deficits by gearing them to the dietary variations in the major food zones.[6] Nine zones have been delineated by the FAO with countries grouped according to main food sources, e.g. rice, wheat, maize, etc., and the percentage contribution of different foods in these zones to the population's intake of energy and protein. (Fig. 27, 28)

Using this food zone approach to dietary requirements we have estimated the additional production needed in calorie deficient regions in 1976. (Fig. 29) This gives a deficit for the poorer regions of some 73 million metric tons of which approximately 28 million tons should be made up of grains.

The deficit is also expressed as a percentage of supply over current production in Fig. 30 which emphasises the relatively small amount needed in aggregate terms.

The projected food production for the 32 poorest countries, those in our E group, in Fig. 31, assumes only that the increase in productivity will rise in proportion to the population through 1980, 1990 and 2000. The additional projection (Fig. 32) shows what will be needed if these countries are to satisfy the minimum calorie requirements according to the specific foods associated with food zones. This projection shows a marginally smaller requirement for cereals and starchy roots but a significantly greater need for meat and fish, eggs and milk.

MAJOR SOURCES OF NUTRITION : By Food Zone, and Population in Need

Food Zone	% Contribution of Different Foods To Total Intake	Cereals	Starchy Roots	Meat & Fish	Eggs & Milk	% of Calorie Intake From Other Sources *	% Population in Need (Average Estimate)
1. Animal Foods/Roots/Cereals/Pulses	Calories	36	25	6	3	30	25
	Protein	37	12	19	8		
2. Rice	Calories	71	7	3	2	18	28
	Protein	64	3	13	5		
3. Mixed Cereals	Calories	68	8	4	2	18	27
	Protein	60	4	9	5		
4. Millet	Calories	73	2	4	3	18	26
	Protein	62	—	11	6		
5. Maize	Calories	56	3	6	4	20	25
	Protein	54	1	17	9		
6. Animal Foods/Cereals Other Than Wheat	Calories	51	7	8	6	28	26
	Protein	41	2	27	13		
7. Wheat	Calories	64	1	3	2	28	30
	Protein	67	1	13	5		

* Other sources required to meet calorie needs are : Sugar; Pulses and Nuts; Fruits and Vegetables; Fats and Oils.

Data : Based on estimates in The State of Food and Agriculture, FAO, 1974.

Fig. 28

Source : Center for Integrative Studies.

ADDITIONAL PRODUCTION REQUIRED IN CALORIE-DEFICIENT[1] WORLD REGIONS, 1976
(In Thousand Metric Tons)

Region \ Food Type	Cereals	Starchy Roots	Sugar	Pulses & Nuts	Fruits & Vegetables	Meat & Fish	Eggs & Milk	Fats & Oils
North Africa	826	108	130	68	734	144	287	42
West Africa	780	1,373	129	189	961	267	213	42
East Africa	961	570	103	142	536	211	181	31
Mid Africa	478	1,077	96	129	739	195	151	32
Mid-South Asia	18,272	7,136	1,454	2,177	7,557	2,781	2,732	495
Southeast Asia	6,725	2,667	553	610	3,545	1,004	1,043	174
Tropical S. America (Less Brazil)	360	286	99	42	430	230	283	35
Total	28,402	13,217	2,564	3,357	14,502	4,832	4,890	851

1. On basis of calorie per capita estimates, World Food Conference, Assessment of World Food Situation - Present and Future, FAO, 1974.

N.B. By calculating the aggregated short-fall per region from 2370 calories per capita per day in terms of 1975 food production. East Asia, which includes China, is technically a calorie deficient region, but it is not included in the total.

Source : Center for Integrative Studies.

Fig. 29

Even with the projected increase in volume to meet the deficit and that required for a more balanced diet, the aggregate amounts are not excessive in terms of both world and local production.

One important protein source within the deficit range is, of course, fish (Fig. 34), providing about 10 percent of the protein available to the present world population but only a small part of overall food energy. Recent estimates suggest that, "The maximum sustainable fish yield is probably not more than twice the present one."[7]

The actual total fish catch in 1973 was 65.7 million metric tons, of which the freshwater catch was 9.8 million metric tons with China accounting for 4.6 million metric tons, i.e. 47% of the total freshwater catch.[8]

Though the sea catch may be limited in yield, local freshwater fish farming could, and does, add significantly to the availability of fish protein.

It is clear that much current malnutrition in the poorer countries is due to low income often directly associated with local production well below possible yields. Closing both the income and the production gap is clearly within the desirable basic needs strategies of those countries, accompanied by stronger regional cooperation and international assistance directed specifically to these ends.

CALORIE - DEFICIT REGIONS, 1976

Percentage of Additional Supply Required Over Current Production

	Cereals	Starchy Roots	Sugar	Pulses & Nuts	Fruits & Vegetables	Meat & Fish	Eggs & Milk	Fats & Oils
Africa	7.0	4.0	18.0	9.0	9.0	16.0	12.0	4.0
South Asia	10.0	21.0	18.0	21.0	13.0	24.0	11.0	6.0
South America	0.5	0.5	0.5	1.0	0.5	2.0	1.0	1.0

Data: FAO Production Yearbook, 1974

Source: Center for Integrative Studies

Fig. 30

Food Production Required: To feed future population of 'E' Group countries at same standard as 1974. (Million Metric Tons)

	1974	1980	1990	2000
Total Cereals	157	184	237	293
Starchy Roots	52	61	81	107
Meat & Fish	7	8	11	14
Eggs & Milk	17	20	26	33

Poorest Countries ('E' Group)
32 Countries 919 Million Pop. (1976)

Data: Projected from 1974 data in FAO Production Yearbook, 1974 using for population growth rate the medium variant in World Population Prospects, 1970 – 2000, As Assessed in 1973, U N ECOSOC, 1975.

Source: Center for Integrative Studies Fig. 31

Food Production Required: To provide a more balanced diet for population of 'E' Group countries at average daily per cap. calorie intake of 2370. (Million Metric Tons)

	1976	1980	1990	2000
Total Cereals	150	167	218	272
Starchy Roots	51	57	74	91
Meat & Fish	26	29	38	48
Eggs & Milk	22	24	32	40

Poorest Countries ('E'Group)
32 Countries 919 Million Pop. (1976)

Data: Population from 1976 World Population Data Sheet of the Population Reference Bureau. Diet balance is according to food zone of each country as suggested by FAO, The State of Food and Agriculture, 1974. Population growth rates from medium variant in World Population Prospects 1970 – 2000 As Assessed in 1973. UN ECOSOC, 1975.

Source: Center for Integrative Studies Fig. 32

FOOD DEFICIT ESTIMATES

Note : Food deficits in meeting current needs may be estimated as 73 million metric tons, of which approximately 28 million metric tons should be made up of grains. Other recent estimates of the world food gap are :

	Million Metric Tons Cereals	Region	Source
1969 – 71	5.0	Total Developing Countries	FAO, 1974.
1969 – 71	23.5	Total Developing Countries	USDA, 1974.
1969 – 71	16.0	Developing Market Economies	FAO, 1974.
1969 – 71	20.5	Developing Market Economies	USDA, 1974.
1985	76.0	Total Developing Countries	FAO, 1974.
1985	58.8	Total Developing Countries	USDA, 1974.
1985	85.0	Developing Market Economies	FAO, 1974.
1985	54.7	Developing Market Economies	USDA, 1974.
1975	19.0	Cereal import requirements for 44 most seriously affected countries	FAO, 1976.

Sources : FAO, 1974 Assessment of the World Food Situation, Present and Future, FAO, 1974.
USDA, 1974 The World Food Situation and Prospects to 1985, U.S. Dept. of Agriculture Foreign Agricultural Economic Report No. 98.
FAO, 1976 Monthly Bulletin of Agricultural Economics and Statistics, FAO, May 1976.

Fig. 33

Protein Available From Domestic Fish Caught For Food

	Catch, 1975 Estimate (Million Tons)	Total Available Protein[1] (Million Tons)	Grams Protein Per Cap Per Day
World	51.9	5.2	3.6
More Developed Regions	28.8	2.9	7.0
Less Developed Regions	23.1	2:3	2.2

1. Assuming 10% of fish catch is consumed as protein. (calculated from average of 12 countries in FAO, Agricultural Commodity Projections, 1970-1980, 1971.

Data : Provisional Indicative World Plan for Agricultural Development, Volume I, FAO, 1970, page 292.

Source : Center for Integrative Studies.

Fig. 34

HEALTH

We have customarily gauged health negatively in terms of relative freedom from sickness or debilitating disease. Yet, as other needs are satisfied, 'positive' health comes to be regarded as an attainable standard and basic right—even where it may be difficult to define or substantiate. Curative health measures are broadened to include programs of preventative medicine and health maintenance.

To a certain extent, health is a purchasable commodity. Those above the economic level of deficiency tend to be healthier than those in chronic poverty; they are better provided with health safeguards such as good sanitation, clean water and more salubrious environmental conditions. Those in the more affluent countries benefit from large and long-term investment in public health, medical research and wide ranging health services.

Definitions of 'positive' health still vary considerably from culture to culture as do attitudes and aspirations regarding general health. Apart from life expectancy, our statistical indicators of health are largely those of ill-health—death rates, infant mortality, physician:population and hospital:bed ratios. Though we use such available indicators for our present purposes, we should recognise that they are, in most cases, surrogate indicators for complex conditions of health maintenance. The expectation of life in years from birth may appear to be a useful index of general health for a society but such condensed indices may not reflect the actual multi-dimensional nature of health assessment.

For easy reference, some key conventional indicators are summarised for our averaged reference countries, (Fig. 35). They serve to indicate the contrasts in available services, life expectancy and health expenditures per caput.

In pursuing more positive health measures, as well as the reduction of disease, we should really seek for indicators that include variations in perceptions of health, and the attitudes and aspirations of those peoples under consideration. Like many of our needs, health is a moving target. Its definition, therefore, rather than being conceived in absolute terms may be better accommodated by considering changes in its perception and by transitions in health status brought about by indirect means.

> "It is widely and explicity recognised that transitions from one stage of health to another can be and often are brought about by means—such as changes in the provision of food, water, clothing and shelter—other than the application of or withholding of medical care."[9]

Health and Environment

Environmental dimensions of the health and disease patterns in the poorer countries are clearly paramount. Many of these countries are located in tropical

HEALTH INDICATORS : Averaged Reference Country Group*

	Life Expectancy at Birth: Male	Life Expectancy at Birth: Female	Infant Mortality per 1,000 Live Births	Hospital Beds (Pop. per)	Physicians (Pop. per)	Nurses and Midwives (Pop. per)	Crude Death Rate per 1,000	Crude Birth Rate per 1,000
A	69	76	14	84	716	264	15	9.7
B	66	70	34	268	837	638	24	7.7
C	57	58	79	388	2,810	1,747	37	11.4
D	48	48	128	817	12,196	2,957	45	16.9
E	39	39	164	2,971	32,584	7,462	46	21.6
USA	67.4	75.1	17	138	621	187	15	9
USSR	65	74	28	89	390	174	18	9
China	50	50	NA	NA	NA	NA	27	10
India	42	41	139	1,571	4,795	8,165	35	15

NA : Not Available

Data : 1974 UN Statistical Yearbook.
1976 World Population Data Sheet.
World Health Statistics Annual 1972, WHO, 1976.

* The average of the seven reference countries in the appropriate A, B, C, D, E classifications.

Source : Center for Integrative Studies.

Fig. 35

and semi-tropical climates which have endemic disease problems due to specific environmental vectors. And other aspects of their physical, social and economic environment render them prey to the ills of poverty. Unsafe water supplies, lack of sanitation and adequte drainage, food contamination by flies, inadequate housing, poor nutrition and low general hygiene contribute to a synergism in the ecology of poverty which accounts directly, and indirectly, for the majority of deaths amongst the young and high incidence of debilitating ill health and chronic conditions in adults.

Many of these environmental conditions can be adjusted and health improved without recourse therefore to elaborate and costly programs of remedial health and their attendant physical facilities. Efforts towards better environmental management and in the general improvements of living standards would not only contribute to general health but reduce the incidence of specific water and airborne diseases prevalent in the poorer regions, e.g., hookworm, amoebic and bacillary dysentery, tuberculosis, trachoma and schistosomiasis.

Malnutrition should also be underlined as an environmental determinant of health in the poorer countries, which in turn is attributed to ecological and agricultural limitations to food production, low income, poor nutritional knowledge and inadequate food hygiene. It is estimated that severe malnutrition affects about 10 million children under five and another 90 million suffer from moderate malnutrition. Apart from being in itself a cause of infant and child mortality, this also increases the vulnerability of the child to infectious diseases. Of all recorded deaths of infants and children, 50 to 75 percent are caused by a combination of malnutrition and infection.

> "Every year hundreds of thousands of children are blinded by Zerophthalmia, a disease particularly frequent in Southeast Asia and caused by a lack of Vitamin A (found in green leafy vegetables or yellow vegetables like the carrot). Prevention includes periodical distribution of large doses of the Vitamin to infants and children and efforts to alter eating habits and stimulate home gardening."[10]

Nutritional anemia particularly affects women of childbearing age and at least 700 million people are estimated to be victims of iron deficiency, serious enough to affect their productive capacity. Vitamin deficiencies are also a large cause of ill health and mal-development. Not only is this closely associated with severe malnutrition but it is also present in moderate malnutrition due to lack of balance in poor diets.

Intestinal parasites, rife in the poorer countries, can bring about the effects of malnutrition even where the victim has a relatively good diet. Roundworm is among the most prevalent and is a major cause of iron deficiency anemia, estimated to affect more than 500 million people, hookworm and tapeworm infestations are also common among the poor, reducing the absorption of protein and certain vitamins. Other diarrheal infections contribute to this diminishment of adequate nutrition which increases susceptibility to other diseases and general malaise.

The General Pattern of Disease

The emphasis above on the forms of disease prevalent in tropical and semi-tropical regions should be somewhat redressed by underlining that many of the major diseases of the developing world are still those which were once common in the developed regions—the communicable infections abetted by undernutrition and poor living conditions.

Generalising broadly on the changes in disease occurrence incident upon development, one author notes,

> "In the time relationship there is observable a continuous and gradual change in the epidemiological picture from an endemic infectious disease situation with a high prevalence of parasitosis, gastro-enteritis, respiratory disease and malnutrition and the vector borne disease; through a state where epidemics of measles, whooping cough, polio-myletis and other bacterial and virus diseases dominate the picture due to rising standards of

DEATHS ACCORDING TO CAUSE , IN LIFE CYCLE, :
Using Typical D Group Country As Example . (Phillippines)

UNDER 1	15 – 24 YEARS	45 – 54 YEARS
1. Ill-defined diseases peculiar to early infancy and immaturity 2. Bronchopneumonia 3. Infections of the new born 4. Gastro-enteritis and Colitis 5. Avitaminosis and other deficiency states 6. Ill-defined and unknown causes	1. Ill-defined and unknown causes 2. Tuberculosis 3. Heart Diseases 4. Primary, atypical, other and unspecified pneumonia 5. Bronchopneumonia 6. Congenital malform-ations of the circulatory system	1. Tuberculosis 2. Ill-defined and unknown causes 3. Heart Diseases 4.Cancer 5. Hypertension 6. Stomach Ulcers
1–4 YEARS	**25 – 34 YEARS**	**55 – 64 YEARS**
1. Bronchopneumonia 2. Gastro-enteritis and Colitis 3. Ill-defined and unknown causes 4. Avitaminosis and other definciency states 5. Bronchitis 6. Measles	1. Ill-defined and unknown causes 2. Tuberculosis 3. Heart Diseases 4. Cancer 5. Congenital malformations of the circulatory system 6. Primary, atypic al, other and unspecified pneumonia	1. Tuberculosis 2. Ill-defined and unknown causes 3. Heart Diseases 4. Cancer 5. Hypertension 6. Vascular lesions affecting central nervous system
5 – 14 YEARS	**35 – 44 YEARS**	**65 AND OVER**
1. Bronchopneumonia 2. Ill-defined and unknown causes 3. Gastro-enteritis and Colitis 4. Avitaminosis and other deficiency states 5. Primary, atypical, other and unspecified pneumonia 6. Tuberculosis	1. Tuberculosis 2. Ill-defined and unknown causes 3. Heart Diseases 4. Cancer 5. Hypertension 6. Primary, atypical, other and unspecified pneumonia	1. Senility without mention of Psychosis 2. Ill-defined and unknown causes 3. Heart Diseases 4. Tuberculosis 5. Cancer 6. Hypertension

Source: World Health Statistics Annual, 1972, Vol I, Sect. 4.1.1, WHO , Geneva, published 1975.

Fig. 36

living; to a final state where the degenerative diseases of a cerebrosclerotic nature, hypertension, heart failure, diabetes, psychosomatic diseases, and cancer comprise the major portions of ill health. Undernutrition gives way to overnutrition and the severity of the disease pattern shifts from the child to the aged.''[11]

This pattern is recapitulated in some measure in considering the life cycle incidence of principal causes of death compiled for a group of the poorer countries in the D reference group. (Fig. 36)

The principal worldwide disease distribution can be seen in the accompanying tables and maps of specific disease occurrences. (Figs. 39-43 at the end of this section.)

Of the approximately 60 million deaths in the world annually, about one-half (30 million) are infants and small children, the majority in Africa, Asia and Latin America. One-quarter (15 million) are caused by infections such as dysentery, typhoid and cholera, tuberculosis, measles and pneumonia. One-sixth are caused by cancer and cardiovascular disease.

For many disease conditions found in the poorer regions, high fatalities may not be the most immediate cause for concern. More important is the high incidence of debilitating conditions which do not kill swiftly or directly but erode the general health of people, impair their social and productive capacities and generally lower the span and quality of their lives. This is particularly the case with many of the parasitic infections such as worms, bilharzia, filoriasis, yaws, trachoma, malaria and leprosy. Specific countries, such as in Africa, carry a heavy burden of these kinds of diseases to the point where some suggest that 'sickness is the norm',[12] with many individuals carrying concurrent infections of one or more disease.

Many of these conditions of disease and debilitation are amenable to preventive environmental improvements with accompanying expansion of health services to aid those afflicted.

Environmental Health and Development

We have emphasised that socio-economic development is crucial to promoting better health. Many specific projects, however, if not accompanied by good environmental understanding and management can actually exacerbate ill-health conditions.

This can occur in different ways. For example, by increasing mobility from and to areas where certain infections diseases are endemic; by altering habitat relationships between disease vectors and hosts; by disturbing traditional patterns of activity which may have kept some diseases in check; by introducing new patterns of ill health such as psychosocial disorders that accompany disruption in ways of life, as in induced urban migration; and by the new ranges of occupational health problems.

> ". . . the evidence is replete with examples of development interventions that inadvertently increase disease hazards. In regard to infectious diseases, examples of such evidence are: (1) increased incidence of trypanosomiasis (sleeping sickness) along new road networks in Liberia and Nigeria; the cycling of trypanosomes by migrant labor between Ghana and the Upper Volta Republic; and an outbreak of trypanosomiasis near the manmade Lake Kariba; (2) increased incidence of bilharziasis (schistosomiasis), especially the more serious intestinal form, schis-

tosomiasis Mansoni, around irrigation schemes, with example ranging from the Gezira cotton scheme in Sudan to sugar schemes in Nigeria and Tanzania and tobacco farms in Rhodesia, with the dangers of further spread of the disease through presently planned agricultural schemes; and (3) an increasingly complex epidemiology of malaria in which, as a result of development activities, and the emergence of insecticide-resistant vectors, sociocultural factors are playing a more involved role."[13]

More projective environmental monitoring is required to assess the likely second and third order consequences of such developmental intervention. This would be similar to, and could draw upon, the techniques of technology assessment now being used to determine the side effects of current and predicted technologies being introduced into societies.

We should also realise, however, that development is a process for accelerating change in which there are some unavoidable social costs. It is the trade-off between costs and benefits which is important; whether, "it is more demoralising to die of hunger than to die of bilharzias."[14]

Other kinds of development projects can also engender increased dangers of a different order.

> "For example, industrial or mining projects obviously involve pollution risks but may also involve unusual risks of work accidents among workers not accustomed to machinery. Again the borrow-pits left by a construction project, if there are not suitable precautionary measures, can become breeding grounds for mosquitoes (vectors of malaria), and snails (vectors of schistosomiasis). In particular areas, there can also be special hazards. For example, a lumber mill or land settlement scheme, may, if wrongly planned, create just the critical density of population which creates the greatest risk of African trypanosomiasis ("sleeping sickness").[15]

These 'hidden costs' of failure to take cognizance of the environmental health aspects of development practices may, in the end, result in a much higher 'remedial price' having to be paid. It may also have more unfortunate and longer lasting effects not only on health but on public attitudes to development itself.

It is extremely important, therefore, not only in assessing health costs and needs alone, but for all areas of development, that sound environmental management criteria be closely involved with developmental planning at the earliest stages.

Health Services and Facilities

Whilst the availability of health services may not wholly indicate 'positive' health conditions, their absence, or low level of availability and access, certainly contributes to ill health for many.

COMPARABLE HEALTH RESOURCES, 1972
C, D, E Country Groups *

Country in reference Group*	Population per Physician	Physicians per 10,000 Population	Support Personnel per Physician	Pop. per Hospital Bed	Beds per 10,000 Population	Pop. per Nursing Personnel	Nursing Personnel per 10,000 Population
C[1]	2,117	4.7	2.7	376	54.6	1,894	16.2
D	6,577	1.5	5.5	692	20.4	2,797	4.8
E[2]	17,271	0.6	8.8	1,459	16.5	12,436	2.7

* All countries in the world assigned to C, D, E, classifications, not the average of the 7 reference country set.

Data: World Health Statistics Annual 1972, WHO Published 1976, Health Sector Policy Paper, World Bank, March 1975, Annex 6.

1. Excluding China.
2. Excluding India.

Source: Center for Integrative Studies.

Fig. 37

In one area of preventive medicine alone, lack of adequate facilities, physicians and other services is critical. Their shortage precludes more than 95 percent of the 80 million children born into the developing world from being vaccinated against such diseases as diptheria, measles, tetanus and poliomyelitis. Where some, such as measles, are rather mild when they occur in the developed countries, hence vaccine use is low, they are killing diseases in many of the poorer countries.

Fig. 37 gives some comparative ranges of health resources available around 1970 for all the countries in the C, D and E categories.

We have used Norbye's set of assumptions to assess the more specific needs of the poor as comprising 90% of the population in our total D and E group of countries.

Norbye assumes that for each million persons in the poor sector, i.e. as 90% of the population in the poorer countries, there is a requirement for:

5 reference hospitals
20 rural or urban slum hospitals
100 health centers
1,000 community health clinics totalling 3,750 hospital beds
215 physicians
900 nurses
1,500 medium level personnel
6,000 community health workers[16]

These assumptions are projected for the years 1980, 1990 and 2000 in terms of population growth. (Fig. 38)

PROJECTED NEEDS ON HEALTH FACILITIES AND PERSONNEL IN 62 D & E COUNTRIES*
(Thousand Units)[1]

	1972	1980	1990	2000
Population: in Poor Sector[2] (Millions)	647	828	1,095	1,415
Referral Hospital (Thousands)	3	4	5	7
Rural or Urban Slum Hospitals (Thousands)	13	17	22	28
Health Centers (Thousands)	65	83	110	142
Community Health Clinics (Thousands)	647	828	1,095	1,415
Hospital Beds (Thousands)	2,427	3,013	4,107	5,307
Physicians (Thousands)	139	178	235	304
Nurses (Thousands)	583	745	986	1,274
Medium Level Personnel (Thousands)	971	1,241	1,643	2,123
Community Health Workers (Thousands)	3,884	4,965	6,571	8,491

* All Countries in the world assigned to D, E, classifications, not the average of the 7 reference country set.

1. Based on the assumption that for 1 million people in the poor sector, the following are required:
   - I 1,000 Community Health Clinics with 5,000 Community Health Workers.
   - II 100 Health Centers with 100 physicians, 500 Nurses, 500 other medium level personnel and 1,000 Community Health Workers
   - III 20 Rural or Urban Slum Hospitals with 40 Physicians, 100 Nurses, 500 other medium level personnel and 2,000 beds.
   - IV 5 Referral Hospitals with 75 Physicians, 300 Nurses, 500 other medium level personnel and 1,750 beds.

2. Poor sector assumed to comprise 90% of population .

Data: World Population Prospects, 1970 - 2000 As Assessed in 1973, UN ECOSOC, 1975 (Medium Variant) Ole David Koht Norbye, "Health and Demography", World Development, Vol.2, February, 1974, pp.13-17. United Nations Demographic Yearbook, 1973.

Source : Center for Integrative Studies

Fig. 38

In general terms, of the same two and a half million physicians in the world, only half a million approximately 20 percent are in the developing nations. Of the world's dentists, only about 15 percent, approximately eighty thousand are in the poorer countries. These figures exclude China, North Korea and former North Vietnam.[17]

These sets of conventional assumptions and projections of personnel and facilities needed do not cover the extended range of ancillary clinics, health centers and the various other kinds of health care workers and technicians who might be required. They are given only to provide a baseline measure both for comparison—and to depart from.

MAJOR DISEASES PREVALENT IN POORER REGIONS

DISEASE	NUMBERS AFFECTED	DISEASE	NUMBERS AFFECTED
Amoebiasis	Extensive	Measles	100 Million Cases each Year
Ascariasis (Large Roundworm Infection)	Approx. 25% of World Population	Onchocerciasis	20 Million
Bacillary Dysentery	Numbers of Cases in the millions	Plague	Fewer than 1500 Cases Per Year (1960's)
Cholera	Approx. 250,000 Cases (1971–2)	Schistosomiasis (Bilharzia)	Approx. 200 Million
Endemic Typhus (Louse-Borne)	(1969) 25,000 Cases	Smallpox	65,000 Cases (1972)
Filariasis	200 Million	Syphillis	Extensive
Gonorrhea	65 Million New Cases A Year (1964 est.)	Trachoma	400 Million (1960)
Leprosy	11–12 Million	Trypanosomiasis and Leishmaniasis, and American Trypanosomiasis (Chagas Disease)	Endemic in Central Africa At Least 7–10 Million in South America
Hookworm Disease	500 Million	Tuberculosis	15–20 Million
Malaria	Approx. 100 Million Cases each Year, 1 Million Deaths	Whooping Cough	70 Million Cases a Year

Data: G. W. Hunter, ed. Tropical Medicine, Fifth Edition (W. B. Saunders Co., 1976); P. E. Sartwell, ed. Preventive Medicine and Public Health, Tenth Edition (Appleton–Century–Crofts 1973); J. S. McKenzie–Pollock, Planning A Healthier World, Unpublished manuscript. Health Sector Policy Paper, World Bank, March 1975. 1974 Report on the World Social Situation, U. N. Published 1975. Fifth Report on the World Health Situation 1969–1972. W. H. O. World Health, July 1976.

Source: Center for Integrative Studies.

Fig. 39

As we shall discuss later, in "Meeting Needs", such a conventional projection of health requirements may not only be unfeasible for the poorer countries—in terms of the level of social and economic investment implied, in a relatively short time span—but it may also be necessary to explore more radical ways of meeting their health needs.

EDUCATION

The problems of education in the developing world are of a different kind and scale from those in the developed.

The one overwhelming problem is illiteracy which constitutes a considerable brake on the overall development of the poor nations. The illiterate individual

SCHISTOSOMIASIS : Seriously Affected Areas

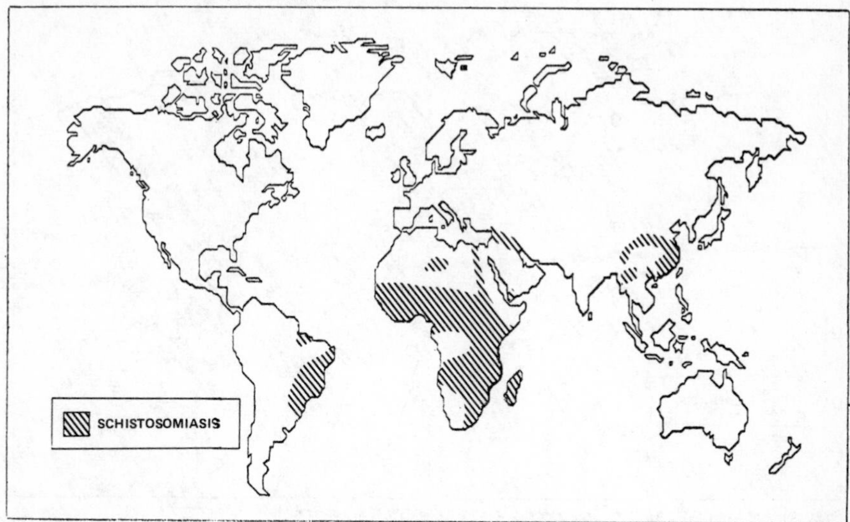

Data: Adapted from G.W. Hunter, ed. Tropical Medicine, Fifth Edition, (W.B. Saunders Co., 1976) Fig. 40

Source: Center for Integrative Studies

CHOLERA : Seriously Affected Areas

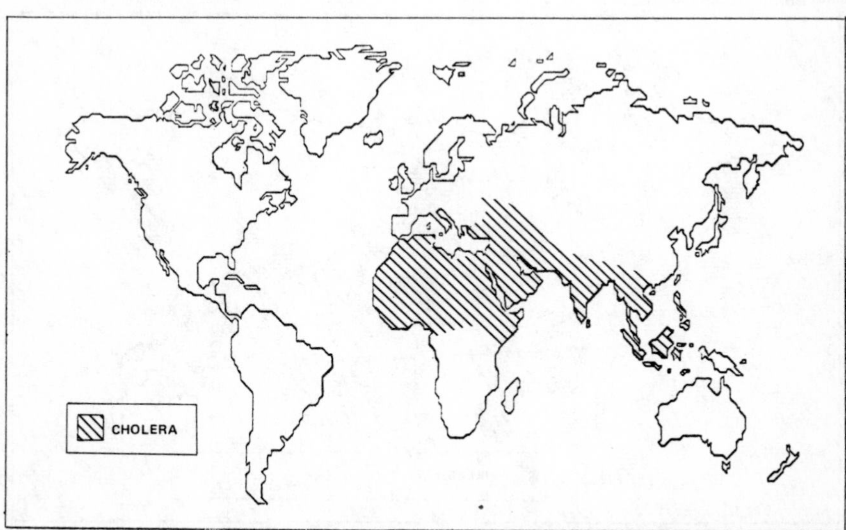

Data: Adapted from P.E. Sartwell, ed. Prevantive Medicine and Public Health, Tenth Edition, (Appleton-Century-Crofts, 1973) Fig. 41

Source: Center for Integrative Studies

FILARIASIS: Seriously Affected Areas

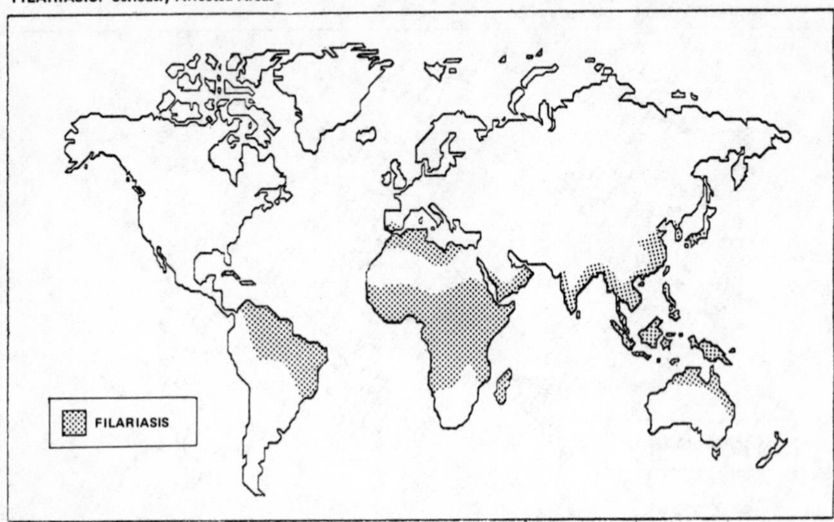

Data: Adapted from G.W. Hunter, ed. Tropical Medicine, Fifth Edition, (W.B. Saunders Co., 1976)
Source: Center for Integrative Studies

Fig. 42

MALARIA: Seriously Affected Areas

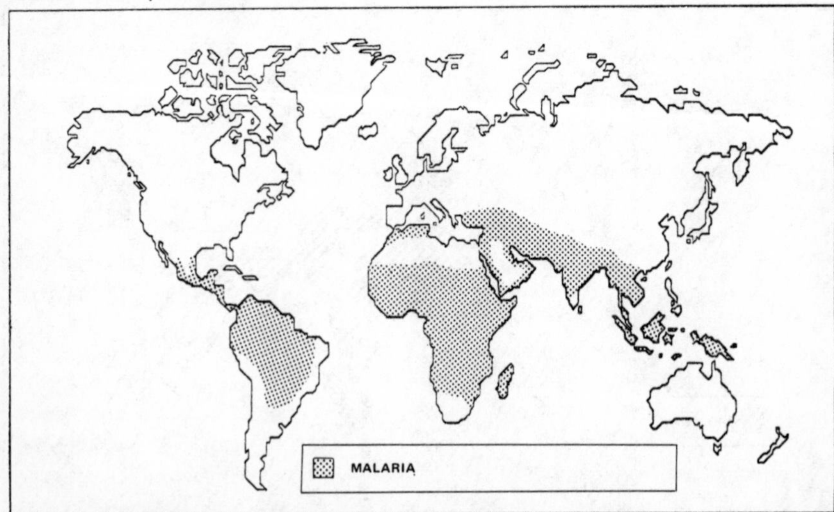

Data: Adapted from G.W. Hunter, ed. Tropical Medicine, Fifth Edition, (W.B. Saunders Co., 1976)
Source: Center for Integrative Studies

Fig. 43

ADULT ILLITERACY (15 yrs. and older): 1970

	NUMBER OF ILLITERATES (in Millions)			ILLITERATES AS % OF ADULT POPULATION		
	Male	Female	Total	Male	Female	Total
Developed[1] Countries	9	18	27	2.4	4.3	3.5
Developing[2] Countries	306	450	756	40.4	60.2	50.2
Total	315	468	783	28	40.3	34.2

1. All Europe, USSR, USA, Canada, Japan, Israel, Australia, New Zealand and South Africa.

2. All other countries excluding China, North Korea and North Vietnam.

Data: 1972 UNESCO Yearbook, p.47-48

Fig. 44

Source: Center for Integrative Studies

increasingly finds him or herself disenfranchised from effective participation in the contemporary world. He or she is not only constrained from participation in the larger world but denied the access, in many ways, to much of local national culture and effectively barred from the social and economic paths towards a better and more secure life.

Taking the need for minimal literacy as a priority, one may gauge the basic level of need in world terms. Accurate estimation of the number of illiterate people is impossible because census data is far from complete, and often not comparable because of different definitions of literacy. However, the numbers of illiterate persons are undoubtedly very high.

> "Although illiteracy at the world level dropped, proportionately, from 44.3 percent in 1950 to 39.3 percent in 1960 and 34.2 percent in 1970, the number of illiterates throughout the world still stands at some eight hundred million. Whereas illiteracy is decreasing in relative terms, as a result of the action taken in many countries, the population explosion and the inadequacy of educational systems are encouraging its growth in absolute figures."[18]

Illiteracy is not wholly confined of course to the developing world. In the developed countries there is a proportion of 'semi-literates', and disadvantaged groups at minimal literacy levels who are dropouts from the educational system. By and large, however, the incidence of illiteracy follows closely the distribution of affluence and degree of development. (Fig. 44)

> ". . . the map of illiteracy coincides almost exactly with that of poverty and . . . in the 25 least developed countries the proportion of illiterates

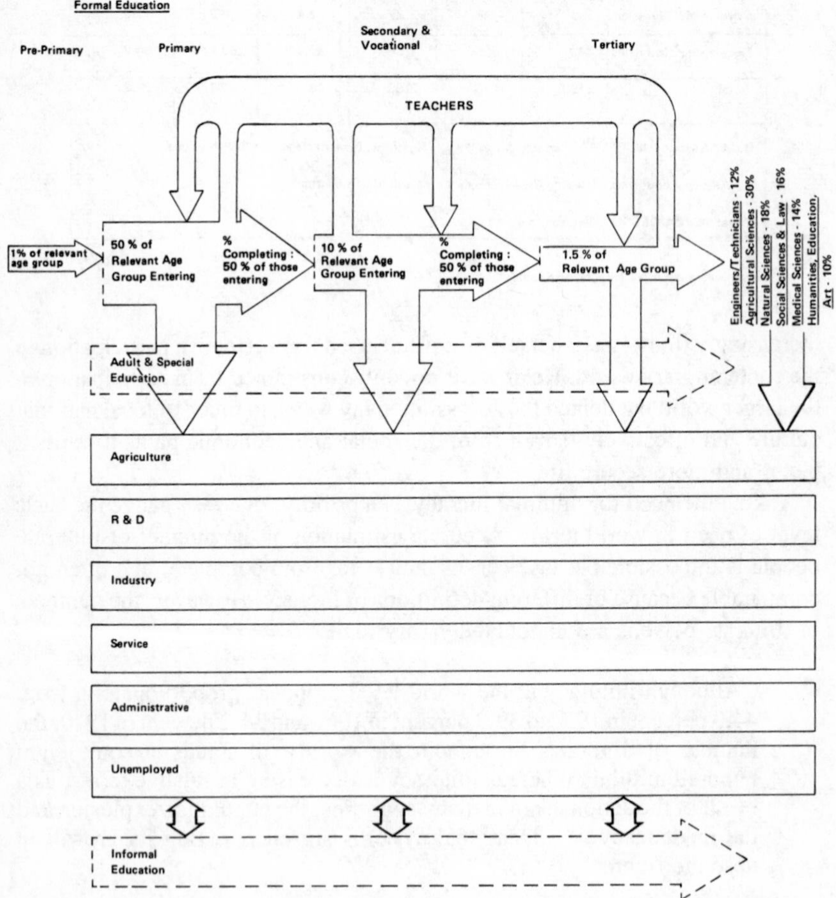

Source : Center for Integrative Studies.

Fig. 45

still exceeds 80 percent. Despite the prodigious efforts made by so many countries of the Third World in the field of education, it is forecast that in 1980 there will still be 240 million children in the world between the ages of 5 and 14 not attending school, and in all, 820 million illiterates, 20 million more than at present."[19]

Literacy is closely related to meeting many of the basic needs. For example, information on health and family planning is hampered where literacy does not exist; improvements in nutrition and agricultural development is much harder to disseminate; self-help in shelter and services provision slows with the inability to read simple instructions; and job training for skill improvement is made much more difficult.

Other Levels of Educational Need

Our assessment of further educational needs in terms of numbers of teachers, schools and facilities, requires certain caveats.

a) Most data and calculations are for *formal* educational systems. Such formal systems are needed at different levels but it is equally obvious that other kinds of systems both formal and informal may also meet similar needs.
b) Educational systems themselves are undergoing a critical re-appraisal period as to content, methods and curricula. Our estimates of projected need do not reflect the internal quality of what is projected nor the changes which ought to be incorporated.
c) The question facing both developing and developed countries is 'education for what?'. Of necessity the emphasis in many developing countries has had to be on the training of much needed technicians and professionals in many fields. Such education has often been oriented more to urbanised developed situations than to the needs of agrarian developing societies. Often the highly trained look for employment abroad and join the "brain drain" thus causing disaffection at home, or they join the ranks of the over-educated unemployables.

Our working assumption here is that the overall conventional and informal 'needs' should be initially stated. A rough guide to this quantitative assessment is given in Fig. 45, "Schematic Profile of Educational Process", which would be appropriate for an average D and E type country. The diagram concentrates primarily on education as training in ways that contribute to the society—rather than on education as an individual developmental process.

In terms of comparative public expenditures for education, there is little variation between countries in the percentages allocated either of GNP or of all

Comparative Public Expenditures for Education

Group*	Public Expenditures Per Caput U.S.$	As % of GNP	As % of All Public Expenditure	Current Public Expenditure on on Education Distribution		
				Pre-school 1st Level	2nd Level	3rd Level
A	260	5.7	16.6	40.1	31.8	17.2
B	72	4.3	12.7	44.6	28.6	15.4
C	31	4.8	17.3	49.6	26.7	13.1
D	15	4.4	18.6	46.1	27.0	14.8
E	5	3.3	16.5	49.3	30.8	13.3

* All countries in A,B,C,D,E groupings excluding USA, USSR, China, India

Data: World Military and Social Expenditures 1976, by Ruth Sivard
UNESCO Yearbook, 1974, Tables 6.1 and 6.3

Source : Center for Integrative Studies

Fig. 46

public expenditures—but, of course, the actual amount available to expend varies considerably. (See Fig. 46 for all countries in the world assigned under our A, B, C, D, E groups).

The next indicator is the average percent enrollment in the various first, second and third levels of education. These are combined together in Fig. 47. This gives some idea of the numbers of students in the formal educational process between the ages of 5 to 24 years. Pre-primary education though obviously a need, is not included here as the numbers in formal programs in the developing countries is very low.

> "Of an estimated 435 million children in the 7-12 years age group in the less developed countries, approximately 201 million were enrolled in primary schools in 1970, i.e. less than 50 percent. In several of the least developed, and the more backward areas of same, only one-sixth to one-third of the children of primary school age were enrolled. These low enrollments can safely be attributed to poverty and to the paucity of facilities available to the majority in the rural areas."[20]

Projection of Needs

Given the variability of needs in formal education, even normative comparison of one group of countries leveled against another is hazardous. Projection or

EDUCATION: Percentage of Appropriate Age Groups Enrolled by Level. (1970)

Average Reference Countries*	6-12 yrs approx. 1st Level	13-19 yrs approx. 2nd Level	20-24 yrs approx. 3rd Level
A[1]	106%	84%	17%
B[1]	114%	44%	11%
C	86%	27%	5%
D	76%	15%	2%
E	43%[2]	6%	1%

* The average of the seven reference countries in the appropriate A, B, C, D, E classification.

1. Percentages also include a proportion of overaged students.

2. This figure includes Zaire. Without Zaire, the percentage would be 31% which is more representative of E Countries.

Data: UNESCO Yearbook, 1974.

Source: Center for Integrative Studies

Fig. 47

forecast on this basis, in aggregate terms, is equally difficult so we may only indicate some provisional targets.

> "The purpose of target-setting is not to make a prediction of what will take place; nor is it to make projections on the basis of limited assumptions of attainment of one or two specific courses of development . . . A target indicates a *direction* for action. Its precise quantitative dimension is far less important than its function of indicating the direction of activity for achievement of specific goals."[21]

Using given provisional targets,[22] we have projected a conventional set of attendance figures for different educational levels in 1980, 1990, and 2000. (Fig. 48)

PRIMARY EDUCATION: Percentages and Approximate Number in Attendance, Age Group (6–12) (Numbers in Thousands)

Group**	1970[1]	1980[2]	1990[3]	2000[3]
A[4]	106% 41,662	100% 38,077	100% 40,635	100% 43,642
B	114% 46,169	100% 43,713	100% 50,387	100% 57,015
C[5]	86% 70,898	100% 102,494	100% 126,751	100% 150,773
D	76% 62,922	85% 93,611	100% 145,812	100% 177,649
E[6]	43%* (31%) 14,980	85% 53,382	100% 84,158	100% 107,812

1. Percentages established from reference countries. Percentages over 100% indicate a large number of overaged students. World Bank estimates that in 1970, 10-20% of the student body consists of over-aged students. Education Sector Working Paper, Dec., 1974, p. 17.
2. Approximate target levels for D & E countries modified from World Plan of Action For The Application of Science and Technology to Development, p. 63.
3. Suggested target from World Plan of Action for the Application of Science and Technology to Development p. 63.
4. Excluding USA & USSR
5. Excluding China, Vietnam (1980-2000), North Korea
6. Excluding India

* This figure includes Zaire, which is oneof our 7 reference countries. Without Zaire, the percentage is 31% which is more representative of E countries, thus the 31% figure is used. See Education Sector Working Paper, World Bank, Dec., 1974, p. 27.

** All countries in the world assigned to A, B, C, D, E classifications, not the average of the 7 reference country set.

Data : Education Sector Working Paper World Bank, December, 1974. UNESCO Yearbook, 1974.
World Plan of Action for the Application of Science and Technology to Development, U.N., 1971.
World Population Prospects 1970 – 2000 As Assessed in 1973, U.N. Medium Variant. UN ECOSOC, 1975.

Source : Center for Integrative Studies.

Fig. 48

SECONDARY EDUCATION: Percentages and Approximate Number in Attendance, Age Group (13–19) (Numbers in Thousands)

Group *	1970[1]	1980[2]	1990[3]	2000[3]
A[4]	84.0% 34,150	90% 42,643	95% 42,664	100% 50,288
B	44.0% 16,625	55.0% 22,294	65% 28,127	80% 41,576
C[5]	27.0% 17,451	40% 33,968	50.0% 52,863	65.0% 88,630
D	15.0% 9,678	33.0% 29,663	40.0% 48,001	50.0% 79,074
E[6]	6.0% 2,322	33.0% 16,810	40.0% 26,582	50.0% 45,497

N.B. Percentages also include a proportion of overaged students.
1. Percentages established from reterable countries.
2. Approximate target for D & E countries modified from World Plan of Action for the Application of Science and Technology to Development, p. 63.
3. A.B.C. countries percentages arrived at by extrapolating with some modification, World Bank school enrollment ratio figures, as they appear in Education Sector Working Paper, Dec., 1974.
A modified extrapolation of the 1970-1980 growth rate as it appears in above chart.
4. Excluding USA & USSR
5. Excluding China, Vietnam (1980-2000), N. Korea
6. Excluding India

* All countries in the world assigned to A, B, C, D, E classifications, not the average of the 7 reference country set.

Data : World Plan of Action for the Application of Science and Technology to Development, UN, 1971.
Education Sector Working Paper, World Bank, December, 1974. UNESCO Yearbook, 1974.
World Population Prospects 1970 – 2000, As Assessed in 1973, UN Medium Variant.

Source : Center for Integrative Studies.

Fig. 48A

TERTIARY EDUCATION: Percentages and Number in Attendance, Age Group (20–24) (Numbers in Thousands)

Group*	1970 [1]	1980 [2]	1990 [3]	2000 [3]
A[4]	17.0% 5,353	25.0% 7,683	33% 10,548	40% 13,242
B	11.0% 2,631	14.0% 3,924	17% 5,117	20% 6,852
C[5]	5.0% 1,822	8.0% 4,107	11% 7,062	14% 11,727
D	2.29% 797,000	5.0% 2,576	8% 5,576	11% 10,394
E[6]	0.61% 137,000	5.0% 1,472	8% 3,125	11% 5,832

N.B. Percentages also include a proportion of overaged students
1. Percentages established from reference countries. Population figures are the percentages taken from World Population Prospects, 1970-2000, As Assessed In 1973, Prepared by the Population Division, Department of Economic and Social Affairs of the United Nations Secretariat.
2. Approximate target levels for D & E countries modified from World Plan of Action, For the Application of Science and Technology to Development, p. 63.
A,B,C, countries percentages arrived at by extrapolating with some modification, World Bank school enrollment ratio figures, as they appear in Education Sector Working Paper, Dec., 1974.
3. A modified extrapolation of the 1970-1980 growth rate.
4. Excluding USA & USSR
5. Excluding China, Vietnam (1980-2000), N. Korea
6. Excluding India

* All countries in the world assigned to A, B, C, D, E classifications, not the average of the 7 reference country set.

Data : Education Sector Working Paper, World Bank, December,1974. UNESCO Yearbook, 1974.
World Plan of Action for the Application of Science and Technology to Development, UN, 1971.
World Population Prospects 1970 – 2000, As Assessed in 1973, UN Medium Variant.

Source : Center for Integrative Studies.

Fig. 48B

TEACHERS NEEDED IN D & E* COUNTRIES TO MEET C LEVEL (IN MILLIONS)

YEAR	Primary	Secondary	Third Level	Totals
1980	4.3	2.1	0.3	6.7
1990	6.8	3.4	0.7	10.8
2000	8.4	5.7	1.2	15.3

* All countries in the world excluding India assigned to D, E, classifications, not the average of the 7 reference country set.

Data: World Plan of Action for the Application of Science and Technology, 1971.
World Bank, Education Sector Working Paper, December, 1974.
World Population Prospects 1970 - 2000 As Assessed in 1973 U.N. Medium Variant.
1974 UNESCO Yearbook.

Source: Center for Integrative Studies.

Fig. 49

PRIMARY SCHOOLS NEEDED IN D & E COUNTRIES TO MEET C LEVEL (IN MILLIONS)

YEAR	Number of Primary School Students	Number of Institutions Needed
1980	147.0	0.9
1990	230.0	1.4
2000	285.5	1.8

1. Based on Current 'C' Level Ratio of Teachers per Institution (4.7 to 1) and 'C' Level Student / Teacher Ratio (34 to 1).

* All countries in the world excluding India assigned to D, E, classifications, not the average of the 7 reference country set.

Data: 1974 UNESCO Yearbook
World Population Prospects, 1970-2000 as assessed in 1973 UN ECOSOC 1975 Medium Variant

Source: Center for Integrative Studies

Fig. 50

More practically, perhaps, one could set the target at the present level of the average C country and project the poorer countries needs for teachers on that basis. (Fig. 49) This kind of educational projection is inherently unreliable as the educational requirements for teachers vary considerably. In many of the developing countries the majority of primary school teachers may have no more than a primary school education themselves—whilst it is generally held that a teacher at a given level should have been trained, at least partially, at the next highest level.

In terms of educational priorities for literacy the primary level is most important. Using the C level again, we may target the numbers for primary school enrollment and schools needed in the poorer countries by 1980 through 2000. (Fig. 50)

The value of figures on which projected targets can be based here is actually negated by the relative ineffectiveness of primary education for many in the poorer countries, due to the difficulties of attending school and the lack of an externally supportive educational environment.

> "A phenomenon general to the primary system in these countries is the large number of drop-outs in the initial year. This is variously attributed to the family's inability to continue to clothe and equip the child for school or to circumstances requiring the child's help at home or in the fields. Additional causes of drop-out may be the uninteresting content of the curriculum, ineffective methods of teaching, and over-all, the irrelevance of what was taught to the pupil's environment and family life-style."[23]

It is clear that even based on the modest C level, the educational task is a formidable one for the D and E countries requiring almost one million primary

DISTRIBUTION OF SCIENTISTS, ENGINEERS AND TECHNICIANS (1972)

Total Nos. of Scientists, Engineers and Technicians (Thousands)

Group*	Scientists Engineers	Technicians	Total
A & B	5,565	11,601	17,166
C	651	856	1,507
D	42	66	109
E	19	15	34

As Percentage of World Totals (Derived from accompanying chart)

Group*	Scientists Engineers	Technicians	Total
A & B	89%	92%	91%
C	10%	7%	8%
D	0.7%	0.5%	0.6%
E	0.3%	0.1%	0.2%

*97 countries for which data available assigned to A,B,C,D,E categories excluding USA, USSR, China, India

Source: Center for Integrative Studies.

Fig. 51

schools by 1980 as against the 379,000 currently available. Were we to work through such needs in more detail down to the amounts of buildings, libraries, auxiliary personnel and transportation required in conventional educational terms it would become clear that indicated targets may not be reached in traditional ways but will require more radical approaches.

Reflecting the general educational imbalance, and thereby prospects for development, is the availability of scientists, engineers and technicians. Fig. 51 gives the comparative world stock and percentage in various country groups.

The targetted requirement in bringing the poorer countries up to the level of the average C country in this regard is shown in Fig. 52. Again this follows traditional lines of education and training assumptions, but the conventional means may be more difficult to circumvent in professional fields.

As far as satisfying educational needs in general is concerned, it may be necessary for the developing countries to move away from established methods and recast their educational systems to meet their specific needs. Education, traditionally, has been mainly concerned with preparing people for relatively fixed roles and those that are associated with status. The poorer developing societies require different approaches so as to meet modes of skill acquisition and self determination. Integrating education modes of skill acquisition and self determination. Integrating education within their overall basic needs strategies will require greater emphasis on the wider participation in, and development through, such a changed educational process. Including formal and informal elements, this change may take the process beyond formal schooling so that education is incorporated more directly into the overall development process itself.

SHELTER

Adequate shelter is one of the core human needs since so many of the other basic needs are satisfied in relation to the household or home—food preparation and

PROJECTED NOS. OF SCIENTISTS, ENGINEERS AND TECHNICIANS TO BRING D & E COUNTRIES TO C LEVEL. (MILLIONS)

	Population	Scientists and Engineers	Technicians
1980	919.4	3.1	3.1
1990	1,216.8	4.1	4.1
2000	1,572.3	5.2	5.2

*All countries in the world excluding India assigned to D, E classifications, not the average of the 7 reference country set.

N.B. 'C' Level ratio of 3000 to 1.

Data. 1974 UNESCO Yearbook
World Population Prospects 1970–2000 as assessed in 1973 U.N. Medium Variant

Source: Center for Integrative Studies

Fig. 52

storage, primary health maintenance, child care, early socialisation and education. Much of the satisfaction of those larger psychosocial needs, beyond the basic and constituting the 'quality of living' are also clustered around the household.

Though most countries have various standards for housing and their governments have more or less clearly expressed housing policies, the implementation of adequate standards and policies, on a large scale, has been singularly difficult for the poorer countries. This is due in part to low resources availability; changes in perception and attitudes to what constitutes adequacy as levels of aspiration change; the increase in numbers to be housed; the growing pressure on urban settlements, ill prepared to accommodate larger numbers; and the cost of investment in suitable low-cost housing, both fiscally and in terms of skilled manpower, as against other developmental priorities.

With regard to standards themselves these obviously vary considerably. A recent survey of existing standards and criteria in countries in Latin America, Asia and Africa, states that,

> "In most of the countries investigated, the accommodation and performance were formed in considerable detail in legislation. Only in a few countries such as India and Zambia, were there many standards of the threshold type.[24] However, because of the legal style in which most of these standards have to be specified, their scientific rationale was seldom stated beyond broad claims of health, safety, privacy and easy accessibility. Attempts to investigate the scientific rationale behind a few of these standards revealed that either these were non-existent or, where they did exist, they had little basis in local experience."[25]

The lack of scientific criteria noted is not surprising as, even in the more advanced countries, housing is one of the last areas of human needs to come under scientific review. Though one of our main 'environmental control' facilities it still develops rather haphazardly on a combination of local traditional precedent, slow accretion of craft knowledge and economic constraint. The family dwelling particularly still bears little relationship to our developed scientific and technical capacities—in its construction, environmental and service functions and flexibility of adjustment to human needs—even though we mass-produce, with ease, several other related technical facilities, such as the automobile weighing around two and a half tons with approximately five thousand component parts.

The provision of some basic structure is only the first step in adequate shelter.

> "Housing is a complex product, providing a combination of services; space, environmental services (water supply, water disposal, energy use) and locational services (access to jobs and social infrastructure such as education and health facilities)."[26]

Estimates of need, therefore, though concentrating more specifically on the availability of basic shelter should be expanded to include these larger requirements already discussed in the description of the unit household approach.

Most information of a generalised nature on the current status of housing in the world is derived from census data. But, as emerged particularly in work done for the 1976 Habitat Conference, many of these data are only available for the relatively developed countries.

> "Housing censuses have been undertaken during the past ten years (1965-1974) on 60 percent of the inhabitants of the world. Very little or nothing is known about the housing conditions of the remaining 40 percent who are located in entirety in the developing countries. Only 44 percent of the African population and 51 percent of the Asian population have been covered by a housing census, while almost the total population for Europe (99 percent) and North America (96 percent) and a high proportion of South America (93 percent) and Oceania (81 percent) have been covered. This means that on this planet there are 1.6 billion inhabitants whose housing conditions are not reported in housing censuses."[27]

Despite the paucity of census data, reports on housing projects and surveys indicate that housing conditions particularly in the poorest countries have worsened rather than improved during the past decade, and that the numbers of those unable to afford even the cheapest dwellings has increased.

The lack of substantive data is reflected in the comparative set of indicators for D and E countries. Little information is available for the poorest countries, and that which is may well reflect only those people in situations above the poverty level. The provisional quality of all data in the estimates which follow should, therefore, be kept constantly in mind.

HOUSING NEEDS : Projection of Population, Number of Households and Percentage in Urban Areas

AFRICA				
	1975	1980	1990	2000
Age in Years	Population (millions)			
0 – 19	218.8	251.8	336.1	436.7
20 – 44	127.2	145.3	193.1	263.0
45 +	55.3	63.8	84.9	114.0
Households				
Number (millions)	63.6	72.7	96.6	131.5
Population per Household	6.3	6.3	6.4	6.2
of Which Number 45 years and over	0.9	0.9	0.9	0.9
Urban Population				
%	24.5	27.1	32.5	37.7

ASIA (Excluding China P.R., Japan, Korea, Mongolia, Hong Kong)				
	1975	1980	1990	2000
Age in Years	Population (millions)			
0 – 19	670.6	761.4	947.0	1,076.4
20 – 44	397.4	454.4	613.2	827.7
45 +	181.8	211.0	276.1	363.2
Households				
Number (millions)	198.7	227.2	306.6	413.9
Population per Household	6.3	6.3	6.0	5.5
of Which Number 45 years and over	0.9	0.9	0.9	0.9
Urban Population				
%	23.0	25.0	29.6	35.0

LATIN AMERICA				
	1975	1980	1990	2000
Age in Years	Population (millions)			
0 – 19	170.6	193.0	244.4	296.6
20 – 44	102.3	120.1	164.3	217.5
45 +	51.2	58.5	76.9	105.8
Households				
Number (millions)	51.2	60.1	82.2	108.8
Population per Household	6.3	6.2	5.9	5.7
of Which Number 45 years and over	1.0	1.0	0.9	1.0
Urban Population				
%	60.4	63.8	69.7	74.8

MORE DEVELOPED REGIONS (Europe, USSR, N. America, Japan, Australia, New Zealand)				
	1975	1980	1990	2000
Age in Years	Population (millions)			
0 – 19	381.9	381.4	396.7	410.1
20 – 44	398.6	426.2	467.9	478.2
45 +	351.2	373.4	412.8	471.9
Households				
Number (millions)	199.3	213.1	234.0	239.1
Population per Household	5.7	5.5	5.5	5.7
of Which Number 45 years and over	1.8	1.8	1.8	2.0
Urban Population				
%	69.2	71.9	77.0	81.4

Source : Center for Integrative Studies

Data : World Population Prospects 1970 – 2000 As Assessed in 1973, UN ECOSOC, 1975.
Global Review of Human Settlements Statistical Annex, UN ECOSOC, 1976.

Fig. 53

Standard housing needs estimation is generally determined by the relationship of population size to household formation. The household forming age group is theoretically taken as 20-44 years, and each household is presumed to consist of two persons of that age group plus their dependents.

The average size of household in Asia, Africa and Latin America calculated in this way is given as 6.3 persons.[28] Comparison with the developed regions shows that the household size is roughly the same with 5.7 persons per household. The essential difference lies in the age mix of the households. The number of younger people per household in the developing world is close to twice the number of those in the developed regions. (See Fig. 53)

CUMULATIVE INCREASE (FROM 1976) IN URBAN/RURAL POPULATION AND HOUSEHOLDS[1] (in millions) Due to Population Growth in E,D, and C Countries*

		1980		1990		2000	
		Urban	Rural	Urban	Rural	Urban	Rural
E	Total Population	48.0	60.9	187.9	209.9	215.6	345.1
	Households	8.0	10.2	31.3	35.0	35.9	57.5
D	Total Population	36.6	41.3	131.8	136.3	261.3	227.6
	Households	6.1	6.9	22.0	22.7	43.6	37.9
C	Total Population	46.0	19.7	159.0	89.7	309.9	144.5
	Households	7.7	3.3	26.5	15.0	51.7	24.1
Total	Total Population	130.6	121.9	478.7	435.9	786.8	717.2
	Households	21.8	20.4	79.8	72.7	131.2	119.5

*All countries in the world assigned to the E,D,C, classification, not the average of the 7 country reference set.

1. Assuming average of 6 persons per household.

Data : Global Review of Human Settlements, Statistical Annex, UN ECOSOC, 1976.
World Population Prospects 1970-2000 As Assessed in 1973, UN ECOSC, 1975

Fig. 54

Source : Center for Integrative Studies

This increase in the younger age groups is particularly marked in projecting the relative cumulative increase in urban/rural populations and households of the C, D, and E countries. (Fig. 54). It also gives some suggestion of the massive increase in housing needs in these populations for the years 1980 through 2000.

Estimates of Dwelling Needs

The procedure used here is modified from that used in the U.N. document, *World Housing Conditions and Estimated Housing Needs 1965*.[29] Due to the

ESTIMATED NUMBER OF DWELLING UNITS REQUIRED * IN AFRICA, LATIN AMERICA, AND SOUTH ASIA BY 1980, 1990, AND 2000 (in millions)

	By 1980	By 1990	By 2000
Due to Population Increase			
Africa	9.5	33.3	66.7
Latin America	7.7	27.4	51.9
South Asia	28.1	97.6	184.9
To Replace Obsolescent Housing Stock			
Africa	5.5	16.5	27.5
Latin America	4.5	13.5	22.5
South Asia	17.0	51.0	85.0
To Remedy Existing Shortages			
Africa	6.3	19.0	31.8
Latin America	4.9	14.5	24.2
South Asia	19.0	56.8	94.6
TOTAL			
Africa	21.3	68.8	126.0
Latin America	17.1	55.4	98.6
South Asia	64.1	205.4	364.5
GRAND TOTAL	102.5	329.6	589.1

* Requirements as of 1975

Data: World Population Prospects 1970 -2000 As Assessed in 1973, UN ECOSOC, 1975.
Global Review of Human Settlements Statistical Annex, UN ECOSOC, 1976.

Source : Center for Integrative Studies

Fig. 55

varied nature of the available data, estimates are not given in the reference country mode but for the U.N. regions, Africa, Latin America, South Asia in the developing world. (Fig. 55; and 56).

(i) *Additional dwellings needed due to population growth*. This is calculated from an estimated average size of household of 6.3 persons, larger than that used in the 1965 U.N. report in which household size was taken as 5.3 persons. Slight fluctuations in the size of households because of changes in group ratios have been taken into account. The major need area in the immediate future in Africa and South Asia is for rural housing, but their later needs become more pressing for urban populations. In

PROJECTED HOUSING NEEDS: URBAN/RURAL

ADDITIONAL DWELLINGS (million units) Required to Remedy Existing Housing Shortages *

		Current Estimated Deficit for 1975 (%)	Additional Dwellings Required per Year (million)	Additional Dwellings Required		
				By 1980	By 1990	By 2000
Africa	Urban	50	0.3	1.5	4.5	7.6
	Rural	50	1.0	4.8	14.5	24.2
Latin America	Urban	45	0.6	2.8	8.3	13.9
	Rural	50	0.4	2.1	6.2	10.3
South Asia	Urban	40	0.7	3.7	11.0	18.3
	Rural	50	3.1	15.3	45.8	76.3
Total	Urban	—	1.6	8.0	23.8	39.8
	Rural	—	4.5	22.2	66.5	110.8

* Requirements as of 1975.

ADDITIONAL DWELLING UNITS REQUIRED (million units) Due To Population Increase *

		Dwellings Required per Year 1970 – 1980	Additional Dwellings Required		
			By 1980	By 1990	By 2000
Africa	Urban	0.9	4.4	15.6	34.4
	Rural	1.0	5.1	17.7	32.3
Latin America	Urban	1.4	7.1	24.7	47.5
	Rural	0.1	0.6	2.7	4.4
South Asia	Urban	2.2	11.0	43.8	91.8
	Rural	3.4	17.1	53.8	93.1
Total	Urban	4.5	22.5	84.1	173.7
	Rural	4.5	22.8	74.2	129.8

* Requirements as of 1975

ADDITIONAL DWELLINGS (million units) Required to Replace Obscolescent Housing Stock *

		Additional Dwellings Required per Year (millions)	Additional Dwellings Required		
			By 1980	By 1990	By 2000
Africa	Urban	0.3	1.5	4.5	7.5
	Rural	0.8	4.0	12.0	20.0
Latin America	Urban	0.6	3.0	9.0	15.0
	Rural	0.3	1.5	4.5	7.5
South Asia	Urban	0.9	4.5	13.5	22.5
	Rural	2.5	12.5	37.5	62.5
Total	Urban	1.8	9.0	27.0	45.0
	Rural	3.6	18.0	54.0	90.0

* Requirements as of 1975.

Data: World Population Prospects 1970-2000 As Assessed in 1973, UN ECOSOC, 1975.
Global Review of Human Settlements Statistical Annex, UN ECOSOC, 1976

Source: Center for Integrative Studies

Fig. 56

Latin America, where over 60% of the current population is urbanised the most urgent priority is for urban housing.

(ii) *New dwellings to replace obsolescent housing stock* are calculated on the assumption that all buildings are to be replaced after 30 years.

(iii) *Additional dwelling required to remedy existing shortages*. This calculation is based on an estimated deficit in 1975 for 50% of the population, and assumes that housing to meet this deficit would have to be built over the next twenty-five years.

The *Report on the World Social Situation*, U.N., 1974, indicates that the goals set for the late 1960's and early 1970's have not been realised. In Africa, the estimated need was for 10-13 units per 1,000 population but, in fact, housing only increased at the rate of 3 units per 1,000 annually; in Western Asia, with similar needs, less than 1 unit per 1,000 inhabitants have been added annually.

With regard to the standard of such projected needs, the common aim expressed by many countries is that, by 1980-85 each family has a separate dwelling and, by 1985-90, each family member should have a separate room.

A standard living space per urban dweller was suggested in 1960 as 8.8 sq. metres; in 1970 and 1972 this was successively expanded to 11.4 and 14.15 sq. metres. Possibly a median target standard might be 10 sq. metres as allocated in our Unit Household Indicators table assuming 50 sq. metres of living space for a five person family.

It is difficult to envisage how all of the estimated housing needs—to accommodate population increase, replace old stock and meet present shortages—can be met without a considerable readjustment in national and international priorities. Overall, over 1,000 million new dwellings need to be built by the year 2000, i.e., 47 million annually—whereas the actual rate achieved during the First Development Decade was 1-3 units per 1,000 people, and in the past five years 2-4 dwelling units per 1,000 in the developing countries and 6-7 per 1,000 in the developed.

Even to meet the situation halfway, within conventional construction and institutional practices, will require a much greater investment in money, manpower and other resources than is presently allocated—and more deliberate policies for the provision of housing for the masses of poor. To go further will require a radical overhaul of the whole framework of housing not only in terms of design and construction but even more with regard to financing, land tenure and ownership/rental practices.

Increases in urban and squatter settlements make this task even more difficult. Although the developing world as a whole is not yet highly urbanised in comparison to the developed, the pressure of rural in-migration is already quite marked and causing stress in many areas. Increases in population in the coming decades will exacerbate this trend towards more congestion and over-

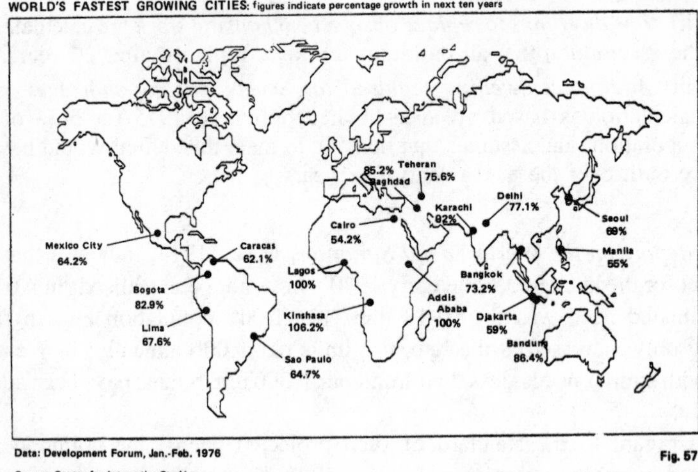

Fig. 57

crowding in many of the towns. Such urban areas are calculated to be growing at the rate of 3 percent a year with some individual centers often twice as fast. (Map Fig. 57)

The present and projected urban and rural balance for the world and the developed/developing regions is given in Figs. 58/59.

On this basis, specific urban requirements within overall housing needs would be:

Africa, Latin America and South Asia	**1975-90**	**1975-2000**
Due to Population Increase	84.1	173.7
To Remedy Existing Housing Shortages	23.8	39.8
To Replace Obsolescent Stock	27.0	45.0
Totals	134.9	258.5

For large numbers of poor urban dwellers in the developing countries, environmental conditions are worse than the rural situations which they have left in search of a better life. Even those fortunate to live in 'standard' housing are, in most cases, overcrowded in unsanitary and slum conditions. But they are better off than those in the proliferating shanty communities.

At present, such squatter settlements and peripheral shanty towns are estimated to account for 30 to 40 percent of the urban concentrations in the developing countries—where the poorest have been pushed out due to lack of housing construction and to their lack of means to buy, or rent, such housing as might be available.

Little detailed information is available on overall squatter populations though, in many countries, the practice is semi-legitimised and efforts are being

URBAN / RURAL BALANCE : Estimated and Projected Population in Urban Areas (in millions)

		1975	1980	1990	2000
World	Total	3,968	4,374	5,280	6,254
	Urban	1,548	1,793	2,376	3,127
More Developed Regions	Total	1,132	1,181	1,277	1,360
	Urban	781	850	983	1,102
Less Developed Regions	Total	2,836	3,193	4,003	4,894
	Urban	766	958	1,401	2,007
Africa	Total	401	461	614	814
	Urban	96	124	196	309
Latin America	Total	324	372	486	620
	Urban	194	238	340	465
South Asia	Total	1,250	1,427	1,836	2,267
	Urban	288	357	551	793

Data : Global Review of Human Settlements Statistical Annex, UN ECOSOC, 1976.
World Population Prospects 1970-2000 as assessed in 1973, UN ECOSOC, 1975.

Source : Center for Integrative Studies

Fig. 58

URBAN / RURAL BALANCE : Estimated and Projected Percentage of Population in Urban Areas (%)

	1975	1980	1990	2000
World	39	41	45	50
More Developed Regions	69	72	77	81
Less Developed Regions	27	30	35	41
Africa	24	27	32	38
Latin America	60	64	70	75
South Asia	23	25	30	35

Data : Global Review of Human Settlements Statistical Annex, UN ECOSOC, 1976.
World Population Prospects 1970-2000 as assessed in 1973, UN ECOSOC, 1975.

Source : Center for Integrative Studies

Fig. 59

made to provide essential municipal services for them. Data presented at the U.N. Habitat Conference, 1976, show,

> ". . . that 60 percent of rooms in such non-conventional dwellings have more than two persons living in them and that 35 percent of the rooms have more than three persons."

In more specific examples quoted, the numbers per room run as high as 10 persons per room, with a median range of 4 to 6—with average living space of 3 square metres per person.

Though many of these settlements are considered as 'transitional' where their inhabitants are presumed to move up to better housing as their situations improve, it seems problematic how long such transition periods may last given the trends in overall growth.

Groups in more permanent transition, normally omitted in housing considerations, are the relatively large numbers of nomadic peoples, e.g. in Somalia they probably constitute a majority. The plight of these nomads and the fragility of their living margins was highlighted in the recent drought.

Water supply and sanitation services are two of the most critical dimensions of housing. The waterborne sewage systems are often the only satisfactory method for removing human waste but are costly and less immediately apparent as necessities than potable water supply, so in poor conditions the problems are

GROWTH RATES OF URBAN POPULATION, SLUMS AND SQUATTER SETTLEMENTS : Selected Countries

		Annual Growth Rates	
		Urban Population (%)	Slum & Squatter Population (%)
AFRICA			
Ghana (Total)	1970	4.6	17.5
Kenya (Nairobi)	1970	10.0	22.5
Morocco (Total)	1971	5.3	7.0
Tanzania (Dar Es Salaam)	1970	7.0	35.7
Zambia (Lusaka)	1969	12.0	45.0
LATIN AMERICA			
Brazil (Rio De Janeiro)	1970	4.4	5.5
Colombia (Buenaventura)	1969	0.4	0.4
(Cali)		7.4	7.4
Guatemala (Guatemala City)	1971	5.3	28.0
Honduras (Tesucisalpa)	1970	5.2	5.2
Mexico (Mexico, Ciudad De)	1966	2.3	12.0
Panama (Panama City)	1970	5.9	5.9
Peru (Arequipa)	1961	3.5	50.0
(Chimbote)	1961	5.0	60.0
(Lima)	1971	5.9	13.7
Venezuela (Caracas)	1974	4.5	5.7
(Ciudad Suyana)	1969	13.7	13.7
(Maracaibo)	1969	7.2	7.2
EAST ASIA			
Korea (Republic) (Pusan)	1969	3.7	32.2
(Seoul)	1966	6.7	56.6
SOUTH ASIA			
Cambodia (Phnom Penh)	1972	10.4	16.4
India (Bombay)	1971	3.6	17.4
(Calcutta)	1971	2.5	9.1
Indonesia (Jakarta)	1972	4.2	4.6
Jordan (Ayman)	1972	9.5	19.1
Malaysia (Kuala Lumpur)	1969	2.5	8.0
Pakistan (Karachi)	1971	5.6	10.0
Philippines (Manila)	1972	4.0	5.5
Turkey (Total)	1971	4.9	7.0
(Ankara)	1970	5.0	9.5
(Istanbul)	1970	6.5	11.6

Data : Global Review of Human Settlements, Statistical Annex, UN, ECOSOC 1976.

Fig. 60

Percentages of Inhabitants Served by Sewerage Facilities in Developing Countries

Regions	Coverage (% inhabitants of each region)	Urban			Rural with adequate disposal	Total population with sewage disposal
		Connected to public sewerage system	Household system	Total		
Total 58 developing countries	59	28.1	44.2	72.3	7.6	24.5
of which : [1]						
22 in Africa	43	18.2	32.2	50.5	14.3	21.4
17 in Latin America	94	34.5	28.4	62.9	20.1	43.1
17 in Asia	51	25.8	55.5	81.3	4.9	20.6
2 in Oceania	3	13.7	56.1	69.8	90.9	84.1

1. The countries for which information was available are :
Africa : Algeria, Benin, Burundi, Central African Republic, Chad, Ethiopia, Guinea, Ivory Coast, Kenya, Liberia, Libyan Arab Republic, Madagascar, Mali, Mauritania, Mauritius, Morocco, Niger, Tunisia, Uganda, Upper Volta, Zaire, Zambia.
Latin America : Bolivia, Brazil, Colombia, Costa Rica, Dominican Republic, Ecuador, El Salvador, Guatemala, Guyana, Haiti, Honduras, Jamaica, Mexico, Nicaragua, Panama, Peru, Venezuela.
Asia : Afghanistan, Bangladesh, Burma, Indonesia, Iran, Iraq, Khmer Republic, Malaysia, Nepal, Philippines, Republic of Korea, Saudi Arabia, Singapore, Sri Lanka, Thailand, Republic of South Viet–Nam.
Oceania : Fiji and Western Samoa.

Source : World Health Organization, World Health Statistical Report, 1973, vol. 26, No. 11, table 5.

Fig. 61

often compounded where the availability of the latter is contaminated by the lack of the former. (Fig. 61)

Even the availability of a public drainage system does not imply an absence of pollution. Sewage may be discharged locally from drains into streams and rivers virtually untreated or conveyed to more distant sea outlets without treatment. This specific problem is not confined to the developing countries.

Potable water supplies are estimated as available to less than 50 percent of the urban populations in some countries. Where such supplies are not available by nearby piped systems, for the poor there is costly recourse to purchasing water from vendors, daily carrying from distant sources or the use of polluted pond and ditch sources.

Targets set by the World Health Organisation (in 1973) are as follows:

> All regions other than Latin America supply 60 percent of urban population with house connections, the remaining 40 percent with public standpipes; supply 25 percent of the rural population with easy access to safe water. In Latin America, the target is to halve the percentage of citydwellers not supplied with water and to reduce by 30 percent the rural population not supplied in each country.

	Community Water Supply 1970	**Targets 1980 Extra Pop. to be served**	**Costs to reach targets U.S. $ mil.**
Africa	77%	55 million	2,500
L. America	76%	96 million	3,800
S. Asia	64%	239 million	4,300*

*_Development Forum_, January-February, 1976, p. 8.

The disposal of human wastes is one of the key problems in both rural and urban situations in the developing countries. Where populations are widely distributed in rural areas the problem of human waste disposal may not be perceived as critical though pollution of ditches and irrigation courses and through soil drainage may afflict drinking water and spread disease. In congested urban settings, it is immediately more apparent. It constitutes a large burden on the service capacity of towns and cities, requiring increasingly more investment in space, equipment and manpower.

The provision of adequate water supply, sewerage and other services essential to adequate housing adds to the magnitude of the task ahead, and will require relatively massive planning and considerable ingenuity to solve in anything like a reasonable time frame. Again, reliance on conventional approaches, particularly in sewerage where there have been few technical changes in hundreds of years may be wholly inadequate. The more immediately fruitful directions probably lie in the development of more autonomous systems for local treatment and possible recycling and byproduct use than in the single use/disposal systems.

The provision of adequate housing and urban settlements is a crucial area for the harmonious integration of environmental and developmental objectives. It involves the interlocked factors of land, water and air, the provision and use of energy and materials, and a variety of the other core activities that surround the satisfaction of human needs.

CLOTHING

The quantitative estimation of clothing for basic needs is one of the most difficult to deal with in other than wholly functional terms. Apart from the variable effects of climate and activity, the amounts of material worn, the form which this takes and its degree of elaboration is almost entirely dictated by local custom, status and aesthetic preference.

In physiological terms, clothing is a 'portable environment control'. It has been a key adaptive mechanism in enabling human populations to flourish under a great variety of relatively extreme climatic conditions. Adequate clothing including footwear, in all conditions, is an important health criterion with its associated benefits of hygiene and health protection and its protective capacities from insects and other disease carrying organisms.

In our set of Unit Household Indicators we have allocated a rough average 18 kg. of material for clothing, and 2 kg. of leather annually for a five person household. In actual practice, this would vary considerably according to climate. Some indication of clothing layers required under different climatic conditions are given in Fig. 62.

The most detailed attention to the functional quantification of climatic and activity needs for clothing of different kinds has been given by the various

CLOTHING AND CLIMATE

By clothing required for warmth *	By temperature and moisture	By regions and seasons
Less than a complete layer	Hot, humid	Tropical and sub-tropical; temperate, summer; deep mines
One layer (by day), more may be needed at night	Hot, dry	Desert; temperate, summer
Two layers		Temperate, fall and spring, mild winter
Three layers	Cold, dry Cold, wet	Temperate, cold winter; oceanic influence, fog, sun often clouded over
Four layers	Cold, dry	Subpolar, winter; polar, summer
Activity needed for balance with any practicable clothing; shelter needed for rest	Extreme cold dry	Polar winter

* There is a gradation from light to heavy in each layer so that there is overlap.

Source : Clothing: Comfort & Function, Lyman Fourt and Norman R. Hollies, 1970.

Fig. 62

military establishments and a considerable number of field clothing manuals and supporting studies exist for such purposes. They are not very useful in establishing more general needs—but do give some indication of relative research and development priorities!

Measures for basic clothing needs in the general population have been made in the course of poverty surveys, and then focussed on the proportion of income spent for clothing necessities. In a variety of surveys scanned, dating from the late 1950's to 1960's, the average proportion of income so allocated was 10 percent. However, this does not give much help in determining the 'goods' range which might be required to meet basic needs in various conditions.

Apart from the base income necessary to include the satisfaction of clothing needs, a broader consideration for many of the poorer countries would be the price and availability of the various materials required in clothing. This involves the proportion of the economy devoted to the provision of textiles and other products for clothing, household, trade and industry. At this level, a key factor has been the relative competive positions of natural and man-made fibers.

WORLD PRODUCTION OF CERTAIN TEXTILE FIBERS
Thousand Metric Tons & Percent

Type of Fiber	1969	1972	1975
NATURAL FIBERS			
Raw Cotton	11,550	13,372	11,863
Raw Wool	1,614	1,455	1,514
Raw Silk	39	42	20
TOTAL NATURAL ABOVE	13, 203	14,869	13,397
% of World Total	63	60	56
TOTAL MAN–MADE FIBERS			
Rayon, Acetate, and Non-cellulose etc.	7,732	9,925	10,328
% of World Total	37	40	44

Source: Textile Organon, Vol. XLVII, No. 6, June, 1976. **Fig. 63**

The significance of synthetic fibers for clothing goes beyond their market share. In some cases, they provide more fabric by unit weight, and have additional advantages of greater durability and washability, over their natural counterparts. But for meeting the needs of the poorer regions, the energy required for production and the cost of instituting processing facilities tend to make natural materials more appropriate.

We may note from the figures given for world production over the period 1969 to 1975 that man-made materials have gained considerably. Cotton, for example, now supplies less than half of the world's requirement for apparel fibers. (Fig. 63)

This has hit hard at certain of the developed countries whose export trade balance has depended on cotton and wool staples and finished textiles. Whilst it might reduce the internal price for clothes it will also reduce incomes available to purchase them, thus allowing local market inroads for cheaper imported artificial textiles.

In the light of such developments, transition strategies to meeting basic needs may, in some cases, require conversion back to industries using indigenous raw materials. This will not only provide cheaper natural materials for clothing to meet immediate needs, but will also support the kind of self-reliant development that will ensure more long term security for improved living standards.

NOTES

1. Marshall, C.L., Brown, R.E., Goodrich, C.H., ''Improved Nutritions vs. Public Health Services as Major Determinants of World Population Growth'', *Clinical Pediatrics*, Vol. 10, No. 7, July, 1971.

2. Poleman, Thomas T., ''World Food: A Perspective'', *Science*, Vol. 188, No. 4183, May, 1975, p. 511.

3. *Assessment of the World Food Situation, Present and Future*. U.N. World Food Conference, November, 1974, E/Conf./65.3, p. 31.

4. Lappe, F.M., Collins, J., *Where More Food Means More Hunger*. War on Hunger, A.I.D. Report, November, 1976.

5. *Ibid*. *Assessment of World Food Situation*, 1974.

6. *The State of Food and Agriculture*, FAO, 1974.

7. Revelle, R., ''Resources Available for Agriculture'', *Scientific American*, Vol. 235, Sept. 1976.

8. *Yearbook of Fishery Statistics*, Vol. 36, FAO, 1975.

9. *A Conceptual Framework for the Planning of Medicine in Developing Countries*, Staff Working Paper, No. 153, International Bank for Reconstruction and Development; prepared by Peter Newman (Consultant), Johns Hopkins University Press, May, 1973.

10. ''Better Food for a Healthier World'', *Impact of Science on Society*, UNESCO, Vol. XXIV, No. 2, 1974, p. 141.

11. Fendall, N.R., ''Medical Care in Developing Nations'', in *International Medical Care*, ed. by Fry J. and Farmdale, W.A.J., pub. Washington Square East, Wallingford, Pennsylvania, 1972, p. 220.

12. Hughes, C.C., and Hunter, J.M., ''*Disease and Development in Africa*'', Journal of Social Science and Medicine, Vol. 3, p. 445.

13. Hughes, Charles Ca., and Humber, John M., ''The Role of Technological Development in Promoting Disease in Africa'', from *The Careless Technology: Ecology and International Development*, ed. Taghi, Farvar, M., Milton, John P., The Natural History Press, New York, 1972, pp. 69-70.

14. Kassas, M., ''Discussion'', from *The Careless Technology: Ecology and International Development*, ed. Taghi, Farvar M., Milton, John P., The Natural History Press, New York, 1972, p. 143.

15. Sharpston, Michael, *Factors Determining the Health Situation in Developing Countries*, International Bank for Reconstruction and Development, World Bank, Staff Working Paper (Mimeo draft), November, 1976.

16. Norbye, Ole David Koht, ''Health and Demography'', *World Development*, Vol. 2, February, 1974, pp. 13-17.

17. *World Health Statistics Annual*, Vol. III, 1972, WHO, pub. 1976, Sect. 1.

18. ''Adult Education Notes'', UNESCO, Special Issue, 1976.

19. M'Bow, Amadon-Mahtar, Director-General UNESCO, Address on 11th International Literacy Day, September 8, 1976.

20. *Basic Services for Children in Developing Countries*, Report by Executive Director, UNICEF Services, March 12, 1976, p. 18.

21. Harbison, F., ''Human Resource Assessments'', from *Economic and Social Aspects of Educational Planning*:, UNESCO, 1964.

22. e.g., "*World Plan of Action for Application of Scienne and Technology for Development*", U.N., 1971.

23. *Basic Services for Children in Developing Countries*, Report by Executive Director, UNICEF Services, March 12, 1976, p. 18.

24. The 'threshold' standards referred to in the above quotation "... define lower and upper limits of populations, area or distance served by a particular amenity or a community service." *Environmental Issues*, S.C.O.P.E. Report, International Council of Scientific Unions, August, 1976, p. 170.

25. *Ibid.*, p. 171.

26. Lakshmann, T.R., Chatterjee, Lata and P. Roy, "Housing Requirements and National Resources", *Science*, June 4, 1976, Vol. 192, No. 4243. *N.B.* also contains set of estimated housing needs based on the *U.N. World Model* by W. Leontieff.

27. *U.N. Conference on Human Settlements*, Item 10 of the Provisional Agenda, A/Conf. 70/A/1/76, p. 137.

28. Where figures are given in the U.N. Statistical Yearbook 1974, the average size of household was Africa (10 countries) 4.8 persons; Latin America (18 countries) 4.9 Asia (12 countries) 5.5 persons.

29. In this document of 1965, requirements for Africa, Asia and Latin America between 1960-1975 were estimated as:

	Urban	Rural	Total
To provide for population increase	67.5	81.6	149.1
To replace obsolescent stock	22.4	120.4	142.8
To eliminate existing shortages	19.8	80.2	99.0
Totals (Millions)	109.7	282.2	391.9

ENVIRONMENT AND DEVELOPMENT

ALTERNATIVES IN DEVELOPMENT

Development, as process or concept, is not confined to the so-called developing countries but should be viewed as a pattern of ongoing changes which involve all nations as they seek for alternative patterns of sustainable growth.

Traditional environmental concern tended to focus on the impact of industrial growth on the natural environment. Currently it is seen as more an integral part of the whole developmental process. The U.S. Conference on Human Environment, in 1972, was crucial in the recognition of this change of attitude by defining the problems important to the different regions and establishing the common grounds for necessary environmental actions. Whilst national and international concern is still strongly focussed on the physical side of soil deterioration, desertification, deforestation and pollution of the air and waters, it has also broadened to include many aspects of the social environment. Emphases on the outer limits of the biosphere are increasingly balanced by those on the 'inner limits' of the sociosphere—on the social limits of institutional constraints, cultural practices, socio-economic and political preferences.

Attitudes to the process of development itself have undergone similar changes in recent years. The linear model of necessary stages of growth, through which all countries must pass, used to provide the rationale for policies which emphasised international aid, technical assistance, trade and transnational investment as the levers of progress. Internal development focussed on economic expansion of the nation, initially favoring the middle income groups and thereafter, ideally working to the benefit of the poor majority.

Disenchantment with this 'stages' and 'trickle down' approach gradually opened the debate to ideas about alternative modes of development. The 'alternatives' approach whilst it has promise and validity has not yet provided a sufficiently clear idea of what form various alternative societies might take, nor what specific alternatives in development might achieve on a larger scale.

As one commentator notes, unless the value judgment is made as to what a developed society is, it is difficult to determine which changes are part of the development process.[1] Alternatives themselves range from differing, political, ideological or social systems to strategies of development concerned with technical issues, or simply to a notion of the Third World in which things are done in other ways than those pursued in the other two worlds.[2] Many of the alternatives suggested for the Third World have, of course, Western origins, as do the majority of their spokesmen. This is not to denigrate the range of alternatives suggested but to indicate that some may originate in response to external perceptions rather than the expressed internal needs of the actual peoples concerned.

The concept of alternative styles and directions of development is, however, a critically important one. Regardless of which direction may be pursued in terms of ideological, economic or cultural preference, three basic considerations may be underlined:

(i) that the satisfaction of basic human needs, in the largest sense, is central to all developmental purposes and provides a unifying framework and goal orientation for any direction chosen.

(ii) that developmental growth be sustainable with environmental bounds at local, regional and global levels. Sound environmental management is the only optimal strategy within which rational developmental objectives can be attained.

(iii) that greater self-reliance, both individual and collective be a major thrust of developmental policy not wholly in terms of self-sufficiency but towards broad diversification of resource use and, for example, the avoidance of undue dependencies on single crops or products.

Redistribution of world economic advantage as a necessary prerequisite for more balanced development is a clear and objective aspect of the radical changes that are being called for under the banner: "New international economic order".

> "The world has become so interdependent that, for the first time, it requires an economic order that takes into account the needs of the entire globe. It is now abundantly clear that a new world order must of necessity be based upon the recognition of the interdependence between both rich and poor nations and, therefore, on the reciprocity of advantage that this notion implies. This new global economic order requires first and foremost a response to the challenge to the industrialised countries of the North from the developing countries of the South embodied in their call for a New International Economic Order, with particular emphasis on the needs of the world's poorest billion."[3]

A recent initiative, which underlines a key discussion in the development process, is the global emphasis on employment in more direct social development put forward by the International Labor Organisation.

> "A first important objective for the World Development Conference could, therefore, be to reach a consensus on an approach, more effective than that of the present International Development Strategy, for achieving social objectives of development. This new approach, would concern both national and international policies. It would be designed to ensure that the emerging patterns of economic relations effectively contribute to greater social progress for the scores of millions of people who continue to live in conditions of deepest poverty, squalor and deprivation."[4]

THE ECODEVELOPMENT APPROACH

Bridging the objectives of new development directions and environmental management is the concept of 'ecodevelopment'. Policies put forward under this heading are not meant to be part of one exclusive kind of development strategy but rather allow for the more flexible adoption of overall alternative directions according to regional requirements, sociocultural preferences and the demands of specific local situations.

> "In brief, ecodevelopment is a style of development which, in each eco-region, calls for specific solutions to the particular problems of the region in the light of cultural as well as ecological data and long term as well as immediate needs.... As man himself is the most valuable resource, ecodevelopment must above all contribute to his fulfillment. Employment, security, the quality of human relations, respect for the diversity of human cultures—of if one prefers, the development of a satisfactory social eco-system—are all part of this concept."[5]

Thus, eschewing the extremes of the growth and anti-growth debate ecodevelopment aims at outlining forms of development which are centered on the needs of human beings. Although, originally used to consider styles of development more suited to agrarian and semi-industrial countries, it is also applicable to the more developed.

The Ecological Context for Development

We have earlier emphasised the necessary extension of human ecological concepts to embrace not only our agricultural but all of our major industrial activities.

> "Such activities now comprise not only local industrialisation in the sense of mass production factory facilities but all the globally interrelated systems complexes of transportation, communications, production, and distribution facilities. There is no longer a division possible between factory and farm or, in this sense, town and country, all are interlocked in a close symbiotic relation—a man-made ecology which we now see, almost for the first time, as an integrally functioning 'organic' sector within the overall ecosystem."[6]

In considering the environmental and developmental aspects of meeting basic needs, it is this extended context which we must bear in mind. Within this context there is need for both immediate emphasis on local strategies for increased agricultural development and an increasing role for such sophisticated technologies as earth satellite surveying. The electron microscope is as appropriate an 'ecotechnique' as the handhoe or the natural fertilizer plant—and may afford greater leverage in terms of some developmental purposes.

To conceptualise this extended map of human environmental interactions, we may refer to the schematic diagram in Fig. 64. Though merely a labelling device which in no way reflects the relative scales of magnitude or dynamics of the system, this may help illustrate some of the points which follow.

For convenience, the human systems and the physical environ systems have been separated:

a) On the side of the human systems, the arrow linking the biophysical and psychosocial indicates the interactions of the *internal human metabolism* with the environment. Within these columns may be identified the individual and collective human need functions.

b) The arrow-linkage between the psychosocial and technological aspects of the human system and the physical environment constitutes the *external human metabolism*. These columns may be partially viewed as an enlarged mirror image of the metabolic processes which sustain an individual organism—with our digestive system externalised into mining, manufacturing and distribution; our locomotive system into air, sea and land transport; our nervous system into the communications network. They comprise all the extractive, processing, manufacturing, distributing and communicating functions involved in agriculture and industry, and all the other socio-economic and cultural aspects of those environmental transactions through which society supplies human need satisfactions.

A primary focus for environmental management concern may be underlined in the concept of 'external metabolism'. Instead of viewing various resource-using activities as compartmentalised into mutually exclusive functions, we should endeavor to assess them as a regenerative resource system. In other words, agriculture, industrial and service processes should be treated as poten-

HUMAN/ENVIRON SYSTEMS

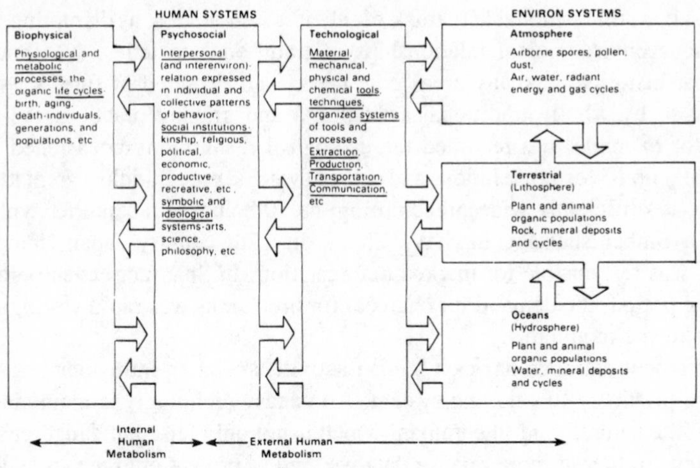

Source: McHale, John, World Facts and Trends, New York, New York, Collier Books, 1972

Fig. 64

tially symbiotic and regenerative systems in terms of their energy and materials flows.

Such an assessment would include not only agri-industrial resource uses, residuals and pollutants but also the flows of energy and materials in all sectors. It would provide a physiological rather than a pathological approach to environmental management—where, at present, we rush to identify economic and environmental malfunctions in one sector without much regard for their relationship to the larger systems.

Within such an approach, social and environmental factors in development planning may be found to be economically advantageous rather than the reverse. Piecemeal attention to pollution, wastes and residuals is often costly. We have no systematic ways in which to extract valuable materials and by-products labelled as pollutants. We therefore burn, bury or void into rivers, lakes and oceans large amounts of economically valuable resources—or engender costs in disposing of the wastes of one activity whilst another may be producing much the same substance as its primary product. Wider and more systematic by-product use and recycling now forms part of the alternative technologies development but it should be made a central theme—particularly in the framing of self-reliance strategies for meeting human needs in limited resource contexts.

This overall conceptual approach also extends to the role of the social and cultural factors in the environmental system. This is not only modified through physical transformations of the earth but also through cultural practices, art, political, ethical and religious systems, and changing perceptions of environmental amenity.

Whilst it is still fashionable to think of 'alien' technologies, as disrupting the harmonious environmental relationships of traditional societies, we should recall that historically, many areas now desert and denuded of forests were rendered so by wholly traditional agricultural and grazing practices. Yi-Fu Fuan,[7] for example, has recorded the ecological disharmony occasioned by specifically non-Western religious and cultural values, e.g. Buddhist cremation practices as sufficiently widespread during the 10th and 14th centuries which created a timber shortage in S.W. China. In 17th century Japan, temple building was responsible for marked deforestation. In Shantung, even before the T'ang period, the demand for charcoal for brush inks was rapidly bringing baldness to the mountains.

Much recent dialogue has cast human activities as alien intrusions into an otherwise pristinely functioning system. An uneasy dichotomy is maintained between 'the natural' and 'the human' which is not only false but dangerously misleading. In lieu of more precise data we tend to project onto the so-called natural system, boundaries of capacity and constraint which are more reflective of individual judgment and socio-cultural preference—than of actual physical bounds. The environment is defined more in terms of preferred qualities rather than essential properties. This is valid providing that we do not treat social judgments as scientific or moral absolutes.

> "... As we come to appreciate that nature's equilibria are transient rather than static, it has become harder to label all changes as adverse ... Some of our most ravaged and degraded landscapes are among the most aesthetically appreciated, the English countryside is a prime example."[8]

Given these caveats, however, there is no doubt that measurable dangerous deteriorations of environmental functions do occur as a result of specific human activities, and that many of our positively conceived developmental modifications such as large scale damming and forest clearing, have often been ill-considered in terms of their eventual human ecological effects. Increased vigilance, both with regard to anticipated impacts and to the conservation, and restoration of environmental systems, is certainly required.

Whilst recognising that many physical limitations imposed by ecological factors are very real, recent thinking has gone beyond the concept of simply sustaining the environmental equilibrium.

> "We must learn to live with a naturally dynamic ecosystem and not make unreasonable demands for short-term stability. Rather, those long term trends that are more likely to determine the survivability of human society

> must be identified and properly managed. In ecological terms, we urge that greater need be given to *resilience* rather than *stability*."[10]

This concept of ecological resilience may be more operationally flexible in determining the compatibility of environmental and developmental objectives in meeting basic human needs.

THE NEEDS/ENVIRONMENT INTERACTION

The accompanying matrices (Figs. 65, 66, 67) provide a schematic framework for considering some of the physical and social environmental interactions with our specified range of basic human needs. The degree of those interactions, noted on a scale from moderate to intense, is given as a provisional guide only.

The harmonising of developmental and environmental directions in the process of meeting needs is not only concerned with the conservation of environmental amenity but with the more positive ways in which the essential economic objectives required for better living standards may be attained without incurring the higher expenses of unanticipated consequences at some later stage in development.

> "... such activities as the construction of roads, dams, airports, irrigation and sewage systems, power plants and industrial facilities sometimes result in concomitant losses of ecological, health or socio-cultural values, or all, and in the long run, increase costs to the society. Such losses, which vary in magnitude, may result from the failure adequately to consider environmental consequences during project planning and design, or from the lack of information and knowledge necessary to predict the eventual impact . . . Higher costs or remedial action may be avoided by prudent planning and early preventative measures."[11]

Clearly, assessing the relationship of such activities with developmental practice needs to be based on different national priorities.

> "A sample of developmental priorities might be: the elimination of hunger, increased material or social welfare, higher employment, marked preference for the short term, the generation of international trade and foreign exchange, industrial development and aesthetic preservation. These would always be mixed in various and changing combinations . . . . Intricately linked to development priorities should be a complimentary set of environmental priorities. Independent factors affecting the objective assignment of environmental priorities are: a) Intensity of the environmentally-degrading activity . . . b) Capacity of the natural system . . . c) Spatial dimensions . . . Developmental and environmental policies will in turn be conditioned by a) Cultural preferences: threatened

INTERACTION MATRIX : Human Needs / Physical Environment

Environ Sectors / Meeting Needs : Basic Human Activities	LAND	Soil	Raw Materials (Minerals)	Arable Land	Meadows and Pastures	Forest	Wasteland	Residential Area	Commercial and Industrial Area	HYDROSPHERE	Oceans	Lakes	Rivers and Streams	Groundwater	Aquatic Plants	ATMOSPHERE	Temperature	Climate	Rainfall	LIFE FORMS Numbers & Growth	Human Populations	Domestic Animals	Wild Animals	Birds	Fish	Insects
FOOD																										
Land Cultivation		■	X	■	/						/	X	X	X	/		■	■	■		■	X	X	X		X
Cropping		X	X	X		/	/	/	/			/	/	/	/		X	X	X		■	■	X	X	X	X
Livestock Production			X	/	/	X	X	/	/		■	■	■		X		/	/	/		X	X	■	■	■	/
Commercial Hunting & Fishing		■	X	■	X	X	X	X	■		/	■	■	■	/		X	X	X		■	■	■	■	X	X
Irrigation		■	X	■	X						/	■	■	■	■		X	X	■		■	X	/	/	X	
Fertilizer & Pesticides		■	/	■	/	/	/	/	/		/	■	■	■	■				/		■	■	/	/	/	
HEALTH																										
Health Facilities			■					■	■								X	X	X		■					
Medicine			/														/	/	/		■	■	X	X		■
Medical Technology			■																		■	■				
SHELTER																										
Buildings & Structures		X	■	/	/	■	/	■	■		/	X	X	X	/		■	■	X		■	X	/	X	/	/
Urbanisation		X	■	X	X	X	/	■	■		X	■	■	■	X		X	X	X		■	■	X	X	X	/
EDUCATION																										
School Buildings		/	■	/	/	X	/	■	■								X	X			■					
Educational Materials			■			/															■					
Educational Technology			■																		■					
CLOTHING																										
Fibre & Clothing Production		/	■	■	■	/		X	■		/	/	X	/	/		X	X	X		■	■	X			X
PROCESSING																										
Resource extraction		/	■	X	/	■	X	X	■		■	X	X	X	X						X	/	/	/	/	
Energy Production		/	■	/		X	/	/	X		X	■	■	■	X		X	X	X		X	X	/			
Industrial Production		/	■	/	/	/	/	/	■		/	X	■	X	/		X	X	X		X	■	/	/	X	/
SUPPORT SYSTEMS																										
Water		X	■	X	/			■	■		X	■	■	■	X		/	X	■		■	X			X	■
Sewage		■	■	X	/	/	/	■	■		■	■	■	■	X		X	X	X		■	■	/	/	X	X
Energy		/	■	X	/	/	/	■	■		X	X	X	/			X	X	/		■	X				
Transport			■					■	■		■	■	■				/	X	X		■	X	/			
Communication								■	■												■					
SOCIO–CULTURAL																										
Human Rights		/	/					X	X		X	X	X	/							■	/	/	/	/	
Employment	■	■	■		/	/		/	■		/	/	/								■	X	/		/	
Security			/	/				/	/		/	/	/								■	/				
Recreation		/	/			/	/	X			/	X	X		/		/	/	/		■	X	X	X	X	
Environmental Protection		■	■	X	X	X	X	X	X		X	■	■	X	/			/	/		■	X	X	X	X	■

N.B. Interactions entered are tentative and provisional for illustration only.

Degree of Interaction : Negligable ☐ (blank)

Slight /

Moderate X

Intense ■

Source : Center for Integrative Studies

Fig. 65

INTERACTION MATRIX : Human Needs/Social Environment

Meeting Basic Needs : Human Activities \ Social Environ Sectors	SOCIAL ENVIRONMENT	Styles of Life	Land Tenure/Property Rights	Kinship Patterns	Community Organization	Religion	Arts & Sciences	Cultural Values	Regulatory Practices	Public Information	ECONOMIC	Income Distribution	Employment : Industrial Sect.	Employment : Agricultural Sect.	Employment : Services Sect.	Social Security	Marketing	Trade : Import/Export	Fiscal Structure	Taxation	Research & Development	Levels of Technology	Incentive Structures	POLITICAL	Legislative System	Environment Policies	Educational Policies	Economic Policies	Health/Welfare Policies	National/Regional Plans	Defense	Ideological Factors	International Aspects	
FOOD																																		
Cropping		/	/	X		/		/		/		/	/	■	/		■	■	/	/	X	X	X		/	X		X		/			X	
Livestock Production		/	/	X		/	/	/				/	/	■	/		■	■	/	/	/	/	X		/	/		X		/			X	
Hunting & Fishing		X	/	/				/				/	/	■	X		■	■	/	/	/	/	/		/	X		/		/			X	
Land Cultivation		/	/	■	/	/		/	/	/		/	/	■	/		X	X	/	/	X	X	X		/	X		X		X				
Irrigation		X	/	X					/	/			/	X	/				/	/	X	X	X		/	X		/	X	X			/	
Fertilizer & Pesticides		/	/	/					/	/			X	X	/		X	X	/	/	X	X	X		/	■		/	/	/			/	
HEALTH																																		
Health Facilities		/	/			/	/	/	/	/		X	/		■	■		/	/	/	■	■	X		/		X	/	■	/			/	
Medicine		/	/				/	/	/	/			X	/	■	■	/	/			■	■	/		/	/			■					
Medical Technology		/						/	/	/			■		■	X	X	X			■	■	/					/	■					
SHELTER																																		
Buildings & Structures		X	■	■	■	X	X	X		/		X	■	/	X	/	X	X	/	X	X	X	X		/	■		■	/	■			/	
Urbanisation		X	■	■	■	■	/	X	/	/		X	■	/	■	X	X	X	/	/	/	X	/		/	X	/	X	X	■				
EDUCATION																																		
School Buildings			/		/	X	/	■	X	X			X		■				X	■	/	/	/		X	/	■	X		■		/		
Education Materials/Technology		/	/				X	■	X	■			X		X		X	X	/	/	X	X			/		■	/				/	/	
CLOTHING																																		
Fibre & Clothing Production		/	■					/					■	■	■	■	■	/	/	/	X	■	X		/	/		X	/	/		/	/	
PROCESSING																																		
Resource Extraction		X	/	X					/	/			■		/		■	■	/	/	■	■	X		X	■		X	/	■	X		■	
Energy Production		X	X	/				/	/			/	■	/	X		■	■	X	X	■	■	X		X	■		■		■	X		■	
Industrial Production		X	■	/		/		/				/	■	/	/		■	■	/	/	■	■	X		X	X		■	/	■	X	X	X	
SUPPORT SYSTEMS																																		
Water		X	X	X		X	/	/	/	/			X	X	X					/	X	X	X		X	■		X	X	■	/	/	/	
Sewage		X	X	/		/		/	/				X	/	X					/	X	X	X		X	■		/	X	X			/	
Energy		X	■			/		/	/	/			■	X	■		/	/	/	X	■	■	X		X	■		X		■	X		■	
Transport		X	■	/		/		/	/	/			X	X	■		X	X	/	X	■	■	X		X	■		■		■	X		■	
Communication		X	■			/	/	/	■	X			X	/	■		X	X	/	X	■	■	X		X	/	X	X	X	■	■	X	■	
SOCIO–CULTURAL																																		
Human Rights		■	X	■	X	X	X	■	X	/		X	X	X	X	■									■	X	X	X	X	X	/	/	/	
Employment		X	■	/		/		/	/	/		■	■	■	■	X	■	■	/	X	X	X	X		X	/	/	■	■	X		/	/	
Security		■	/	X	/	/	/	/	/	/					■	/	/	/	/	X		/			■	/		/	/	/	■	X	■	
Recreation		/	■	/	/	/	/	X	/	X		/			■					/			/		/	/	/	/	/			/	/	
Environmental Protection		■	/			/		/	/	/			/	/	/				/	/	X	X	X		■	■	/	X	X	■		/	X	

N.B. Interactions entered are tentative and provisional for illustration only.

Degree of Interaction : Negligable ☐ (blank)

Slight ⧄ (/)

Moderate ☒ (X)

Intense ■

Source : Center for Integrative Studies

Fig. 66

INTERACTION MATRIX : Interactions of Activities in Meeting Basic Needs

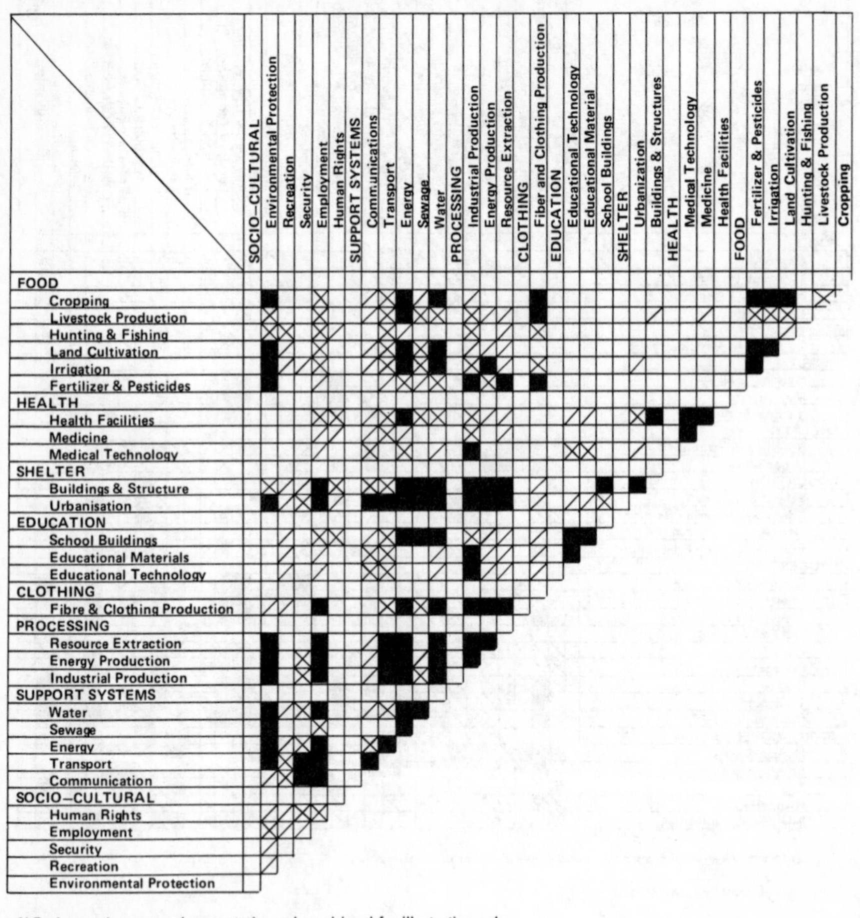

N.B. Interactions entered are tentative and provisional for illustration only.

Degree of Interaction : Negligable ☐

Slight ◪

Moderate ☒

Intense ■

Source : Center for Integrative Studies.

Fig. 67

national or religious symbols or sites will precipitate intervening action. b) The vision of man as a biological as well as an economic entity . . . c) The level of income . . . In Particular, priorities change as a country develops. Amenities, space, cleanliness and other indicators of the quality of life become increasingly more important as the factors essential to life are taken for granted.''[12]

In discussing the strategies for meeting basic needs, we shall again focus more specifically on the objectives within each need area. Given the variety of developmental and environmental situations, and the alternative ways in which needs may be met in different societies, such discussion is of a general nature only and would require more detailed 'on-the-ground' assessment of particular cases for its more effective consideration.

NOTES

1. Horowitz, Irving L., *Three Worlds in Development*, Oxford University Press, p. 59.
2. Streeten, Paul, ''The Concept of Alternatives'', *World Development*, No. 2, February, 1974, p. 5.
3. Grant, James and Ul Haq, Mahbub, ''Income Distribution and the International Financing of Development'', Annex 2, *Reshaping the International Order: A Report to the Club of Rome*, Tinbergen, Jan, Coordinator, Dotman, Anthony I., editor, pub. E.P. Dutton and Co., Inc. New York, 1976, p. 210.
4. *Employment, Growth and Basic Needs: A One World Problem*, I.L.O. Geneva, 1976, p. 5.
5. Sachs, Ignacy, ''Environment and Styles of Development'', in ''*Outer Limits and Human Needs*'', ed. Matthews, Wm. H., Dag Hammarskjold Foundation, Uppsala.
6. McHale, John, *The Ecological Context*, George Braziller, New York, 1970, p. 8.
7. Fuan, Yi Fu, ''Our Treatment of the Environmental Ideal and Reality'' *American Scientist*, May/June 1970.
8. Nisbet, Ian, C.T., ''Ecology, Hard Push on a ''Soft Science'', *Technology Review*, October/November, 1973, p. 17.
9. *Resilience* (after C.S. Holling) is the ability of a system to absorb and even benefit by unexpected finite changes in system variables and parameters, without deteriorating irreversibly. In contrast, *stability* describes the ability of a system to absorb very small perturbations about a state of equilibrium.
10. *Science, Technology and Society: A Prospective Look*, Bellagio Conference, 1976, U.S. National Academy of Sciences.
11. *Ecological, Health and Human Ecologic Considerations in Economic Development Projects*, World Bank, May, 1974, p. iii. *N.B.* This is an excellent handbook which treats many areas of this discussion in considerable detail and provides working checklists for specific types of developmental projects.
12. McLeod, Scott, *Environmental Costs and Priorities: A Study at Different Locations and Stages of Development*, Development and Environment Conference, (Founex), U.N., Geneva, 1972.

MEETING BASIC NEEDS

There are no unique paths or policies which may guarantee that if one set of environmental and developmental objectives is pursued then the basic needs of more people in the poorer countries will be met.

Whilst they do have much in common, countries are different in their social and economic capacities, their resource endowment and their specific geographic and environmental situations. They also differ in the incidence of poverty, in internal income distribution and in their rates of economic and population growth.

Appropriate basic needs strategies should, therefore, be determined by the countries themselves, although these might be helped by degrees of inter-country, regional and international cooperation.

Several current approaches to meeting basic needs focus on increasing income and employment as the core means towards the fulfillment of needs. The World Bank has many studies and projects devoted to this end. The ILO has called for a strategy for increasing and diversifying employment. The Bariloche Study[1] extends such approaches, through use of a mathematical 'world model', to include a wide range of variables, both with regard to needs and the supply levels of resources to meet them, and to consider these in terms of appropriate implementation.

In describing its aims, a recent ILO paper summarises some general characteristics of the above approaches.

> "The paper proceeds by choosing a goal in terms of a defined set of basic needs for each of 15 sub-regions of the world. Then an income is estimated which an individual would need to be able to consume a bundle of goods associated with such needs . . . continues by computing the economic growth and income redistribution needed for each sub-region to enable on average, the poorest 20 percent to satisfy their needs . . . Our aim is to demonstrate the magnitude of the growth and/or redistribution of income required so that as many individuals as possible can receive enough income in order to satisfy basic needs."[2]

All of these directions have the merit of being unitary in their approach and of recognising the essential inter-relatedness of needs.

In this regard Shalaby underlines the need for integrating all dimensions as a basis for new types of development plans.

> "1. Absolute growth goals are replaced by new quantitative growth goals which emphasise the production of those goods and services which satisfy the basic needs of the population.
>
> 2. Provision is made for meaningful opportunities for participation in the development process by the masses of population in the developing countries.
>
> 3. There is an emphasis on self-reliance and collective self-reliance, taking advantage of country's or a group of countries' endowment of human and natural resources.
>
> 4. There is an emphasis on improving patterns of income and wealth distribution."[3]

We propose here to explore some of the components of such a strategy which emerge from considering the materials supply side of needs themselves. I. e., having estimated some needs deficiencies we shall discuss ways to meet them whilst bearing in mind the environmental and developmental objectives within which this would be done.

FOOD AND AGRICULTURE

Food production through sound agricultural practices is one of the prime areas in which environmental and developmental objectives can be mutually supportive and in which maximal utilisation of resources to meet basic needs can be harmonious with the maintenance, and expansion, of productive capacity.

Several objectives present themselves in this area; raising food production in the needy countries, providing a more varied diet, and ensuring more equitable distribution and access to sufficient food.

As we have noted, there is more than enough food produced on the world scale and present land and yield capacities could feed even more. These points have been made many times.

> "Thousands of the world's poorest people eat food as soon as they harvest it. It never enters the market . . . World food supplies have been increasing steadily, and have not yet been outrun by population growth . . . Even in 1972, when weather conditions reduced crop yields in all regions of the world, the marketed grain could have provided 632 pounds for every person . . . in 1960 this would have fed 300 million more people than were thought to exist. By 1973 this figure was 600 million."[4]

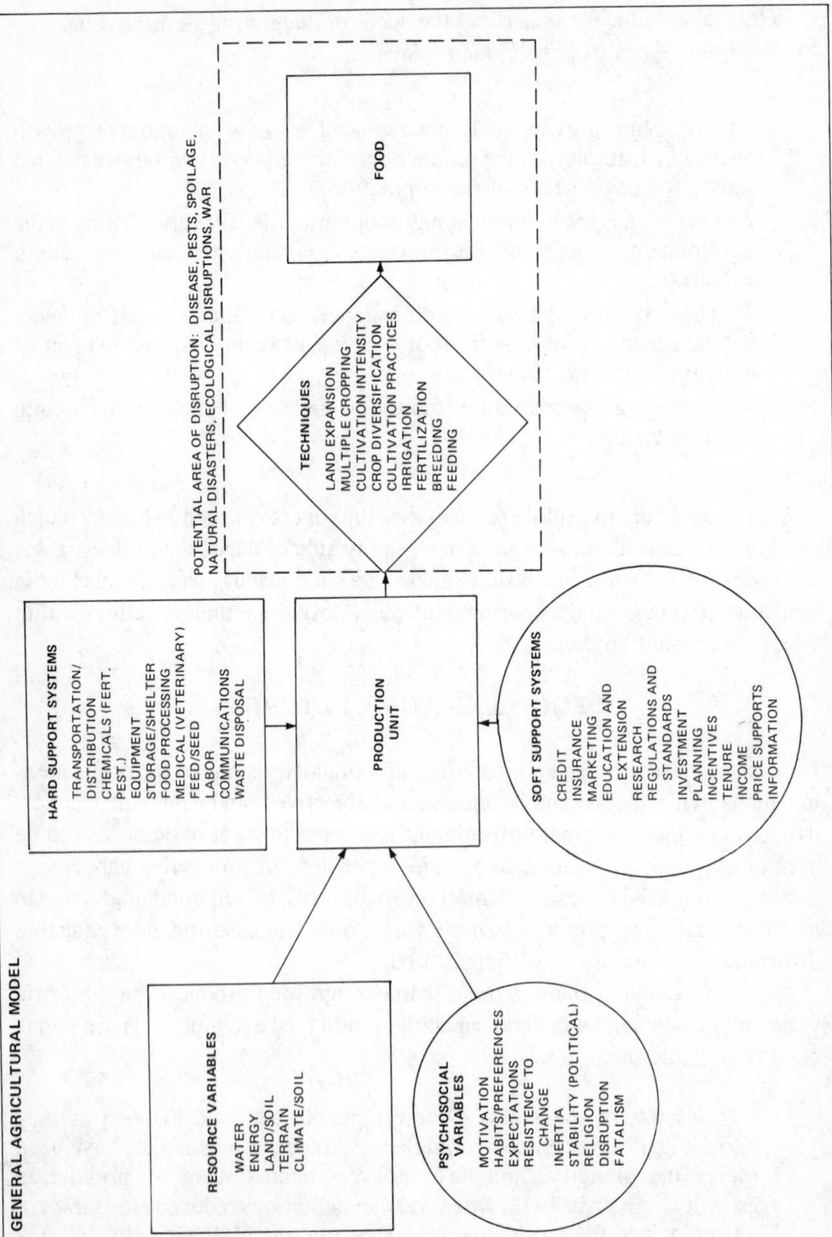

Source: Center for Integrative Studies

Fig. 68

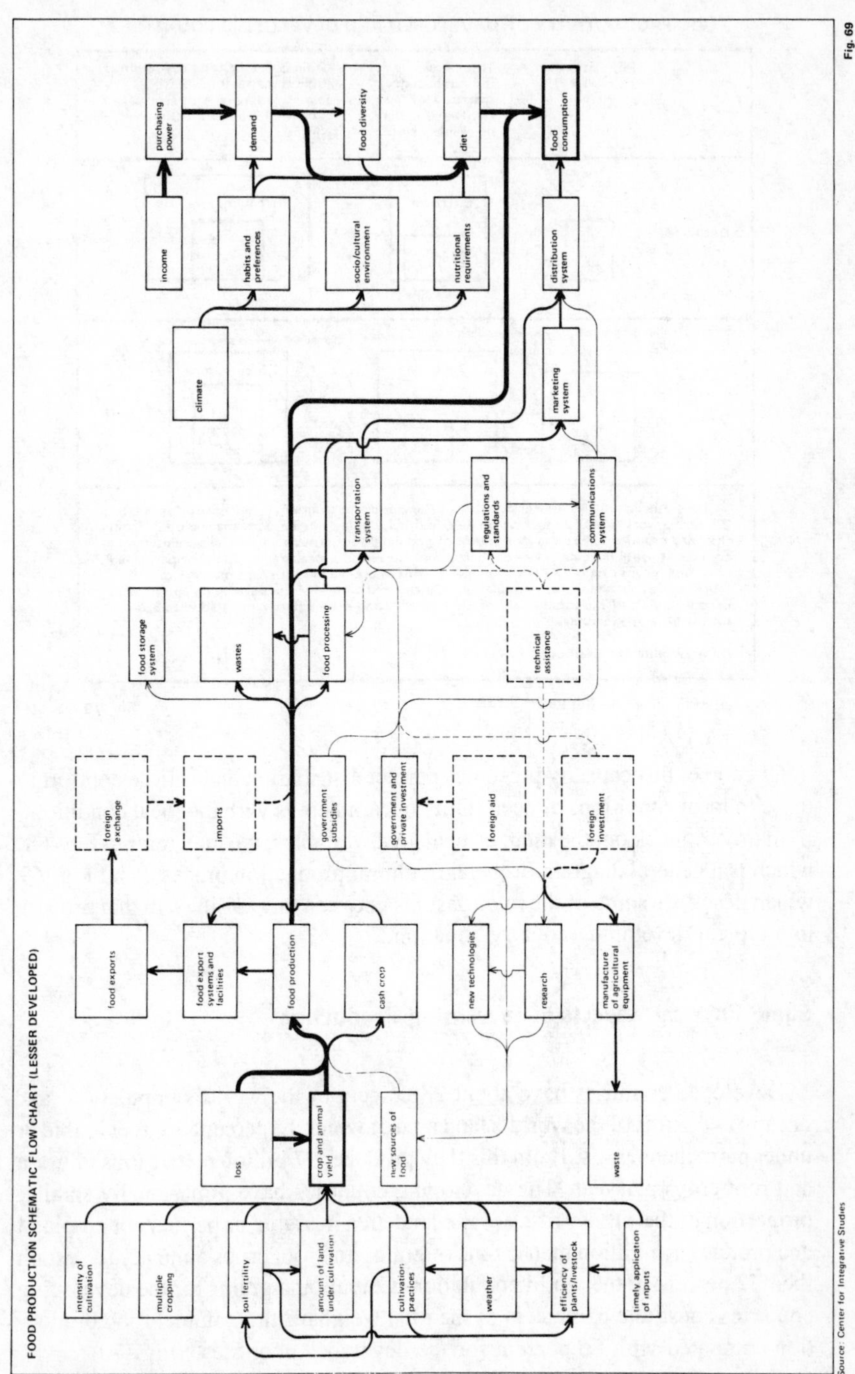

Source: Center for Integrative Studies

Fig. 69

FOOD PRODUCTIVITY OF DEVELOPED AND DEVELOPING COUNTRIES

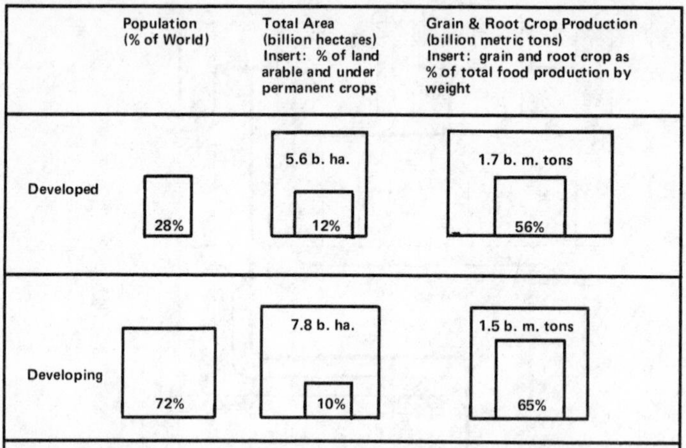

	Population (% of World)	Total Area (billion hectares) Insert: % of land arable and under permanent crops	Grain & Root Crop Production (billion metric tons) Insert: grain and root crop as % of total food production by weight
Developed	28%	5.6 b. ha. / 12%	1.7 b. m. tons / 56%
Developing	72%	7.8 b. ha. / 10%	1.5 b. m. tons / 65%

Developed countries have about 28% of the world's population. They occupy about 2/5 of the world's land area of which 12% is either arable or under permanent crops. From this they produce 1.7 billion metric tons of grain and root crops a year. The developing countries devote marginally less of their 3/5 of the world's total area to arable or permanent crop land, producing only 1.5 billion metric tons of grain and root crops per year to sustain their 72% of the world's population. Cereals and grains for the developing countries constitute 65% of the total weight of their annual food production, compared with 56% for the developed countries.

Data: Production Yearbook 1974, FAO.

Source: Center for Integrative Studies.

Fig. 70

Of course, this capacity presumes perfect distribution and is little comfort to those in local conditions of need. Our concern here is with the local condition.

In order to seek out the more critical local variables, we may refer to Fig. 68, which is a general diagram of the agricultural production process, and Fig. 69 which describes some of the relationships between the variables in that process in a typical developing country situation.

Some Physical Aspects of Increasing Production

Developed countries have about 28 percent of the world's population, and occupy two-fifths of the world's land area of which 12 percent is either arable or under permanent crops. From this they produce 1.7 billion metric tons of grain and root crops per year. The developing countries have a marginally smaller proportion of their three-fifths of the land area in arable or permanent cropland and produce 1.5 billion metric tons of grains and root crops annually to sustain their 72 percent of the world population. Cereals and grains for the developing countries constitute 65 percent of the total weight of their annual food production compared with 56 percent for the developed countries. (Fig. 70)

FACTORS IN PLANNING

Activities to Meet Needs In Agricultural Sector: Increased Food Production

ACTIVITY	NEGATIVE FACTORS	HARMONIOUS POLICIES	
		ENVIRONMENTAL	DEVELOPMENTAL
Intensive Cultivation	Soil Depletion	Soil Rotation and Restoration; Multi-cropping; Crop Shifting	Adequate Land and Soil Conservation and Tenure Policies
Deforestation to Extend Cultivation	Leaching; Slash/Burn Techniques	Planned Forest Uses Reforestation; Terracing	Tree Cropping; Use of Forest Crops and Product-forest Farming
Pest Control	Water Runoff; Contamination of Fish, Drinking Water	Integrated Systems of Biological and Chemical Controls	Agricultural Research; Rural Training, Public Education; Improve Processing Warehousing, Storage of Crops
Increased Fertilizer Use	Water Runoff and Contamination, Nitrate Poisoning of Drinking Water	Use of Biological Sources of Nitrogen and Nitrogen Fixation; Use of Composts and Wastes	Research and Development; Local Systems of Composting Wastes
Increased Irrigation and Daming	Salinization; Water Logging; Modification of Soil Structure; Water Borne Diseases; Loss of Silt; Population Displacement	Comprehensive and Anticipatory Planning of Water Management	Thorough and Integrated Review of Planning Priorities and Alternatives; Mobilization of People to Participate in Control Policies
Introduction of High Yield Crops	Susceptibility to Disease; High Chemical Controls Required	Retain Crop Diversity; Increase Traditional Yields; More Comprehensive Planning of High Yield Crop Use	Yield Incentives for Traditional Crops; Encourage Crop Diversity and Sustained Rather than Short Term Benefits
Intensive Animal Husbandry in Grazing and Feed Lots	Soil Erosion/Depletion; Desertification; Excreta and Waste Concentration Runoff	Diversification of Livestock Use; Desert Reclamation and Use of Saline Agriculture Techniques	Balanced Policies for Livestock Production; Cropping of Wild Species; more Comprehensive Policies

Source : Center for Integrative Studies

Fig. 71

Part of this difference in productivity is due to climatic conditions and the proportional availability of productive soils but much is also due to other more controllable factors.

In many of the poorer countries, traditional agricultural practices often have several deleterious side effects leading to soil degradation and loss of productivity. Land that is worked with little rotation and nutrient replenishment reduces progressive yields; soil erosion due to seasonal flooding and poor irrigation practices is also accompanied by salination and alkalinisation of soils; leaching of soils follows the conversion of forests to farmland; desert encroachment aggravated by overgrazing and loss of ground cover often accompanies the traditional herding practices associated with nomadism.

Attention to the control of these factors could increase productive capacity considerably. Some selected examples have been summarised in Fig. 71. One specific case, the problem of soil erosion in Lesotho may be adduced here. Volunteer groups have been enrolled to assist in terracing and other watershed management schemes, contour ploughing has been vigorously promoted and other directly participative methods have been encouraged. One positive side of this effort has been the establishment of fish farming where eroded land or that unsuitable for cultivation has been used for carp and trout ponds. Such ponds

A MORE NATURAL FERTILIZATION
Quantities of soil nutrients, used or unused, available to the Third World through organic wastes in 1971, compared with the quantities of chemical fertilizers it produced, imported or consumed during the same year (in millions of tons)

	Nitrogenous N	Phosphatic P	Potassic K	Total NPK
Animal	17.80	4.91	14.12	**36.83**
Farm compost	9.54	3.34	9.54	**22.42**
Human	12.25	2.87	2.61	**17.73**
Urban sewage	1.43	0.29	0.86	**2.58**
Urban compost	0.48	0.38	0.57	**1.43**
Other	6.63	4.44	11.35	**22.42**
Available organic waste	48.13	16.23	39.05	**103.41**
Chemical fertilizer production	3.28	1.65	0.30	**5.23**
Imports	2.59	0.96	1.14	**4.70**
Consumption	5.87	2.61	1.44	**9.93**

Sources : Organic materials as fertilizers (SIDA/FAO) and Production Yearbook 1974 (FAO) and CERES, March/April, 1976.

Fig. 72

not only help fight erosion by retaining run-off but provide an additional protein source and a new marketable product. Fish farming, as the by-produce of this integrated program to arrest soil erosion, has also given farmers, particularly women, the chance to acquire new skills.

Such Lesotho-type cases could be introduced where large numbers of under-employed people can be mobilised for terracing, reforestation and similar projects. New land management techniques can be introduced to check over-grazing by upgrading stock, pasture rotation, fencing and in some cases, as in Africa, by the introduction of more systematic cropping and 'farming' of wild species.

Water management, itself, presents special problems. The Asian countries, as a whole, have placed traditional emphasis on irrigation networks but they often work below potential due more to economic and administrative factors than to physical supply.

> ''Even so, one out of every three acres cultivated in Asia is supplied with irrigation water of one kind or another, mostly from rivers, canals, tanks

> or wells. Thus not surprisingly, paddy rice accounts for half the total area under grains, almost three-quarters of all grains harvested and two-fifths of the total calorie intake of Asia's consumers. On dry land, a great number of grains, as well as pulses, oilseeds, and fibres are grown with varying degrees of success and at yields which are often the lowest in the world."[5]

Under appropriate management conditions, multiple cropping could be more widely introduced yielding three to four times the return from a single crop. Likewise, the integration of livestock fodder crops could supplement the traditional one crop system not only adding animal farming but providing additional protein sources.

Increasing production directly through the *high yield grains* has had mixed success. Due to requirements for increased irrigation, fertiliser and better crop management, it has often benefited the richer and larger farmers rather than the poorer. Its extended use should include subsidizing and training of the small farmer, thereby improving his opportunities for self-reliance.

Chemical *fertiliser use* itself whilst it has undoubtedly raised yields now adds to the burden of the poorer countries where it requires scarce foreign exchange to purchase. Many have already equipped themselves to produce their own chemical fertiliser—but more natural fertilisation is feasible with no mineral resources and at less cost. (Fig. 72)

> "In 1971, the tonnage of soil nutrients available to the developing countries was ten times what they used in chemical form during the same year and twenty times what they produced."[6]

Such natural fertiliser processing could provide the basis for local agri-industry development. It may also be linked to village-scale biogas fertiliser plants and thereby to increased local energy autonomy. (Fig. 73)

Some other possibilities for enhancing productivity lie with protected cultivation—(usually considered beyond the economic capacity of farmers in the developing world but more possible now with cheap plastic coverings). Other possibilities include: relay cropping (of one crop sandwiched between the growth seasons of another); the reduced tillage technique which now seems especially applicable for difficult and easily erodible tropical soils; and new types of forage crops for the arid and semi-arid areas.[7]

Crop diversification is a likely strategy for greater self sufficiency at both local and national levels that would provide more balanced diets. As a recent report emphasises,

> "Man has only just begun to take stock of the chemical and genetic possibilities in the plant kingdom . . . The apparent advantages of staple plants over minor tropical plants often result from the disproportionate

Production of 230,000 tons of Nitrogen per Year by Western and Alternative Technologies

	Western technology	Alternative technology
Number of plants	1	26,150 (at 8.8 tons per year per plant)
Capital cost	about $140 million	about $125 million (at 4,825 per plant)
Foreign exchange	about $70 million	nil
Capital/sales ratio (at $510 per ton nitrogen)	1.20	1.07
Employment	1,000	130,750 (at 5 per plant)
Energy	about 0.1 million MWh per year consumption	6.35 million MWh per year generation

Source : CERES, March/April, 1976.

Fig. 73

research attention they have been given. Many indigenous species may possess equal merit but were disregarded during the colonial era when consumer demands in European countries largely determined the cultivation (and research) priorities in tropical agriculture.''[8]

Properties of some thirty-six species are outlined in the above quoted report, ranging through cereals, roots and tubers, vegetables, fruits, oilseeds, forage and other crops. Two of these have recently received wider attention; on, the winged bean[9] has possibilities of becoming a significant food crop of high protein value in the humid tropics, and two, the jojoba, a liquid wax secreting plant, promises to be an important source of industrial oils and waxes.

Fig. 74 gives a list of fifty plants with a high protein content many of which are insufficiently used for food and associated purposes. Of course, protein content is not the only factor, there is ''their biological value, digestibility, protein efficiency ratio and whether they will grow in any soil or climate'', factors which have not yet been established in many cases.

In the arid and semi-arid zones, there is also a great variety of food plants[10] which were formerly used as staples by local peoples, and whose properties are now being reviewed for their use as supplemental crops. Many of these are also suitable for cultivation under conditions where saline irrigation can be used.

The potential for such diversification is considerable though much research and development is still necessary. Such development work in itself should be more directly encouraged as part of countries' basic needs strategies and should

AGRICULTURAL DIVERSIFICATION

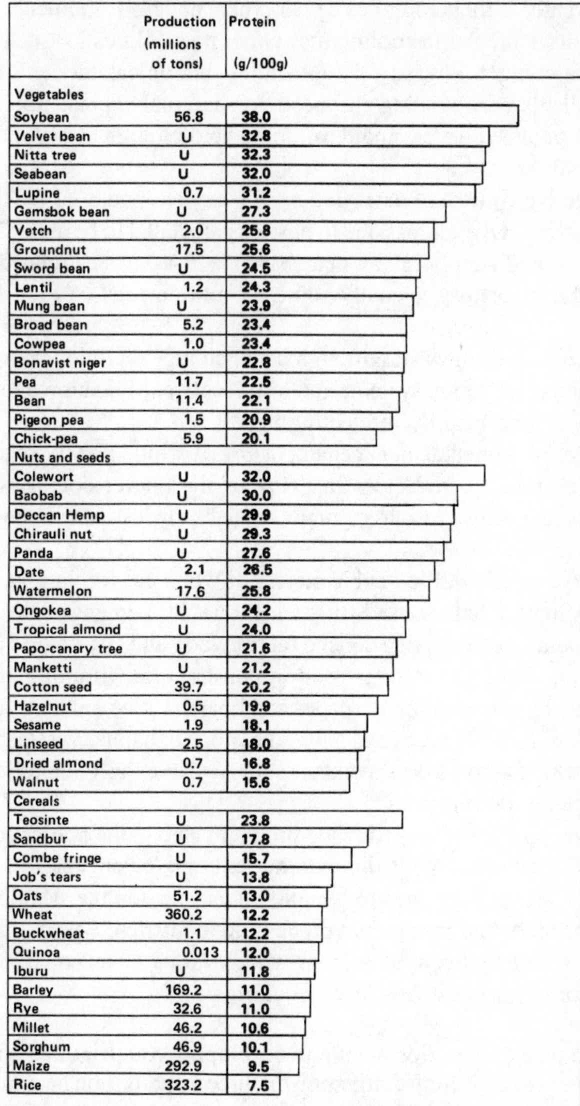

	Production (millions of tons)	Protein (g/100g)
Vegetables		
Soybean	56.8	38.0
Velvet bean	U	32.8
Nitta tree	U	32.3
Seabean	U	32.0
Lupine	0.7	31.2
Gemsbok bean	U	27.3
Vetch	2.0	25.8
Groundnut	17.5	25.6
Sword bean	U	24.5
Lentil	1.2	24.3
Mung bean	U	23.9
Broad bean	5.2	23.4
Cowpea	1.0	23.4
Bonavist niger	U	22.8
Pea	11.7	22.5
Bean	11.4	22.1
Pigeon pea	1.5	20.9
Chick-pea	5.9	20.1
Nuts and seeds		
Colewort	U	32.0
Baobab	U	30.0
Deccan Hemp	U	29.9
Chirauli nut	U	29.3
Panda	U	27.6
Date	2.1	26.5
Watermelon	17.6	25.8
Ongokea	U	24.2
Tropical almond	U	24.0
Papo-canary tree	U	21.6
Manketti	U	21.2
Cotton seed	39.7	20.2
Hazelnut	0.5	19.9
Sesame	1.9	18.1
Linseed	2.5	18.0
Dried almond	0.7	16.8
Walnut	0.7	15.6
Cereals		
Teosinte	U	23.8
Sandbur	U	17.8
Combe fringe	U	15.7
Job's tears	U	13.8
Oats	51.2	13.0
Wheat	360.2	12.2
Buckwheat	1.1	12.2
Quinoa	0.013	12.0
Iburu	U	11.8
Barley	169.2	11.0
Rye	32.6	11.0
Millet	46.2	10.6
Sorghum	46.9	10.1
Maize	292.9	9.5
Rice	323.2	7.5

"Figures in second column show that the largest tonnages are not always from plants richest in protein...of course, proportion of protein is not the only factor... one should not overlook, for example, biological value, digestibility, protein efficiency ratio or the fact that not every plant will grow in any soil or climate."

U = Unknown.

Source : Adapted from CERES, March/April, 1976. Amino -acid content of foods and biological data on proteins (FAO) and Production Yearbook 1974 (FAO).

Fig. 74

involve the poorer countries' own well trained people so that they could contribute greatly to their countries development and also assume leadership in such areas within the world community. Other possibilities for such advanced work are searching for ways of augmenting biological modes of nitrogen fixation in plants so obviating the need for external inputs; improving the efficiency of photosynthesis; and developing acid biological methods for pest and weed control.

More effective control of *pests and crop wastage* would go far to increase usable production. Overall loss due to pests is calculated to be about 20 percent of the world's food supply in any one year. The FAO has estimated that rats, insects and fungi destroy annually some 33 million tons of food in storage alone.

The reduction of such wastes through better storage facilities, more efficient processing and distribution systems and large scale participation and incentive programs, is a clear priority in meeting needs.

Improved environmental management of *forests* would greatly enhance basic needs and self-reliance strategies in many of the poorer countries. Though technically a renewable resource, many valuable forests are being denuded through indiscriminate use.

Of the two and half million cubic meters of wood cut for various uses each year, approximately half is used for fuel. About 90 percent of the people in Asia, Africa and Latin America depend on firewood and charcoal as their main source of fuel; about one-third is used in construction, furniture and related industries and 13 percent in pulp, paper and board. Large amounts are wasted each year due to natural causes and particularly due to haphazard slash and burn cultivation, which ignores the special uses forests have for food production and ancillary agricultural purposes.

Only a fraction of the finished wood product value in the poorer countries is realised, and then usually by the external enterprises engaged in this area. Opportunities are thereby lost for employment and for the development of indigenous primary and by-product processing industries. Possibilities for the production of fuel hydrocarbons from wood wastes have not been pursued except, typically, in more developed countries.

> "More than 250 million people in developing countries eke out a scanty existence from shifting cultivation on three to six billion hectares of land. By combining the establishment of permanent forests with food production, the harmful effects of shifting cultivation can be removed, and instead of the degraded shrub which usually grows on land abandoned by shifting cultivators, people can have forests capable of being utilized for their economic well-being."[11]

The emphasis here on forestry within the topic of food and agriculture is to draw attention to the importance of the overall agricultural sector—not only to provide food, but to provide a large range of raw materials for other industries which rely on agricultural products. Examples of these such as industrial alcohol and fuel hydrocarbons have been mentioned. Others include organic chemicals, beverages, pharmaceuticals, plastics, textiles and other fiber products, leather and rubber. Many of these are used to produce goods which would have to be imported and paid for with foreign exchange. Many countries are hampered by dependence on a few cash crops which absorb much of their agricultural economy. Greater self-reliance may be sought through wider diversification of these agriculturally produced raw materials for use in domestic industries—thereby reducing imports, enhancing lcoal employment, and widening the developmental base of the country.

Institutional constraints on maximising resource use to meet basic needs constitute a further and overriding limitation to sound development. One such constraint is the 'institution' of poverty itself, where a great many of the farmers are close to subsistence and hedged in by small plots, invidious land tenure practices, low or non-existent credit and the lack of an adequate infrastructure to serve their needs. Many are tenant farmers and laborers where, "the family provides the bulk of the labor, consumes most of the produce harvested and buys and sells little to supplement a less than adequate living standard."[12]

In such situations there are few incentives and little opportunity to increase production. The laborer, though hard working, is relatively unproductive and underemployed; the family, and often the whole village group, may be singularly disadvantaged with regard to improving their lot—by lack of education and training, low health, energy, and poor surroundings and by traditional acceptance of their lot.

For example,

> "The total number of rural households in India is 70 million of which 35 percent are below the subsistence category, 30 percent are subsistence farmers and 21 percent are middle class farmers. About 50 percent of the land is owned by the 7 percent classified as rich farmers—a major constraint lies in the division of the country's agricultural economy into two sectors. The sector which controls the major surplus of food grains is developing. This sector which includes relatively few people, is well provided with personal and government-provided services. The less-developed sector comprises the area cultivated by the great majority of the tillers—small scale and marginal farmers, tenants, sharecroppers and agricultural laborers who are also the most disadvantaged in regard to education, housing and public health."[13]

In many Latin American countries, it is estimated that between half to one percent of the landholders own or control more than 50 percent of the land and, in some case, up to 75 percent.

When these conditions are altered as they have been in several countries, by such measures as land reform the capacity for meeting needs locally has increased and there are greater incentives to participate in more innovative and productive agricultural management by the majority of the people. This may be noted, for example, in Mexico, where beneficiaries of redistributed land have shared substantially in the spread of new methods during the past several decades,

> "The ejidatarios achieved this despite the fact that their farms were on average small, their soils were generally of poorer quality than on private farms, their formal education was scant (average of 3.4 years in 1965) and most of them lacked farm management experience before receiving land."[14]

The question of ownership of institutionalised water rights is part and parcel of the land tenure problem. Control over irrigation can be as effective as actually owning the land itself. Associated with these tenure practices of land, water and other facilities, there are rigid hierarchical divisions of class and status which constrain initiative and productivity, particularly in the traditional agricultural sector.

Other institutional barriers to higher local productivity are restrictions which make credit rarely available on an adequate scale for the small and marginal farmers at high risk. Centralised marketing, processing, distribution and transportation facilities and other parts of the agri-industry support infrastructure such as extension services and training facilities are also usually inadequate to the same degree. This lowers possible income and reduces incentive for production when the sale of surplus produce may be on an unstable basis, where foods may not be stored without spoilage and where a good harvest may be 'lost' due to lack of such basic facilities. Sound basic needs directions at this level would seek deliberately for a more integrated infrastructure within which the individual farmer could exercise some due measure of participation and control.

One recurring problem for rural development strategies is the lure of the city. This might be somewhat redressed if the agricultural worker had more stake in the land, and if it were possible to decentralise urban facilities, so that more could be offered at the village level in the way of occupational and recreational alternatives. However, it has to be recognised that in comparison with other activities, labor intensive farming is an arduous and demanding occupation which, were choices equal, might rank low on most individual preferences. It may well be that in the long range, as we begin to consider the satisfaction of human needs beyond the minima, small holdings may not provide the most plausible way of meeting societies' large scale developmental requirements.

The Role of Nutritional Policy

Given adequate local production of food and income to ensure sufficiency, poverty and ignorance may still erode the capacity to select a balanced diet. Many traditional ways of preparing foods are destructive of their nutrient content, and the household distribution of foods often do not favor those most in need, i.e. children and nursing mothers. This, combined with the general paucity of locally available food ranges, suggest that national nutrition policies have a central role in fulfilling basic food needs.

A note is made here of some of the key components that may be considered in the framing of nutrition policy.

(i) *Food balance sheets, consumer expenditure and consumption surveys* identify the problem and begin to specify the target populations in most need.
(ii) *Nutrition objectives* determine where and to whom programs should be directed, e.g. "by 1978 Country X should achieve provision of adequate protective foods and services in types and quantities that will reduce from 30 to 10 percent the number of six to two year old children suffering third degree and second degree protein-calorie deficiency". This may be appropriately adjusted for other target population groups.
(iii) *Adoption of a system approach* helps locate nutritional objectives within the socio-economic environment and provides a broad range of feasible and interrelated targets and programs for nutritional programs at national and local levels of implementation.[15]

The essential elements of an adequate nutrition policy would become part of the overall basic needs strategy that would outline the targets for basic food supply and related services. Just as we have noted that good environmental management plays a major role in forwarding economic development, so adequate nutrition policies play an equally important role in the human resource development which is central to all activities in any society.

HEALTH SERVICES

Approaches to the service of health may be summarised roughly as follows: 1) the curative approach to identifiable disease; 2) attention to poor health that results from such factors as low nutrition, debility, the minor disorders of childhood and chronic conditions of old age; 3) the large area of preventive medicine, expanded even further to the realm of public health and including adequate nutrition and housing, clean water, an hygienic environment with proper sanitation and various standards for community health maintenance for all ages and human activities.

Major attention in the poorer countries is still given to the curative approach. However, it is the public conditions of environmental health which appear to require the highest priority. All three approaches in their present form emerge from medical and public health advances in the developed countries in the past hundred years. Many of their practices are still relatively alien to the more traditional areas in the developing countries though they have contributed greatly to the partial conquest of many diseases in those countries which previously claimed hundreds of thousands of victims.

In settling the context for meeting health needs within overall basic needs strategies, we may consider those categories of health services which contribute to larger socio-economic development as well as to individual health:

(i) Programs whose primary purpose is to maintain and improve the level of health;
(ii) Programs which play a part in the control of health hazards and environmental deterioration;
(iii) Programs whose primary contribution is to increase productivity;
(iv) Programs which play a supporting role or exert a beneficial influence over a wide field of activity.

"As well as personal health care services and traditional public health services, health programs include medical information systems, biomedical research, and the education and training of personnel . . ."[16]

In our estimates of need, we found that most of the poorer countries are low in all of these service areas. The bulk of expenditures and professional services go to curative medicine; hospitals tend to be centralised in the urban areas and most of the prime medical services are mainly accessible to the urban populations and then to those more affluent amongst those populations. The rural poor are largely removed from adequate medical services of this type. Further, the provision of health maintenance and improvement organised along conventional lines, staffed with qualified physicians at recommended levels with all the support systems required, seems to be beyond the present or forseeable capacity of most poor countries. They could neither afford it in physical terms of plant, facilities and equipment nor in terms of the length of time and amounts of money required to train sufficient members of physicians and specialised personnel. This, coupled with their equally urgent needs in the field of environmental health, suggests that quite different approaches are essential rather than incremental extension of present systems.

This has been recognised by the Director-General of WHO in its 1975 Annual Report.[17]

"Drastic and fundamental rethinking of the relationships between communities and their health is necessary if the health requirements of the underserved millions are to be met . . . basic threats to health are unlikely to be countered by conventional health service techniques, however sensitively and intensively they are applied."[18]

This recognition parallels the reconceptualisation of health services already underway in many of the poorer countries and in some of the international assistance programs. Its fundamental premise is expressed in a reversal of health care emphasis from professional curative services to more broadly based programs of preventive and curative systems reaching out into the remotest communities, and predicated on the involvement in, and wider participation of, non-professionals and para-professionals in 'health for the people'.

The only country to provide substantive long-term evidence for the success of such a system is China. But increasingly, dissatisfaction over the levels of rising investment against health returns of conventional systems witnessed in the developed world have encouraged its acceptance.

One of the basic premises of the approach is that health care is essentially social. Even in traditionally 'backward' and remote communities, there was always some person or institution dealing with health problems. Ineffective as these might have been in their relation to mortality or morbidity, their traditional role was important in reducing anxieties, providing curative or palliative remedies and coping with routine 'emergencies' such as childbirth. Building from this base, the new approach to health care attempts to adopt western-type knowledge and skills while retaining the social qualities of the traditional system. It is an approach to *mass* health care predicated on maximising *individual* and social contact with those requiring its services.

Its major organisational characteristics are as follows:

a) Each country or area starts with the formation or recognition of a local community organisation which then has five major health functions—(i) fixing priorities, (ii) organising community action for tasks beyond the individual e.g., water supply and basic sanitation, (iii) controlling the primary health care service by appointing or 'legitimising' the primary health care worker, (iv) assisting in financing the service, (v) linking health actions with wider community goals.

b) A common element is the primary health care worker, frequently a villager selected by the community and trained locally for a brief period of perhaps only 3-4 months initially. This worker is seen as key to the approach, not only as accepted and totally or partially supported by the community but because he or she is *there* when wanted and can also be replaced by, or can call upon, the community itself.

c) There is no separation of the promotional, preventive, and curative health actions at this primary level, as there may be in other systems. In most cases, the primary health worker is also responsible for referral to more specialised help and is the recipient of training, support, drugs, equipment and ideas coming to the community.

d) As a 'total health' approach, this does not mean that all health actions are integrated in a single person at the village level. In many cases, actions traditionally separate, such as family planning or sanitation work, and allocated differently between the sexes, may remain so. Also more than one primary health worker may be needed to play similar roles in heterogeneous communities.[19]

The emphasis on the primary health worker in various descriptions of the new approach[20] does not negate the role of professionals such as doctors and nurses, but suggests further review of their roles, selection, training and integration into the health care system.

> "One physician supported by a number of health assistants, specialist nurses, nursing aids, sanitarians, an administrative assistant and other health auxiliaries properly organised into a team system, can cover the essential preventive and personal medical care needs of a community more effectively than many doctors with individual practices can. This integrated team approach must become the essence of the health system in middle and low income countries for many years to come."[21]

Where most professionals in the developing countries are in centralised facilities, their access to poorer peoples and poorer peoples access to them is severely restricted. This affects the quality of health care both as far as actual curative medicine is concerned and in terms of the wider social requirements of medicine in the community.

> "The combined impact of geographical, administrative and cultural factors seriously limits health coverage in the developing countries . . . most people visiting health facilities come from the immediate vicinity . . . The decline in inpatients' use of health facilities is somewhat less rapid but still rather dramatic . . . A wide cultural gap may exist between the personnel at a modern facility and the tradition-bound people it is designed to serve."[22]

Within the overall approach which we are discussing there is obviously a need for more trained personnel at all levels. Finding the 'right mix' in terms of both urgency and available expenditures is the key problem. The primary health worker at the local level is a low cost component, doctors are the highest expense and take the longest period to train. Many countries now realise that the greatest returns in more immediate service extension will come from larger investment in middle-level and peripheral personnel—nursing assistants, dental auxiliaries, environmental health workers, laboratory, X-ray and other technicians. Problems still exist, however, in the shortage of teachers and teaching aids for these types of personnel, and this is clearly an area where international assistance could well be used in designing intensive, short 'package course' programs for low-cost training. The capacities to do so expeditiously have been well demonstrated in war-inspired emergency conditions.

Training a full-scale medical doctor requires resources of a different order of magnitude.

> "The outlay in training a medical graduate can be estimated by multiplying the annual expenditure on him by the number of years—four to six—that his course will last, and then taking into account investment wasted on students who 'drop out' before graduating. Using this formula, a study some years ago, showed that it cost Nigeria U.S. $33,600 and Uganda $26,000 to train a medical graduate. The size of these figures may be seen even more clearly when they are compared with the per capita annual income of the two countries at the time, $68 and $83 respectively."[23]

The explicit assumption in the above quotation that all medical graduates will be men highlights the under-utilization of women in the overall development process, particularly in the professions but also in middle level paraprofessional roles. Even in the most progressive countries, traditional attitudes will act as a brake on the larger role which women could play, particularly in the area of needs strategies. A more active role on the part of women would not only help meet their individual needs, but would be of advantage to their countries which can hardly afford to disregard the potential contribution of more than half of their population.

In an overall basic needs strategy, the difficulties of finding and training health service personnel should be facilitated through a multisectoral approach. Development workers from other need areas should be drawn upon and vice versa such as teachers, community workers, agricultural extension service personnel, household and housing service workers, and even military personnel whose skills and services may be available and underutilised.

Though primary health care costs may be met at the local community level this should not be regarded as an isolated item attributable to rural communities alone. Rather it should be seen as part of an overall integration of health care programs to which the society as a whole is committed—otherwise the two-tier double standard of present systems will persist.

Four interconnected solutions are suggested:[24]

1) re-allocate health resources more equitably between all segments of the population;

2) introduce a program of self-reliance and self-sufficiency to all segments of the population (urban as well as rural);

3) reserve a larger proportion of national health funds for the development and capital costs of primary health care services;

4) redesign the existing government supported (and other) health ser-

vices to give them a more clearly defined supporting role in relation to a wide primary health care base.

Sound health systems planning at the national and regional level is an important component in reducing overall costs, and at the same time, increasing efficiency. Effectiveness requires hospitals and other facilities to be part of the system and not to operate in isolation.

> "Hospital out-patient departments, health centers and village dispensaries deal with ambulatory cases and act as catchment areas for the hospital system. Where a hospital acts as an isolated unit, it becomes inundated with nonselected cases and cannot operate effectively. It is also an expensive way of delivering medical care because peripheral units can cope at a much lower per unit-of-service cost. Fendall[25] gives cost per illness treated at different echelons of service in Kenya. Dispensary, 23 cents; health center, 56 cents; district hospitals, 7 days average stay, $11.80, regional hospital, 10 days average stay, $24.00; central hospital, 22 days average stay, $52.00."[26]

Notwithstanding the low potential costs of health systems, international assistance both in funds, facilities and training programs will be necessary to meet basic health needs on a large enough scale within the shortest time.

International cooperation may assist by giving access to many of the sophisticated technologies which can decentralise and augment health services even in the most primitive situations. Satellite-relayed communications, for example, where the overall systems are enormous but the local contact instruments are relatively cheap, can potentially channel expert medical advice and consultation even to the remotest hamlet. Complex 'remote' telemetry and automated diagnostic procedures can be deployed as easily for the upper Amazon and the moon as for downtown Detroit. 'Walking on many legs' in the health developmental sense can include aerospace communications as well as the barefoot doctor!

Lest the more detailed considerations of health systems skew the drift of discussion, we should reemphasise the importance of procedures that ensure adequate levels of environment health—which can vastly reduce pressures on the health system and do so at low cost and in ways that rebound immediately to better health. We refer to simple ways of protecting and monitoring well water and other water supplies that provide adequate sanitation and sewage disposal, elementary hygiene measures in the processing and preparation of food, infant and child care training, etc. Singly and in combination such measures can be more effective in promoting better health than many more grandiose schemes for large medical complexes.

The direct effects of health policies and services in developing societies are many including,

a) improvements in agricultural and industrial productivity through increased working time and higher individual output.

b) educational developments.

c) increase in socio-cultural inducements to wider social and economic participation.

d) increase in confidence among the population for a better future.

EDUCATION

The meeting of educational needs involves: one, the needs of the individual for growth, self-competence and self-realisation; and, two, the needs of the society for the skilled contributions of individuals to its growth and development. Both these aspects interact sharply in periods of rapid change, when traditional folkways can no longer provide individuals with the sense of continuity and competence required to meet new perceptions and expectations, and when society requires wider participation in development and a greater number of skilled persons with which to manage its human and physical resources.

The main issues in basic needs strategies for education in the poorer countries, are literacy, primary education and the relative effectiveness of formal and non-formal means in reaching large numbers of people. In the wider context of educational priorities there are also the problems of secondary and tertiary education and the specialised training of professionals. As in health care, the resolution of these issues depends upon the realisation that the problem is less one of incremental extension of existing systems than of redesigning the overall approach, particularly with regard to basic education.

Literacy

The most pressing need in most of the poorer regions is for minimal literacy.

Earlier emphases on technical reading and writing skill standards have been broadened to include 'functional' literacy which sets greater importance on an individual's local experience and needs. The ''Experimental World Literacy Program'' jointly sponsored by UNDP and UNESCO has been assisting eleven projects in the past six years along these lines in Algeria, Ethiopia, Guinea, Madagascar, Mali, Sudan, Tanzania, Ecuador, Iran and Syria. Recent conclusions underline that:

1. full government participation in all phases of operation are essential . . .
2. the integrated approach seems to work better than treating literacy as an isolated problem . . .
3. literacy programs can only be fully functional—and development

efforts fully conducive to literacy—if they accord importance to social, cultural, and political factors as well as to economic growth

4. adult learners must be permitted to define their own needs and direct their own progress.

. . .EWLP proved the worth of three basic adult education practices: a) an inductive approach which gives recognition to adults' experience and insights as a valid starting point for learning; b) learning by doing; c) a diversified strategy for adult literacy using a variety of methods and techniques."[27]

Similar to primary health care, this program emphasises that literacy instructors need not be trained teachers and that it was demonstrably more effective, in many cases, to have students, other workers and farmers conduct the courses—with literacy materials developed indigenously and focussing on actual problems encountered by people in their daily activities.

Integration with Other Basic Need Programs

These findings suggest that such a process might be taken a stage further by combining literacy training within local and national basic needs strategies. In effect, this integrated approach would use the experience of basic needs satisfaction both as the incentive and as the means for attaining literacy.

a) Urban/rural programs for enhancing productivity require specific literacy skills which could be inculcated while learning about agriculture, irrigation, food, storage, processing, marketing and indigenous industry crafts.

b) in rural situations, environmental education that emphasises the role of natural systems in enhancing good husbandry can be a directly advantageous area for aiding functional literacy as well as being an appropriate field demonstration area for primary and secondary education.

c) primary health, nutrition, sanitation, and environmental hygiene projects at the local level provide excellent vehicles for instituting functional literacy.

d) self-help projects in housing and its support services draw upon traditionally available skills whose augmentation can be accomplished through a considerable range of literacy associated activities.

This approach would serve many interrelated need functions simultaneously and would particularly give more immediate reinforcement of learning through observed results and accomplishments. Meeting the peoples' own basic needs within such a coherent framework of traditional skills and newly motivated learning would also generate a sense of greater achievement and aspiration in their own development.

One singular feature of such an approach is the way in which it may draw upon the entire resource range of the community for its 'teachers'. Many older members, for example, may have specific traditional skills, experience or insights which can be utilised; the young can also have much to teach the old and so on.

Within such an integrated approach it might also be found useful to leapfrog over the reading and writing stages of literacy which are often the initial stumbling blocks. Many technical skills can be acquired through visual and other means without formal literacy per se. Given the encouragement of increased competence, literacy itself is then perceived as an easier hurdle and less of a discouraging pre-requisite for participation.

The basic needs direction might also be generalised for other educational requirements, i.e., at the primary, secondary and technical levels. This approach meets the more recent criteria for education as a lifelong learning process and the need to take basic education beyond the limits of formal schooling. It is paralleled, in part by the concept of the ''minimum learning package'' developed by UNICEF[28] whose elements include:

1. Functional literacy enabling persons to have access to sources of knowledge which they personally might find useful . . .
2. An elementary understanding of the processes of nature in the particular area . . .
3. Knowledge and skill to develop self-reliance and for raising a family and operating a household
4. Knowledge of the social environment to allow constructive participation in community affairs.

One specifically interesting example in this general area is the Brazilian MOBRAL (Movimento Brasiliero de Alfabetizacao) project. This is a massive, functional literacy movement operating nationwide and relying on community organisation and local participation. In the first four years from 1970, MOBRAL has reached more than 6 million illiterates to produce about 4 million literate adults at low unit costs.[29]

Primary Education follows and parallels minimal literacy in the scale of priorities since in many developing countries it is not confined to the younger age groups but includes young adults and older learners.

Its failures and successes are due to several interactive factors; the capacity to teach and to learn; what is taught, i.e. the curriculum; and the overall environment for learning within and outside of the school.

Capacities and resources for teaching are usually in short supply in the poorer countries. Teachers themselves may be just above the primary level and the aids and resources they can call upon are limited. In the formal system, this is a difficult problem which might only be resolved by redesigning teacher training programs, upgrading this level of teaching in status and by incentives for teacher recruitment and self development. The number of teachers required is in itself formidable and probably only to be met by some type of compressed emergency training programs such as were used successfully in several countries such as the U.K. after World War II.

An additional problem is that many may not wish to serve in the rural areas of their country, amenities and conditions being much lower than in the towns, and where more incentives may therefore be required.

The capacity to learn is a function of age, maturity, individual health, levels of expectation and aspiration—and is importantly influenced by family and other external environment conditions. Where financial costs are involved parents may be unable to afford schooling or be otherwise unsupportive where a child's contribution is seen as important to the family livelihood. Where these various conditions are unfavorable, there is considerable educational wastage. Drop-out rates[30] and a high degree of repetition of grade levels also cut down on the overall effectiveness of schooling.

An important key to this set of problems may lie in the curriculum. As many studies have noted, curricula and school systems at primary and secondary levels in many developing countries have retained the form and substance of their colonial periods not ill-adapted to their present circumstances.

> "Many . . . have stubbornly refused to change these curricula because they fear that a system based on African (or Indian or Indonesian) needs might be a device aimed at preventing equality between African and European . . . . (such curricula) represent a world and ideals which are generally foreign to the local and family environments in which their pupils belong."[31]

In such cases, lack of curricula revision may prevent education from being the pacemaker and primary agency of change in the society. In the upper levels of the system it can also create a class of unemployables whose mal-education does not fit any of the needs of the local society.

There are many examples of developing countries now endeavoring to expand and improve their primary education as rapidly as possible. Some seek ways in which existing schools can serve more by double-shifts, alternating school days for different groups and by keeping schools open longer. Others have reorganised their school systems' organisation, e.g. the 'godfather' school in Tamil Nadu (India) and the 'nuclear' or 'consolidated' schools of Latin America, which group smaller village schools offering a limited range of instruction under others that offer the full cycle.[32]

Nigeria has recently initiated its 'March to Literacy' program, which aims at universal primary education, by giving free admission to school for those who are currently 6 years old, so that in five years it will cover the entire primary system. In 1975 there were 4.8 million children in primary schools; last year there were 8 million. By 1981, the figure will rise, in theory, to 18 million pupils. Last year the country needed 60,000 new classrooms and 163,000 additional teachers. About 300,000 new teachers will be required over the next five years; to meet this need the government has taken over 156 teacher training colleges and plans to build 74 new colleges with a student population of 1,000 each.[33]

In another mode, India has been using satellite communications to beam basic education programs to schools in remote areas. We might expect these and other technological assisted projects to be more economically available in the next few years. Already in the adult education area there are many universities of the air and open university type projects being developed in various countries, using radio, film, T.V. and tape cassettes. The 'electronic classroom' is still some way off in terms of practicality in meeting the basic needs of the poorer countries though, undoubtedly, many of its applications could be extremely useful in accelerating specific skill training and in augmenting the teacher shortage.

Dissatisfaction with the pace and accomplishments of formal education has also encouraged interest in non-formal approaches in child, youth and adult education. These vary considerably from country to country and have been surveyed extensively by Coombs.[34] Whilst non-formal methods may be more successful in many situations (Fig. 75) in providing new paths for learning, one commentator makes a point about the social and cultural role of the school per se in local circumstances,

> "The clienteles in prospect for the massive efforts in non-formal education have in effect to be offered a substitute for the school . . . the question (to be) considered is of what use the school actually is to a rural community; what do they expect the school to do for their children . . . Perhaps the village school serves a very real need, however imperfect and contemptible it is in the eyes of the outsiders."[35]

Thus reminders of the social and symbolic roles of education in society intrude on even the best conceived 'technical' schemes for reaching larger numbers of people through more innovative means. Again this phenomenon is not at all confined to developing countries but strongly influences educational reform in the developed.

One encouraging note in this area with regard to changing traditional attitudes is the comparatively rapid increase in the number of girls and women, in the developing world who are learning to read, attending various levels of school, and slowly gaining entry into the technical fields and professions. Illiterate women still outnumber illiterate men, however, and much more has to be done to enfranchise more women in their access to general and specialised education.

DIRECTORATE OF NON-FORMAL EDUCATION, MINISTRY OF EDUCATION AND SOCIAL WELFARE, INDIA

MAIN ASPECTS OF NONFORMAL EDUCATION FOR THE AGE GROUP 15 - 25

Given below are the main elements of the non-formal education programme. It should, however, be made clear that these are only intended to be broad guidelines, sufficiently defined to provide a framework, but with considerable scope for adaptability and diversification. Emphasis is now put, along with existing schemes, on programmes for youth in the 15-25 age group. For fuller details, readers are referred to the Government of India publication: 'Main Schemes of Nonformal Education.

FOR WHOM AND WHY?

Nonformal education is not confined to any age-group or any specific category. But limitations of expertise and resources compel the adoption of priorities. Therefore, one of the priority programmes in the first phase is intended for the youth in the age-range 15-25 because:

- a large number of them are illiterate or semiliterate and thus unable to participate fully in socio-economic and developmental processes.
- they are nevertheless active and alert and involved in family, community and societal responsibilities, and need to be helped through education to play these roles efficiently.
- since most of them are living in rural areas, the decrease of rural poverty largely depends on them.

WHAT WILL THE PROGRAMME CONTENT OFFER?

It will be a composite programme of nonformal education including literacy. It will contain:

- information and knowledge about the environment
- knowledge about the social, economic, scientific and technological changes in the midst of which young people live and work
- elementary principles of health and hygiene, child care and nutrition
- basic skills in reading, writing and arithmetic
- introductory occupational and vocational skill programmes to prepare the learner for employment and self-employment

HOW WILL THE PROGRAMME BE ORGANISED?

The programme will start with about 100 centres in each district and will try to reach about 200, in stages, each centre enrolling about 30 learners. Here again the number of centres depends upon the learners available for enrollment.

WHO WILL BE RESPONSIBLE FOR DISTRICT LEVEL IMPLEMENTATION?

One of the existing functionaries at the district level:

- an officer designated for the nonformal education programme
- the Nehru Yuvak Kendra Coordinator
- the full-time Functional Literacy Project Officer
- a voluntary organisation
- another officer considered by the State Government as suitable

WHO WILL BE THE INSTRUCTORS?

A wide range of full-time and part-time arrangements is envisaged (with preference to those who come from the same environment as the learners):

- school teachers
- unemployed educated youth
- NSS volunteers
- skilled workers and technicians
- university and college students

HOW WILL THE CLASSES BE SUPERVISED?

Supervisors may be either part-time or full-time as found convenient by the state education departments and other implementing agencies.

WHAT WILL THE CURRICULUM MATERIALS CONSIST OF?

The learning and teaching materials will consist of:

- sheets with description and explanation of learners problems
- a combined primer and reader
- complementary learning sheets
- a teacher's guide
- a kit of charts
- other audio-visual aids

The reader will consist of 40 to 50 learning units, each consisting of a living or working problem —key words related to it, basic knowledge and knowhow for understanding and solving it.

WHAT WILL BE THE BASIC APPROACH?

- to relate educational content to the needs, interests and environment of the youth
- to make the programme as functionally related as possible
- to help the youth to understand their environment and problems scientifically and to be ready and able to solve them

WHO WILL BE THE IMPLEMENTING AGENCIES?

A variety of existing institutions, resources and agencies will need to be pressed into service:

- State governments
- voluntary agencies
- Nehru Yuvak Kendras
- youth clubs and youth organisations
- rural development and social welfare centres, etc.

HOW LONG WILL THE PROGRAMME BE?

The programme can be organised in a variety of ways to suit the learners:

- as a 9-month course with shorter hours each day
- as a 4-5 month course with longer hours each day
- as a recurrent course over three summers
- or any other arrangement

WHEN SHOULD THE CLASSES BE HELD?

Any time that suits the learners:

- mornings
- afternoons
- late evenings
- holidays

HOW LONG SHOULD THE CLASSES LAST?

Again, this should be left flexible from situation to situation, from season to season, and even from one week to another, according to the occupational and environmental demands of the learner groups.

Fig. 75

Problems of meeting needs in secondary, technical and vocational education are different in kind and scope from those in more basic education, though the demand for educated manpower is as pressing. Some of the internal problems of curriculum design, in accessibility, and in content and skill relevance are, however, rather similar. Many secondary and upper-level educational services in the developing countries are even more strongly oriented to external models than primary education.

This may be partially defensible, in terms of educational parity with other countries because it allows for foreign training and exchange. It does constitute, however, a brake on innovation in, and more indigenous development of, such education. It is also one of the reasons for local unemployability of some of its graduates and for the 'brain drain' to other countries. As a World Bank report notes,

> "... shortages in skills are observed in specific categories such as science and technology teachers, engineers, agronomists and managers, despite unemployment among school graduates. The observation suggests that the content of education must be re-oriented to relate skills taught to jobs, thereby ensuring that graduates can be employed. Emphasis on vocational schools and technical schools and centers, and attempts to 'vocationalise' the curricula of academic schools are illustrations of attempts to achieve such an orientation."[36]

New Directions

1. Though a great deal of ingenuity and money has been devoted, both in developed and developing countries, to the elaboration of new systems and media for communicating the content of education, much less attention has been given to reforming the *content* itself. Much more ruthless pruning and updating of the content would go far to make training more efficient and relevant at lower manpower and equipment costs.

2. The 'equal time' proposition plagues much education and training where each skill area and speciality is presumed by its specialists to be the more important, who then seek to convey as much of their field's information as possible. The question to be asked rather is, what is the minimal set of information essential to gaining a skill or basic working knowledge of a field? How can skills be 'clipped on' more expeditiously?

3. Allied to the above is the underlying moral position that knowledge and skill must be hard won. This proposition becomes rather tenuous when prepackaged skills become cheaply and widely available as with the electronic hand calculator. Arguments are put forward against the superficiality of using sophisticated mathematical transformations by such means, whilst their theoretical

and step-by-step working out has not been required, but such objections are similar to those heard when printed books were introduced.

4. A strong shift in emphasis is indicated—from learning what is known to learning to learn, i.e. learning the means of finding out what one needs to know when the need arises.

5. Reforming the continuous and single entry/exit form of upper level education towards a more flexible mode. Much more could be learned on the job and more practical life experience secured by allowing students to enter and exit the process more frequently, and change skill paths more flexibly. This also applies to the increasing need for updating the knowledge and skills of those who are already graduated.

Given the urgent need for skilled upper level manpower and the lack of available resources to meet this need in many poorer countries education is one area in which much increased international cooperation and assistance will be required.

SHELTER AND CLOTHING

Shelter or housing and clothing, are parcticularly characterised by the ways in which physiological needs are modified by local and traditional values. The house, as home, is not only a basic utilitarian function but the center of social concerns and interactions, a ritual place and the physical locus for the satisfaction of many human needs.

The material requirements for meeting clothing needs can be subsumed under textiles and fibers used for household or home items. Clothing is less in short supply than the other needs but it is price-sensitive due to export demand and the use of imported materials.

Developing strategies for meeting housing needs takes different forms for different countries. After a long period of architectural and planning enthusiasm for variants on the so-called 'international style' in high density building, recent emphasis have been placed on more indigenous ways of meeting the housing needs. This accords with the new developmental directions of self-reliance and self-development, and it is, in most cases anyway, how many poorer people house themselves already in the developing countries.

The term, indigenous, is taken here to mean, (a) the use of locally available materials and energies, (b) local, and often traditional forms of building and design more suitable to specific environments, (c) organisational and planning techniques appropriate to socio-cultural and economic situations. In other words, indigenous building systems constitute "a process intimately related to the users' needs and finances and very much in users' control."[37] In contradistinction to the idea that housing is produced and distributed by governments or private institutions for a relatively passive population.

Indigenous Building

1. Placing emphasis on the use of mud brick, traditional design and elements of more advance technology, Hassan Fathy of Egypt, has developed an 'architecture for the poor' which has attracted considerable attention as a model of its kind. Given mud brick as the most obvious building material available in hot, arid zones, Fathy notes that its water and moisture problems can be "solved by using stabilisers such as bitumen and paraffin emulsions . . . and asphalt for damp courses to stop moisture from seeping up from capillary action from the ground." Roofing needs are dealt with by resort to the traditional concentric vaulting without the need for timber or other supports. Thus materials, technology, energy, and, to a large extent, the design of complete buildings are within the reach of the poorest village communities.

> "The use of the cooperative system in mud-brick building has reached a remarkable scale in recent years. When villages in Nubia were to be flooded after the second elevation of the Aswan Dam the Nubians had to build 35,000 new houses above the new water level . . . (these) were planned and executed in one year by the peasants without the assistance of a single architect or engineer, for the low sum of 75,000 pounds . . . When the region was to be reflooded (for the High Dam), architects were called in to build the new villages. They came up with one identical house type in stone and concrete for the whole region. To build just half of the houses in this way cost 28 million pounds."[38]

This conception of indigenous self-help, therefore, goes beyond single household dwellings to include community buildings, and services as part of a cooperative project.

2. The 200,000 houses produced by the Santiago, Chile, foundation, Hogar de Christo, under Josse Van de Rest, are built from prefabricated wooden parts and so are somewhat in conflict with self-build orthodoxy. They are not designed as permanent but 'provisional' dwellings as the first step to a definitive home. Used actively in disaster relief, 15,000 have been erected in 2 months in Guatemala, and 20 people can erect 200 of them in a day.

This example is adduced here as applicable to situations where wood is plentiful and where the manufacture of such prefabricated housing parts of a more permanent type could be the basis for local industries and employment

3. A community development project of Lorestan, Western Iran is less a specific example of self-help housing alone than of the ways in which such needs fit together in the general context of local self-reliance. Housing was the mud and mud brick style common to the region but with the not unusual problem of unsanitary stables contiguous with or underneath living quarters. Meeting housing needs with more amenity and hygiene, in his case, involved

such innovations as community organisation of collective stables detached from living quarters.

The Lorestan project goes much further as a pilot program in the basic needs area, (a) with its attention to the use of fermented cow dung in biogas plants to provide fuel for cooking and lighting, (b) because it was a move towards cooperative ownership of the flour mill, (c) it revived traditional vault and dome construction in the building of a public bath (also to use biogas for all or part of its heating), (d) it attempted local control of malaria by anopheline habitat manipulation techniques.

The emphasis here was on the people themselves and their participation in the integrated growth and development of the community and on the needs of the majority, particularly the less vocal in the lower strata of the social pyramid. The major effects were; "to identify and implement environmentally compatible and appropriate technologies suited to the resources of the local ecological systems and the cultural characteristics of the region."[39]

Site/Services: Squatter Upgrading

Many of the self-help approaches have emerged not from the rural but the urban squatter settlement situation. Here conditions are different with regard to available materials and community services. But the principles are the same, i.e. inadequate, often makeshift housing has to be improved through individual and collective self-help. In the case of squatter settlements, local collective organisations and initiatives have already taken place, providing building materials and other assistance so as to enable people to help themselves better.

The World Bank's 'site and services' and, 'squatter upgrading' programs are examples of this approach. The former refers to opening up new lots of urbanised land and providing services such as water, drainage, sanitation and electricity whilst leaving people free to build as they wish. In some cases, partially built dwellings, are provided. In this way services are brought to where people are already in ill-equipped squatter settlements.

Metroville, in Karachi, is one of many projects of this type in the site and services program. It is a 205 acre site that will house 30,000 people at the lowest income level. The prospective homeowner buys from the city on a very low downpayment a plot of 80 square yards with concrete utility wall and cemented floor. The wall is partitioned for kitchen, bath and toilet, and fitted with gas, electrical and sewerage connections, running water and latrine. Designed for a second story, also, the buyer can build with whatever materials he can afford. The aim is to make Metroville a self contained community with full health, educational and other services where 30 percent of the employment could be within the community itself.[40]

Slum and squatter upgrading projects are carried out along the same lines. For example, at Mentang Waddis, Jakarta, one of the worst makeshift slums of the city, unemployed laborers were hired to pave footpaths, make drainage ditches and install communal baths and public toilets. These efforts then resulted in considerable self-initiated upgrading of the housing itself and the whole area gained amenity.

Critics of overall self-help in urban squatter settlements focus on two aspects which may be critical in terms of genuine self-development. *One*, is the tendency to romanticise the 'autonomy' aspect in these situations and be over-optimistic about its freedom(s) of choice. "The term autonomy used in contrast to dependency implies an actual freedom of choice. In fact, people in the 'popular sector' are *forced* by *necessity* to provide for themselves in order to survive, while others who have more cash power and knowledge are not forced to do so . . . it does not question the existing situation but reinforces it."[41] *Two*, ". . . squatters and slum dweller were seen as a solution and not a problem, (as) people living in slums of hope rather than slums of despair . . . In the transition from the poetry of slum life to the realism of policy action, the assumptions (self-help, etc.) mentioned above have not been tested."[42]

Whilst self-help may in such urban squatter situations be limited, and limiting, it can and may be useful to examine the reasons for urban migration into such situations and whether it could be stabilised or reversed. The main attractions of the urbs, are (potentially) higher wages better services such as water and electricity, education for children, and access to medical care. Presumably if these could be made available, in better measure, for rural areas, the flow could be reversed. As we have noted earlier, adequate land reform in many countries would, in itself, go far to make rural life more attractive for many of the landless peasants who now swell the urbs. Not only would these factors have to be changed or reversed but additional ways found to make life outside the cities attractive. Many seek escape from the narrow traditionalism and sociocultural poverty of village life. These kinds of structural qualities are more difficult to encourage, but are not without the bounds of genuine self-development policies.

Towards a Shelter Industry

Shelter as basic need is possibly the *one* need for which almost every component is available in terms of local self-reliance.

> "An economic development strategy based on the improvement of human settlements will fulfill (many) requirements in most developing societies and will combine the necessary multiple effects with a fairer distribution of goods and services and sound environmental planning.
>
> The construction and housing industries are the only major economic sectors in developing economies for which all basic materials, at least for traditional designs, are available nationally and for which there is no

heavy import component. Hence, this strategy lays a healthy emphasis on internal reliance and capabilities.''[43]

The importance of 'dwelling' as a core development activity has been grossly underestimated partially because of financial returns on low cost mass housing for investors and by the conventional credit institutions, and partly due to failure of imagination where these constraints do not exist.

Given the contributions and importance of localised self-help schemes it is doubtful if they alone can contribute massively enough to match the scale of need in this area. What is required is an integrated program for producing the range, not only of necessary dwellings, but also of their internal household requirements and external service components.

For physical building itself, there is a match between the need for low-cost housing and low-skilled job opportunities. Building materials such as bricks, cement, gypsum, wood, fibres, tiles and stone, sand, gravel and mud are generally extensively available or can be locally produced. Labor for many purposes is not a problem as the greatest housing needs are often accompanied by the greatest unemployment. There is to be sure usually a shortage of skilled craftsmen, technical building personnel, administrative and intermediate personnel. Some of these defects can be remedied by mobilising student and staff time from the architectural and engineering schools of the country and integrating such work with their educational programs. Other advantages may be gained by gearing more adult education towards skill training in these areas.

This speaks to conventional building *programs* but beyond these there are opportunities for developing a building *industry*, i.e., one which is organised industrially on more advanced technological lines. The technology need not be very advanced as most home building is still craftwork even in the developed countries. A building industries' capacities could run from the mass production of simple 'self-build' housing, school or village clinic components, to the more systematic planning and provision of larger structures and complexes. Such an industry need not be centralised but could consist of many dispersed satellite groups working to common standards and purposes.

Properly conceived, its integration within an overall basic needs strategy would include not only the provision of structures for agricultural, education, and health functions but also the ancillary manufacture of service system components such as drainage pipes and tiles, septic systems, water piping, storage cisterns and plumbing facilities; low-cost energy generation units, cooking and lighting fixtures, etc. The textile and furniture making capacities, in many countries, could also be integrated within this grouping of activities to provide low-cost household furnishings, fabrics and clothing. Many of these items, particularly in Asia, are already produced in quantity for export purposes; diversion of some to internal needs could obviate imports and through local inter-country cooperation could increase mutual self-reliance.

Lest the alternative technologies proponent be put off by the term 'industry' one should emphasise that what is required here is the more systematic planning and utilisation of a variety of small scale cottage industry components to larger purposes. Even where the purpose is large the local scale is relatively small.

Two other conceptual approaches may be important to mention here—the autonomous house and that of resource-conserving settlements.

1. The autonomous house has been pioneered by R.B. Fuller for almost half a century and paces his development of low-cost geodesic structures for dwelling. The fundamental concept views dependence upon extended systems of sewage, water and energy supply as being the least efficient and as having the most harmful impact on the environment of any of the components that go towards satisfying housing requirements. Fuller's concept of the autonomous house, first prototyped in 1927 and now elaborated by many other workers, is of a scientifically designed dwelling fully equipped to take the most gainful advantage of the naturally receiving cycles of sun, wind and rain to power its energy needs, provide heating and cooling and make the most economical use of recycled water, wastes and sewage. It would also be provided with full communications equipment for working at home, for self-education and recreation so that living away from large social centers need not mean deprivation of amenities and social interaction. Recent explorations of this idea by a variety of individuals and institutions have developed into explorations of autonomous communities, relatively self-sufficient as to energy, water and food supply, and self-supportive through various light industries and crafts.

The wholly autonomous 'ecological house' or 'life raft' ecological community is, within certain limits, scientifically feasible but has obvious social, cultural and economic limitations. Its central idea, however, of turning naturally impinging processes to positive advantage begins to gain ground in renewed interest in solar heating, wind generated energy systems and the integration of household heating, lighting and cooling in more efficient and environmentally compatible ways.

2. The resource-conserving settlement, or city, explored by R.L. Meier is based on similar premises of greater autonomy and systemic resource use but underlines that, "One of the essential properties of the stable human habitat of the future is that it have urban characteristics."[44] The desirable alternatives of the resource-conserving urbs are based on the use of low-level technologies together with systematically integrated modes of water, energy and material resource management so that the city would function as an efficient ecosystem in itself. Food supply is envisioned as only partially dependent on the countryside with each component city community augmenting its food by intensive garden cultivation of vegetables, tubers and fruits; by fresh water fish farming, and mariculture where available, and by single cell protein production linked into the local food processing industry. The water and energy economy is designed to make maximal use of resources by recycling and re-use; by mass transit and low-energy local bicycle and pedicab movement; and by encouraging telecommunications as a substitute for transportation.

A side note on clothing which is related to household needs is in order here. Poor people usually have very little clothing so that its life is greatly reduced by frequent washing in cold water, often without soap and by beating against hard surfaces. Noting these elements, one analyst suggests that household technologies should, therefore, include,

> "...four devices which complement each other and can help solve the problem of adequate clothing: the hand-operated spinning wheel (Gandhi's Charkha); the handloom, a simple solar heater, and a hand-operated washing machine."[45]

All of these approaches to meeting shelter needs contribute to the objectives of development and better environmental management in designing and constructing the built environment. The choice of approach will obviously be determined locally by the immediacy of particular problems and the availability of resources.

Satisfactory and rationally appealing as these approaches may be, however, they do not directly address other socio-economic factors which can impede or accelerate the meeting of needs even more than resource availability or design appropriateness. These are institutional questions of land ownership and control, the credit and financing of building development, speculative practices and their effects on rural and urban settlement, taxation structures, and the control of agricultural and industrial enterprise. Such factors can effectively retard even the best conceived initiatives if they are not taken into consideration.

The management of institutional change itself, in this regard, is one of the core problems in meeting the urgent human needs on a sufficiently large scale. In many cases, the physical resources are given, and the manpower available, to carry out even the most ambitious programs but the roadblocks of vested interest bureaucratic inertia and lack of political control may render them ineffectual.

Much of what has been touched upon with regard to the physical possibilities of needs satisfaction requires, therefore, to be considered within the context of the ways in which the allocation of power and control over resources is vested in various groups and institutions within the society.

NOTES

1. *Catastrophe or New Society? A Latin American World Model*, Herrera, Amilcar O., and others, Fundacion Bariloche, Argentina, pub. International Development Research Centre, Canada, 1976.
2. Hopkins, M.J.D., Scolnik, H. with McLean, M., "Basic Needs, Growth and

Redistribution: A Quantitative Approach,'' *World Employment Background Papers Vol. I: Basic Needs and National Employment Strategies*, ILO, Geneva, June, 1976.

3. Shalaby, Ahmed A., ''Scientific and Technological Cooperation in the Interests of Economic and Social Development'', *Labor and Society*, Geneva, Vol. 1, No. 3-4, July/October, 1976.

4. Marstrand, P., Rush, H., *Food and Agriculture*, S.T.A.F.F. paper, Science Policy Research Unit, University of Sussex, U.K., 1976, (mimeo), p. 1, 2.

5. Klatt, W., ''Matters of Food and Farming in Asia'', Food Policy, U.K. February, 1976, p. 155.

6. ''New Paths'', *Ceres,* FAO, March/April, 1976, p. 20.

7. Wittwer, S.H., ''Food Production, Technology and the Resource Base'', *Science*, Vol. 188, No. 4188, May, 1975, p. 580.

8. *Underexploited Tropical Plants with Promising Economic Value*, U.S. National Academy of Sciences, 1975, p. 1.

9. *The Winged Bean: A High Protein Crop for the Tropics*, U.S. National Academy of Sciences, 1975.

10. Felger, R.S., Naphan, G.P., ''Development Barrenness'', *Ceres*, 50, Vol. 9, No. 2, March/April, 1976, pp. 34-37, provides a useful summary.

11. Aggarwala, Narinder, *Boosting Forest Resource Earnings*, Action U.N.D.P., July/August, 1975.

12. *Op Cit.* Klatt, ''Matters of Food and Farming in Asia'', p. 155.

13. Sigurdson, Jon, ''Development of Rural Areas in India and China'', *Ambio*, Vol. V, No. 3, 1976.

14. Crosson, Pierre, ''Institutional Obstacles to Expansion of World Food Production'', *Science*, Vol. 188, No. 4188, May, 1975, p. 520.

15. Berg, Alan, *The Nutrition Factor: Its Role in National Development*, The Brooking Institution, 1973, pp. 233-247. *N.B.* paraphrased extract.

16. *Interrelations between Health Programmes and Socio-Economic Development*, Public Health Paper 49, WHO, Geneva, 1973, p. 10.

17. *Official Records of the World Health Organisation*, No. 229, 1976.

18. *WHO Features*, No. 36, April, 1976.

19. Summarised from Newell, Kenneth W., ed. *Health for the People*, WHO, Geneva, 1975, pp. 192-194.

20. *Joint Study on Alternative Approaches to Meeting Health Needs of Populations in Developing Countries*, Annex 11, WHO/UNICEF Services, December, 1974, pp. 53-56. *N.B.* A recent WHO/UNICEF study has also laid out in detail the different types of such health services that can be adapted to different degrees of development and described their physical and personnel components—these include the tasks of the primary health care worker, their facilities, equipment and drugs to the referral centers and hospitals with their professional specialties and technicians.

21. McKenzie-Pollock, James S., *Planning a Healthier World*, unpublished Manuscript, p. 141.

22. *Health Sector Policy Paper*, World Bank, Washington, D.C. March, 1975, pp. 35-38.

23. Bland, John, ''Health Manpower Development: Basic Skills'', *World Health*, WHO, July, 1976.

24. Newell, Kenneth W., ed. *Health for the People*, WHO, Geneva, 1975, p. 196.

25. Fendall, Nire, ''Planning Health Services in Development Countries'', *Public Health Reports*, 78, 1963, pp. 977-988.

26. McKenzie-Pollock, James S., *Planning a Healthier World*, unpublished Manuscript. p. 196.

27. *The Experimental World Literacy Programme: A Critical Assessment*, UNDP/UNESCO, 1976.

28. *Basic Services for Children in Developing Countries*, Report by the Executive Director, UNICEF, March 12, 1976, p. 20.

29. Education, Sector Working Paper, World Bank, Washington, D.C., December, 1974, p. 25.

30. This phenomenon is not restricted to the developing countries but is also prevalent, albeit at the later age ranges, in the developed countries. Its high incidence may be due to many factors but one is undoubtedly the apparent irrelevance of school to society where what is taught may have little linked relationship to changing conditions in the external world.

31. Serge, D.V., *The High Road and the Low*, Allen Lane, 1974, pp. 58-59.

32. Phillips, H.M., *Basic Education: A World Challenge*, John Wiley and Sons, London, 1975, Chapter 10.

33. *New York Times* Report, November 10, 1976.

34. Coombs, Philip H., with Prosser, Roy C., and Manzoon, Ahmed, *New Paths to Learning for Rural Children and Youth*, Non-formal Education for Rural Development Series, UNICEF, 1973.

35. Oxenlpan, John, Institute of Development Studies, Sussex, ''Review of New Paths to Learning for Rural Children and Youth'', *World Development*, Vol. 2, No. 4/5, April-May, 1974, p. 92.

36. *Education*, Sector Working Paper, World Bank, Washington, D.C., December, 1974, p. 22.

37. Cain, Afshar F., Norton J., ''Indigenous Building in the Third World'', *Architectural Design*, April, 1975, p. 207.

38. Fathy, Hassan, ''Self Help/Mud Buildings'', Egypt, *Architectural Design*, (U.K.) October, 1976, p. 596. *N.B.* see also, Fathy, *Architecture for the Poor, An Experiment on Rural Egypt*, University of Chicago Press, 1973.

39. Summarised from Farvar, Mohammed Taghi and Rasavi-Farvar, Catherine, ''The Lessons of Lorestan: Achievements and Shortcomings of a Project in Endogenous Development'', *CERES*, 50, Vol. 9, No. 2, March/April, 1976, pp. 44-47.

40. Orvis, Pat, ''Low-Cost Housing: A Self-Help Approach'', *Action UNDP*, New York, May-June, 1976, p. 111.

41. Harms, Hans, ''Limitations of Self-Help'', *Architectural Design*, (U.K.), April, 1976.

42. Laquian, Aprodicia A., ''Whither Site and Services'', *Science*, (U.S.), 4 June, 1976, p. 50.

43. Penalosa, Enrique, ''The Need for a New Development Model'', *Finance and Development*, World Bank, Vol. 13, No. 1, March 1976, p. 7.

44. Meier, R.L., ''A Stable Urban Ecosystem'', *Science*, (U.S.), June 4, 1976, pp. 962-967. *N.B.* also *The Design of Resource Conserving Cities*, Institute of Urban and Regional Development, University of California, Berkely, November 1973.

45. Makhijani, Arjun, ''Solar Energy and Rural Development'', *Bulletin of the Atomic Scientists*, June, 1976, p. 21.

RESOURCES, TECHNOLOGIES AND TRADE

Central to the problem of meeting human needs in the developing countries is the amounts of energy and materials which may be required, the directions of technological development, and the role of international trade in determining the degrees of self-reliance and inter-dependence of these countries.

Energy, in one form or another, is the essential commodity. Any increase in physical standards of living will entail some concomitant increase in energy production and consumption. The supply of other non-fuel material resources can, to a certain extent, be defined in terms of the energy available for their extraction, processing and end-uses.

Where energy is the measure of other resources, information is, in turn, the measure of energy. Access to resources is conditioned, therefore, on the levels of scientific and technical knowledge which may be applied. Resource adequacy is a function of those technological alternatives determining the energies and materials that can be used, and that are adaptable to particular country situations.

The harmonising of developmental and environmental objectives in meeting needs entails closer specification of the mix of resources, the appropriate technological directions and the external interdependencies which may best forward these objectives.

Our discussion of these topics outlines the bounds of the area in question in a way that may suggest directions for further exploration. The separation of energy, materials and technologies is for textual convenience only, in principle they should be discussed together, and there is considerable overlap from one area of such discussion to another.

ENERGY

An initial distinction can be made between capital and income energies. *Capital* sources are the non-renewable fossil fuels; coal, oil and natural gas with shale and tar sands. Nuclear fuels might also be included though their reserves relative to the developing technologies in their use may put them into the

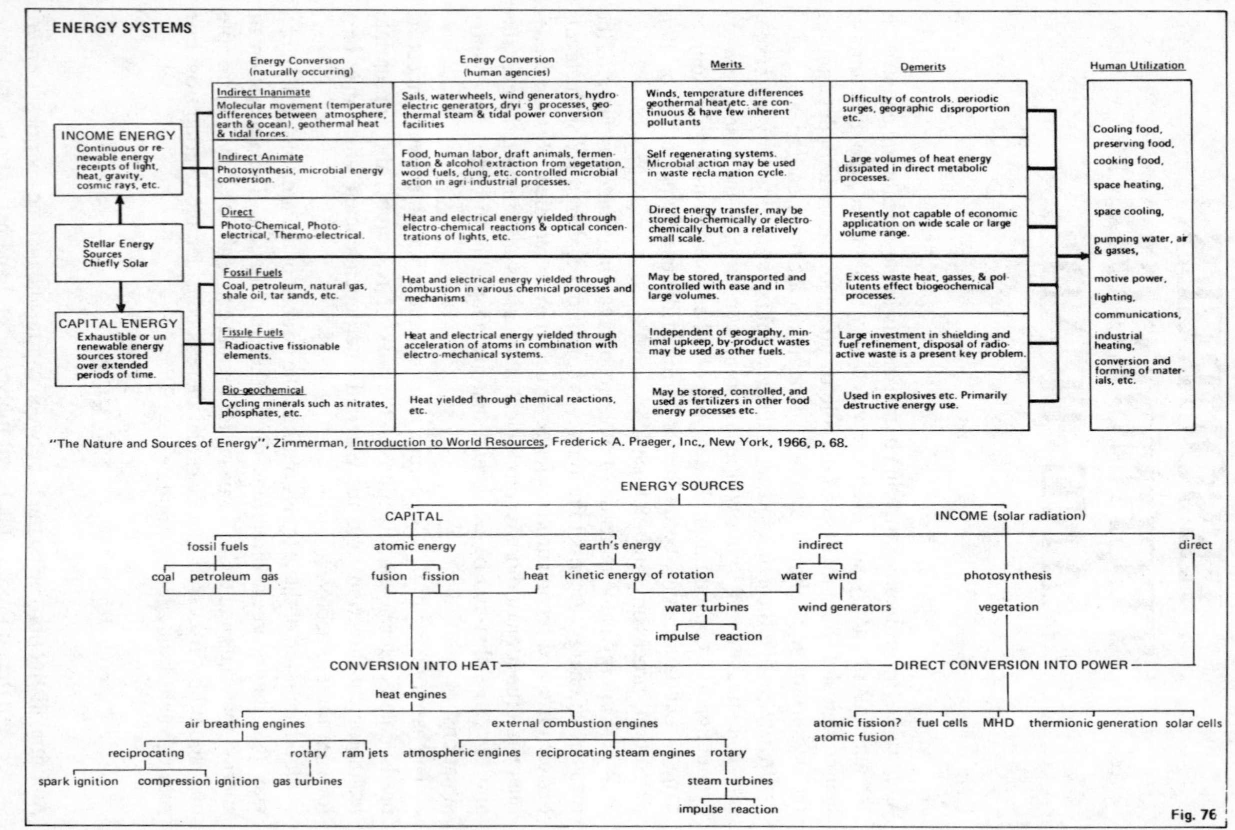

Fig. 76

Energy Into Power, E. G. Sterland, National History Press, Garden City, 1967, pp.120–121.

income class. *Income* energies are self-renewing and relatively inexhaustible sources that derive from those wind, geothermal and other forces recurrent in the environmental system. (Fig. 76)

The accelerated development of the past hundred or so years in the developed regions has been based mainly on the fossil fuels. There, oil and natural gas have gradually displaced coal as the major fuel source for many industrial purposes.

Despite recent alarms about the energy crisis and impending world scarcities, this is not so much an energy crisis as an oil crisis, then still not a crisis in terms of immediate world shortage, but in terms of price and purchasing ability. Whilst the oil and natural gas reserves of the oil producing countries may have varying 'years of supply' (at present use rates) between 30 and 50 years, the recoverable reserve figures themselves are under fairly constant revision—as new discoveries are made and technological developments give access to more oil in present fields. Reserves of coal have many more years of supply, extending beyond a hundred or more years of current estimates.

In advancing such figures, it should be underlined that data in the energy field are unreliable for reasons such as national and corporate security, limitations of physical survey techniques, and the paucity of present knowledge.

Whilst reducing cause for undue alarm, this should not lead to underestimation of the critical nature of energy supply, for both developed and developing countries. Apart from the gross environmental impacts of fossil fuel use, oil and natural gas are too valuable to continue burning wantonly as they are also a major source for a vast range of chemical products such as fertilisers, pharmaceutical drugs and plastics. The upward pricing of oil and natural gas is also likely to decrease its availability for those developing countries which do not possess their own supplies.

In considering overall world development, it is clear that the greatest efforts should be made to increase the use of, and investment in the range of renewable energy sources whilst continuing to pursue other options deriving from fossil fuels which may stretch supplies without increasing environmental spoilage.

The comparative energy uses of countries classified in our reference groups is given in Fig. 77. It will be seen that industrial or commercial energy production and use is extremely low in the poorer countries. For most of them, human muscle energy and firewood are still the major sources particularly in the agricultural sector. Any attempt, therefore, to project their attainment of higher living standards will require attention to how they can produce more energy—and at the same time become more energy self-reliant.

The Conventional Route

In the comparative table the developing countries in the D and E group exclude those in OPEC. If we deal first with their capacities for conventional energy development through fossil fuel supplies their local resource situations

REFERENCE COUNTRY* COMPARISIONS – Population / Energy / GDP

1974

Averages – Reference Country	A	B[2]	C[3]	D[3]	E[4]	USA	USSR	China, P.R.	India
Population (Millions)	37.2	22.0	30.8	38.7	24.2	211.9	252.1	824.96	586.3
Gross Domestic Product (Billion $)	162.9	31.1	17.3	7.5	2.6	1,398	462.2	245.8[7]	73.4[7]
Per Caput Gross Domestic Product ($)	4,916	1,961	452	277	114	6,597	1,833	298	125
Energy Consumption (Million Metric Tons, Coal Equivalent)	170.9	42.9	18.1	7.9	1.1	2,443.5	1,323.7	525.6	117.7
Per Caput Energy Consumption Kg. Coal Equivalent	5,074.3	2,251.1	582.6	327.9	53.4	11,485	5,252	650	201
Energy Used To Produce [1]Unit GDP	1.05	1.38	1.05	1.05	.42	1.7	2.9	2.1	1.6
Energy Sources – By Category[5]	Solid- 24.9% Liquid- 59.8% Natural Gas- 12.3% Hydro- 2.4% Nuclear- .6%	S.- 15.3% L.- 57.9% NG- 24.5% H.- 2.5% N.- .3%	S.- 9.2% L.- 81.6% NG- 2.0% H.- 7.5% N.- 0.0%	S.- 8.6% L.- 60.8% NG- 26.6% H.- 4.0% N.- 0.0%	S.-11.9% L.- 57.9% NG- 21.0% H.- 9.0% N.- 0.0%	S.- 20.6% L.- 43.9% NG- 33.3% H.- 1.6% N.- .6%	S.- 35.8% L.- 40.0% NG- 26.0% H.- 1.1% N. .1%	S.- 84.5% L.- 13.9% NG- .8% H.- .8% N.- 0.0%	S.- 71.8% L.- 24.3% NG- .8% H.- 2.9% N.- .2%

1960 – 1974

1960 – 1974	A	B[2]	C[3]	D[3]	E[4]	USA	USSR	China, P.R.	India
Energy Consumption Average Yearly Growth Rate- Reference Country	5.5 %	9.4 %	6.1 %	5.9 %	8.8 %	3.6 %	5.2 %	1.4 %	4.7 %
Per Caput Energy Consumption Average Yearly Growth Rate	4.8 %	9.0 %	3.4 %	3.2 %	2.7 %	2.5 %	4.5 %	-.4 %	2.5 %
Energy Consumption Average Yearly Growth Rate – G.P.	**4.8 %**	**6.4 %**	**7.8 %**	**6.4 %**	**6.1 %**				
GDP – Average Yearly Growth Rate	12.1 %	12.9 %	8.5 %[6]	7.9 %[6]	7.3 %[6]	8.5 %	6.6 %	4.2 %[8]	6.2 %

* The average of the seven reference countries in the appropriate A, B, C, D, E classifications.

** All countries in the world assigned to A, B, C, D, E, classifications, not the average of the 7 reference country set, for this line of percentages only.

NB.: A. Energy from fuelwood, dung, etc., is shown separately due to lack of data.
B. Data is for commercial forms of energy only.

1. Kilogram per U.S. $1.
2. GDP figures for two reference countries are for 1973.
3. GDP figures are for 1973.
4. Figures are for 1974 GNP and PC GNP.
5. Computations of Hydro and Nuclear percentages are based on electrical power data given for countries concerned.
6. Growth rates for GDP are for the period 1960–1973 for C and D countries and 1960 – 1970 foe E country reference group.
7. Estimated.
8. Estimate based on PC GNP Growth Rates for 1960 – 73 and 1965 – 73.

Data : United Nations Statistical Yearbook 1975 (United Nations Publishing Service, New York, 1975) Tables 18 and 193; World Bank Atlas, Population, Per Capita Product, and Growth Rates (World Bank, Washington, D.C., 1975) and, World Energy Supplies, 1950 – 1974 (Statistical Papers, Series J, No. 19, United Nations, New York, 1976).

Fig. 77

Source : Center for Integrative Studies.

vary considerably as to type of fuel and capacity. Some have coal of various qualities, others have actual and potential hydropower.

Although the non-OPEC developing countries use less than 10 percent of the world's energy consumption for almost half of its population, recent estimates note that, together they have enough economically recoverable reserves to reduce their dependence on energy imports from other groups of countries from about 30 percent of total consumption in 1974, to between 12 percent and 6 percent in 1980. "The author here also notes that this would require annual investments that are twice as high in real terms as those made in 1968-1973."[1]

India may be a useful case example, in which most energy requirements with the exception of oil and petroleum products, 70 percent of which are imported, now come from domestic sources—i.e. coal, coal derived electricity and fuelwood. Such imports, however, probably account for only about 10 percent of total energy use. A large part of India's energy consumption still comes from firewood and other noncommercial fuels such as dried cow dung and vegetal wastes.

> "The most important is firewood, the present annual consumption of which is put at no less than 130 million tons, which exceeds the current output of the coal industry."[2]

Much of the fuelwood and noncommercial fuel use is accounted for by the large agricultural sector which is comparatively ill-served by other commercial energies. Hydropower is another important source providing some 40 percent of total electrical generation—with considerable unused hydrocapacity, nuclear power accounts for less than 5 percent of electrical generation.

Projecting requirements forward, a recently detailed study by Revelle notes that in order to provide for India's needs and produce enough food for population increase by 2000:

> "... considerable increase in energy use will be essential primarily for three purposes: irrigation, chemical fertilizers and additional draft power for cultivating the fields ... With present technology (this) would have to be provided largely by fossil fuels and hydroelectrical power. If the requirements were met by using petroleum products, 43 million tons would be needed, more than twice the quantity used at present. Alternatively 95 million tons of Indian coal could be used. These figures might be significantly reduced by development of the Indian and Nepalese hydroelectric power potential."[3]

In addition to these latter sources, there is the possibility of larger offshore and land production of Indian oil, with proven and indicated reserves estimated at 250 million tons—further estimates suggest 1 billion tons offshore and some 3 billion on land.[4]

India may be atypical by virtue of its size and indigenous energy endowment. Other developing countries however, have conventional resources in development and are potentially capable of meeting more of their needs. More natural gas for example may be made available than is at present because of its hitherto restricted market. Current production is still inefficiently utilised. For example, ten countries in our C, D, E categories (including Gabon, Malaysia, Nigeria and Peru) used less than 15 percent of their gas production; the rest was wasted, reinjected for repressuring or for driving turbines in the gas field.

Hydroelectrical power is one of the main sources of industrial energy for the developing countries, but though they have 44 percent of the world's hydro capacity only about 8 percent of their potential has been developed so far. The use of *tidal* power is still very much in its infancy. *Nuclear* power is highly restricted and unlikely to take up more than 10 to 15 percent of the developing countries' power needs in the next ten to fifteen years; in terms of current technology and its overall value as an energy source, it may not represent a significant option for many developing nations.

Geothermal sources of energy have been little exploited other than in the form of hot springs. Some power generation is being carried out in the developed countries and there is increased interest in many areas; e.g., in 1972, the U.N. reported one of the world's largest potential sources of geothermal energy in Ethiopia as potentially capable of generating large amounts of electrical power. A side attraction of geothermal energy is that its occurrence usually coincides with rich mineral deposits such as potash and magnesium chloride.

The presently accelerated exploration for oil and gas could open more offshore and land fields in the poorer regions, but the lead time for full utilisation would place this somewhere in the late 1980's or 1990's—and then probably as expanding their trade capacities rather than being directly usable domestically.

Given the present status of these sources and the preponderance of their agricultural sector many of the poorer countries will have to expand their use of alternative energy supplies—whilst at the same time they should endeavor to improve their use of conventional sources. Unfortunately, this is often hampered by lack of technical manpower, machinery, and spare parts, and by poor maintenance levels as a result of these. The technologies needed in conventional energy production are also capital intensive and labor saving, whereas in poor countries the reverse would be more useful. And these countries' low level of industrial infrastructure means that even if more plentiful amounts of such energies were immediately available they could not be fully used.

We should note, however, that though environmental considerations are advanced to support the argument against more development of such conventional industrial energies, this argument may not be very helpful in terms of the developing regions essential growth from present low levels. Pollution is not 'built in' to increased energy use even of fossil fuels but depends upon the degree of effective controls exercised by the society. Many of the more affluent industrial economies have significantly healthier and 'cleaner' environs than their poorer agrarian counterparts.

Alternative Energy Directions

So far we have been discussing large scale, relatively centralised, energy supply at the overall society level, whilst poorer countries have large rural sectors which may be least helped by such directions in the shorter term. The basic question, therefore, is "What kind of energy supply and delivery systems are feasible and economic for widely dispersed populations such as usually characterise rural areas?"[5] Even fractional amounts of increased energy may provide enormous leverage in the poorer regions, supplying energy for increasing food yield, for individual purposes and community utilities.

If, as seems likely, the expansion of mechanical or biochemical energy converters is slow, then firewood will continue to be an important source of domestic heating and cooking fuel. This suggests priority consideration should be given to the reduction of waste in such uses by more efficient cheap stove design, better housing insulation at low cost and by methods for converting wood supply as a more renewable resource. Attention should be directed towards,

> Large scale reforestation programs.
> Organising fuel wood supply for entire villages so that cutting can be done with minimum drainage to the soil and accompanied by replanting efforts.
> Organising and planting village wood lots so that within a 10-15 year period the necessity for cutting trees in areas outside the village is entirely eliminated.
> Reforestation programs can be a source of employment for large numbers of people, including those who will lose income from the sale of wood. Many poor people in all poor countries depend on gathering wood in the forests for sale in villages, towns and cities.[6]

A useful typology of other local power needs is as follows,

> "Group 1—Units delivering a fraction of a watt up to several watts, such as power supplies having roughly the capability of a standard flashlight battery and slightly larger, can run radios, transistorized T.V. receivers and small transmitters—providing news, education, entertainment as well as vital communication linkage where telephones and other units are not available.
>
> Group 2—Units from several watts up to one kilowatt, with the capability of an automobile battery, might be used for a microwave relay station, for refrigeration, and for larger communications apparatus.

> Group 3—Units comparable to the power of a gasoline lawnmower engine or larger, providing power for the pumping of water and other agricultural and productive purposes.''[7]

This suggests a much wider spectrum of energy source options which are, in many cases, environmentally benign and well-suited to local indigenous development. Many of those now under consideration are not wholly new but have been used in different forms for a long time.

Wind Power was once a primary energy source which helped spur industrialisation in the developed world. Its present potential is far from realised but may be extremely beneficial in suitable localities. Wind generators can be tied into local electrical power grids or used on a smaller scale for local purposes.[8]

Solar Energy is already the main energy source used in poor countries—through growing plants and eating them or by using fuelwood derived from photosynthesis.

Other ways to use solar energy take many forms, and have been explored for a long time. The recent 'energy crunch' has accelerated technical developments ironically in the more affluent countries, particularly for household systems, using solar panels to heat and cool or photovoltaic cells to generate electricity. These still tend to be too costly for use in the poorer countries, but many local centers are working on cheaper alternative systems as well as components such as solar cookers and water heaters. There are also many promising directions being explored for the indirect uses of solar energy to produce fuels by various methods. (Fig. 78) One longer range approach is the redirection of photosynthesis by using plants, algae and micro-organisms to produce hydrogen which can then be used in gaseous form or liquefied as a gasoline substitute.

The more immediately usable indirect methods in current review are those grouped around the anaerobic fermentation of organic wastes to produce methane.

For example,

> ''A crude estimate of energy needs of a 200 house, 500 population village is . . . about 180 MWh per year . . . (which) can be easily met by a plant which can generate out of available cattle and human wastes about 500 cubic feet of biogas (50 to 80 percent methane) per day . . . or 240 MWh per year. In contrast, one large-scale coalbased fertiliser plant consumes the energy needs of about 500 villages . . . the bio-fertiliser output of each village plant can service the cropped-land area of 290 hectares per village with two and a half times the present level of nitrogen consumption which is about 12 kg. per hectare.''[9]

Emphasising the ecological soundness and development appropriateness of this method, the author of the above notes that it not only reduces fossil fuel and wood use but renders disease-carrying wastes harmless, has low environmental

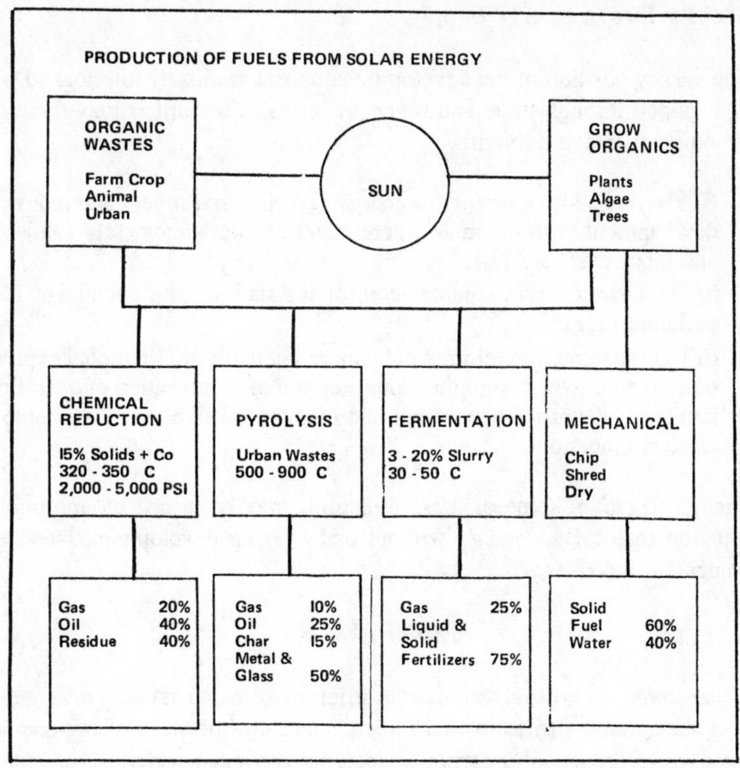

Source: Heronemus, William E., The Case for Solar Energy, The Center Report, February, 1975, Center for the Study of Democratic Institutions.

Fig. 78

impact and that cooperative manufacture and maintenance can stimulate local self-development.

Interestingly enough, these kinds of 'bio-directions' in alternative technologies coincide with many of the more sophisticated interests in industrial microbiology and advanced scientific development. The large amounts of human, animal and agricultural wastes are a relatively vast source not only for energy supply and its fertiliser by-products but of other ranges of usable by-product materials. The scientific and technological potential of this area goes far beyond a more immediate provision of rural low cost fuel.

Small scale hydro-power and geothermal energy sources may be more widely used where conditions are appropriate. Though these are usually thought of as being used for larger scale energy generation, their local uses, e.g. in watermills, have been traditional in many areas and traditional utility can be augmented with more modern technics.

Others Factors in Energy Supply

The energy position of the developing countries is closely interlocked with the developed through trade and other processes. The former may therefore gain some advantage through,

(i) the competitive pricing of energy favoring investment and industrial development in those areas where materials are strategically available, and labor costs are low.
(ii) less strict environmental control legislation may encourage high pollutant industries.
(iii) these trends are reinforced by more intensive multinational exploration for energy in developing countries and their relocation of operations into those countries where fuel and labor supplies become available in close conjunction.

Though negative, some of these directions may be turned by appropriate negotiation to local advantage without endangering developmental and environmental objectives.

MATERIALS

The assessment of non-fuel resources is different from that of energy. There is a much greater range of metals and minerals and the spectrum of options and alternatives to the use of a particular material are much wider.

One important difference is that we 'consume' energy in use, whilst we do not consume materials—they are employed for a specific purpose then discarded in various forms which can then be reemployed for the same or different purposes. The potential, if not the actuality, of recycling makes several of the key metals renewable resources, e.g., iron, copper, aluminum, lead, tin, antimony, silver, gold, mercury and nickel.

When we refer to material resources, we are really describing the range of physical elements as they occur in different combinations, and concentrations in the earth's crust, the oceans and the atmosphere. The periodic table of the elements is, as it were, the overall menu for materials use.

The growth of materials use in the past century has been characterised not only by greatly increased quantities but, even more, by expansion in the range of elements coming into use.

> "Since 1900, a host of new substances, metals and minerals have come into use. Germanium, thorium, vanadium, beryllium, tungsten, selenium, molybdenum, and titanium are a few examples of odd elements that only a 100 years before were either unknown or recognised only as mineralogical curiosities. Today a great number of them are components

of our industrial technology and it is an unusual element indeed that does not have a scientific or industrial application.''[10]

The disposition of material deposits around the earth is quite uneven hence no nation is wholly self-sufficient in the metals required by a modern industrialised economy. Sheer continental size has a good deal to do with relative self-sufficiency. The USSR, USA and China, for example, come close to being able to supply almost all their material needs from within their own borders. The uneven disposition of resources has disadvantages for many of the smaller and poorer countries unless they are fortunate enough to possess some key deposit of an important material.

Overall Adequacy of Resources

A commonly voiced opinion is that raising living standards may be unfeasible due to material resource limitations.

Recent price changes on the world market combined with political uncertainities and the energy crisis has encouraged such neo-Malthusian predictions. Little factual evidence however can be found for these predictions.

> ``The argument that the world is running out of resources rests on two assumptions. One is that reserves are not only finite which, of course, is a truism but that they are limited in the sense that resources can only sustain present rates of growth in consumption for a relatively short period of time. The second assumption is that the growth rate of consumption, if left to itself, is not able to respond to the reduction in that of supply. For even if prices rise sharply, the response to this through substitution or raw materials savings, would take too long to prevent ultimate depletion.''[11]

Reserves estimation is hazardous. Available estimates are generally revised upwards over time due to more extensive exploration and improved extraction techniques. For example,

> `` . . . reserves of copper have risen 3.5 times since 1935; of bauxite 7 times since 1950; metals and minerals available data suggest that, in many cases, these are ample for almost every material in the next fifty to a hundred years.''[12]

The extension of reserves is not only a function of exploration and extraction technology but also of use rates, functional resource competition and substitution. The costs of extraction may cause higher prices as our levels go down but even this has not effected availability to any real extent. The 'in-use' reserve of materials is often very large particularly in the case of those with only a few years supply like silver, mercury, lead and tin.

Use and growth rates estimations are based on primary processing from which it is difficult to assess actual use rates. Evidence suggests that factors such as growing intensivity-of-use, i.e., doing more with less, is quite marked in advanced industrial practice. Increased economic growth in recent years has *not* been accompanied by the increased use of materials per product function but by considerable gains in higher performance per unit of material used; and this has also been paced by a decline in energy used per production unit in many cases. Possibilities for recycling and increased substitution from man-made and other materials has also been a factor in restraining growth use rates in key metals and minerals.

Fears of projected inadequacy due to increased growth rates by major users in the advanced countries seem similarly unfounded. Population growth rates are declining in these countries and we have earlier shown that increased affluence alone is not necessarily paralleled by a consistent increase in materials' use.

This is not to say that the use of materials should be profligate or that present use rates in advanced countries should not be slowed. There are quite enough reasons for greater materials efficiency and conservation without advancing impending world scarcities.

Relative Country Positions

An overall indication of reserves, production and major imports for some sixteen important metals and minerals is given in Fig. 79

It shows that for many metals and minerals the larger countries such as USSR, USA and China have major reserves and production. In selected items such as titanium, vanadium, cobalt, molybdenum, chromite, and tungsten, for example, reserves and major production are the province of a handful of countries.

> "Developing countries are estimated to have roughly 40-45 percent of the world's major non-fuel mineral reserves, with 35 percent in developed countries and 25-30 percent in centrally planned economies . . . Reserves of phosphate, tin and bauxite are concentrated in the developing countries which also account for about half of the copper and nickel reserves, whereas the reserves of iron ore, manganese, zinc, lead and silver are concentrated in the developed and centrally planned economies."[13]

Though the developing world as a whole has a large percentage of the general reserves of some of the major metals and minerals, many developing nations are not so well endowed. Such is the case, of course, with several of the developed countries, Japan being a key example. However, the reserve picture does not take into account the changing profiles of resource needs in technical development, and the changes in industrial growth themselves.

MATERIAL RESOURCES, Reserves, Production, Imports : Zinc, Lead, Nickel

ZINC

Reserves — in million metric tons — World Total 135,100,000 m.t (1973–74)

Other	Africa	Asia	Western Europe	Australia	Eastern Europe and U.S.S.R.	U.S.A.	Canada
13.0	6.4	10.9	14.4	16.3	16.4	27.2	30.8

Production (Mine) — in thousand metric tons — World Total 5,703,000 m.t. (1973)

Other	Japan	Mexico	Peru	U.S.A.	Australia	U.S.S.R.	Canada
1,938	264	271	412	434	478	670	1,236

Imports (Ore, Concentrates, Refined) — in thousand metric tons — World Total 2,916,000 m.t. (1973)

Other	France	U.K.	W. Germany	Benelux	Japan	U.S.A.
254.8	210.3	282.0	410.2	515.7	523.9	714.6

LEAD

Reserves — in million metric tons — Total 149,700,000 m.t. (1973 – 74)

Other	Africa	S. America	Australia	U.S.S.R.	Canada	Europe	U.S.A.
13.6	4.5	5.4	16.3	16.3	17.2	22.7	53.5

Production (Mine) — in thousand metric tons — World Total 3,532,000 m.t. (1973)

Other	Mexico	Peru	Canada	Australia	U.S.S.R.	U.S.A.
1,345	179	199	386	406	470	547

Imports (Ore, Concentrates, Bullion, Refined) — in thousand metric tons — World Total 1,176.500 m.t. (1973)

Other	France	Japan	W. Germany	U.K.	U.S.A.
150.8	114.4	188.6	223.9	244.4	254.4

NICKEL

Reserves — in million metric tons — World Total 45,259,000 m.t. (1973)

Other	Cuba	Canada	U.S.S.R.	New Caledonia
11,156	3,809	7,256	9,070	13,967.8

Production (Mine) — in thousand metric tons — World Total 658,495 m.t. (1973)

Other	New Caledonia	U.S.S.R.	Canada
179.6	98.9	136.1	243.9

Imports (Ore, Matte, Unwrought) — in thousand metric tons — World Total 3,701,152 m.t. (1972)

Other	U.S.A.	Japan
324.6	199.2	3,177.3

Fig. 79

MATERIAL RESOURCES, Reserves, Production, Imports : Cobalt, Molyodenum, Tungsten

COBALT

Reserves — in thousand metric tons — World Total 2,450,714 m.t. (1973)

Other	Canada	U.S.S.R.	Cuba	Zambia	Oceania	Zaire
	175.1	204.1	337.4	347.4	671.2	680.3

Production (Mine, Metal Content) — in metric tons — World Totals 25,627 m.t. (1973)

Australia	Finland	Morocco	Cuba	U.S.S.R.	Canada	Zambia	Zaire
762	1,270	1,421	1,633	1,678	1,790	1,995	15,079

Imports (All Categories) — in metric tons — World Totals 23,806 m.t. (1972)

Other	W. Germany	U.K.	Japan	U.S.S.R.	France
1,955	1,252	2,032	3,636	6,447	8,484

MOLYBDENUM

Reserves — in thousand metric tons — World Totals 5,986,200 m.t. (1973)

Other	P. R. China	Chile	Canada	U.S.S.R.	U.S.A.
167.8	113.4	816.3	861.7	907	2,961.4

Production (Mine) — in metric tons — World Total 82,152 m.t. (1973)

Other	P.R.China	Chile	U.S.S.R.	Canada	U.S.A.
1,301	1,492	5,884	8,481	12,449	52,542

Imports (Ore, Concentrate, Metal) — in metric tons — World Total 58,212 m.t. (1972)

Other	France	Italy	U.K.	Belgium	Japan	W. Germany
3,147	5,558	5,759	9,213	9,560	10,501	14,474

TUNGSTEN

Reserves — in thousand metric tons — World Total 1,777,720 m.t. (1973)

Other	N. Korea	S. America	U.S.A.	N. Korea	U.S.S.R.	Canada	P.R. China
125.6	45.8	59	107.9	113.4	158.7	215.9	952.4

Production (Contained Tungsten) — in metric tons — World Total 38,693 m.t. (1973)

Other	Canada	North Korea	R. Korea	Thailand	U.S.A.	Bolivia/Peru/Brazil	U.S.S.R.	P.R. China
6,864	2.083	2,154	2,252	2,601	3,435	3,930	7,392	7,982

Imports (Ore, Concentrate, Metal) — in metric tons — World Total 37,126 m.t. (1972)

Other	France	Sweden	Japan	Benelux	U.S.S.R.	U.S.A.	U.K.	W. Germany
2,237	2,014	2,418	2,496	4,318	5,249	5,256	6,567	6,571

Fig. 79 cont.

MATERIAL RESOURCES, Reserves, Production, Imports : Tin, Chromite, Manganese

TIN

Reserves — in thousand metric tons
World Total 10,137,648 m.t. (1973)

Other	2,739.0
Brazil	609.6
U.S.S.R.	629.9
Bolivia	1,000.8
Malaysia	1,236.5
Thailand	1,524.0
Peoples Republic of China	2,397.8

Production (Mine) — in thousand metric tons
World Total 236,574 m.t. (1973)

Other	24.4
Nigeria	5.8
Australia	10.5
P. R. China	20.3
Thailand	20.9
Indonesia	22.5
U.S.S.R.	29.5
Bolivia	30.3
Malaysia	72.3

Imports (Ore, Concentrate, Oxide, Unwrought) — in thousand metric tons
World Total 276,303 m.t. (1972)

Other	51.5
Italy	3.0
France	4.3
Benelux 4	14.4
Malaysia	15.5
W. Germany	22.5
Japan	31.1
U.S.A.	53.3
U.K.	67.8

CHROMITE

Reserves — in million metric tons
World Total 1,692.5 million m.t. (1973)

Other	85.3
Southern Rhodesia	558
South Africa	1,048.5

Production (Mine) — in thousand metric tons
World Total 6,808,849 m.t. (1973)

Other	1,017.9
Southern Rhodesia	544.2
Turkey	559.6
Philippines	580.5
Albania	653.4
South Africa	1,648.9
U.S.S.R.	1,904.7

Imports (Ore,Oxide, Hydroxied) — in thousand metric tons
World Total 3,758,802 m.t. (1972)

Other	952.7
Sweden	148.3
Poland	169.3
France	279.7
W. Germany	375.0
Japan	875.96
U.S.A.	957.8

MANGANESE

Reserves — in million metric tons
World Total 1,814 million m.t. (1973)

Other	81.6
Gabon	90.7
Australia	145.1
U.S.S.R.	680.3
South Africa	816.3

Production (Mine) — in thousand metric tons
World Total 22,153,000 m.t. (1973)

Other	1,844
P.R. China	1,000
Australia	1,522
India	1,535
Gabon	1,919
Brazil	2,157
South Africa	4,176
U.S.S.R.	8,000

Imports (Ore, Concentrate, Oxide) — in thousand metric tons
World Total 9,434,396 m.t. (1972)

Other	1,920.5
U.K.	368.8
Benelux 4	433.6
W. Germany	481.5
Poland	507.4
France	1,127.8
U.S.A.	1,678.6
Japan	2,921.2

Fig. 79 cont.

MATERIAL RESOURCES, Reserves, Production, Imports : Titanium and Vanadium

TITANIUM

Reserves – Ilmenite (in thousand metric tons)

World Total 245,797,000 m.t. (1973)

Other	Australia	South Africa	U.S.A.	Norway	Canada	India
5,400	10,884	19,047	25,396	38,094	49,885	97,956

Reserves – Rutile (in thousand metric tons)

World Total 94,509,400 m.t. (1973)

Other	U.S.A.	Australia	India	Brazil
1,905	3,265	5,079	20,498	62,130

Production – Ilmenite (in thousand metric tons)

World Total 2,581,131 m.t. (1973)

Other	Sri Lanka	Finland	Malaysia	U.S.A.	Norway	Australia
102.8	92.9	139.5	156	619.5	641.4	829.1

Production – Rutile (in thousand metric tons)

World Total 384,409 m.t. * (1973)

Other	Sierra Leone	Australia
5.8	11.9	366.6

Production – Titaniferrous Slag (in thousand metric tons)

World Total 779,200 m.t. (1973)

Japan	Canada
5.5	773.7

Imports – (All categories) (in thousand metric tons)

World Total 2,550,76 m.t. (1972)

Other	Benelux	France	Italy	W. Germany	Japan	U.S.A.
562.6	95.3	171.3	180	477.3	502	562.3

VANADIUM

Reserves (in thousand metric tons)

World Total 9,704,900 m.t. (1973)

Other	Chile/ Venezuela	South Africa	U.S.S.R.
398.1	226.8	1,814	7,256

Production (contains Vanadium) (in metric tons)

World Total 19,306 m.t. (1973)

Other	Chile	Finland	U.S.S.R.	U.S.A.	South Africa
1,532	961	1,259	3,357	3,970	8,227

Imports (Pentoxide, Oxide, Hydroxied, Metal) (in metric tons)

World Total 5,258 m.t. (1972)

Other	Spain	Italy	U.S.A.	Japan
144	400	881	1,794	2,039

Fig. 79 cont.

MATERIAL RESOURCES, Reserves, Production, Imports : Nitrogen, Phosphate Rock, Potash, Fertilizer Materials

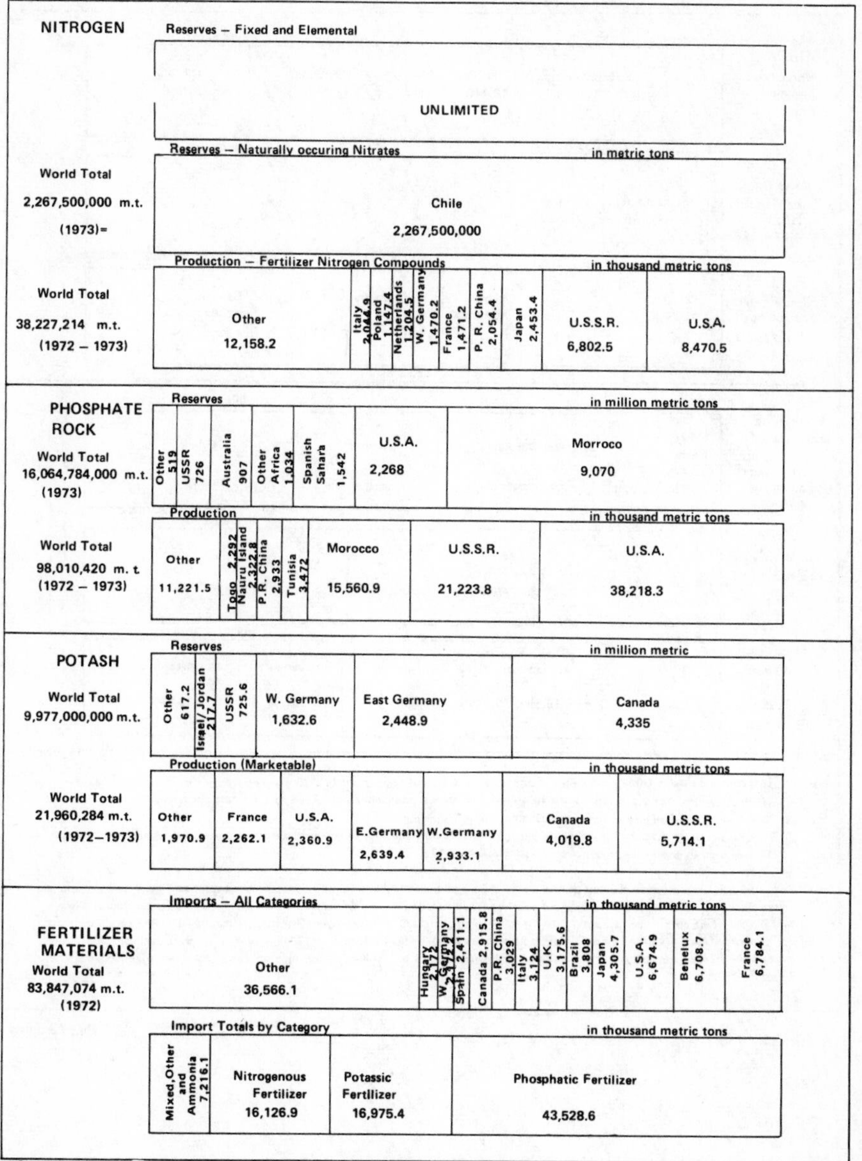

N.B. Imports for 1972 are shown for all categories of fertilizer materials. The 36,566, 100 m.t. of imports shown under "other" reflects total imports by 80 countries.

Fig. 79 cont.

MATERIAL RESOURCES, Reserves, Production, Imports : Boron Kyanite

BORON

Reserves (in thousand metric tons) — World Total 72,560,000m.t. (1973)

Chile	Argentina	P.R. China	Turkey	U.S.S.R.	U.S.A.
4,540	4,540	9,100	18,140	18,140	18,140

Production (Contained Boron) (in metric tons) — World Total 310,194 m.t. (1973)

P.R.China	Argentina	U.S.S.R.	Turkey	U.S.A.
4,540	9,070	36,280	72,560	187,750

Imports (Crude, Oxide, Acid) (in metric tons) — World Total 978,264 m.t. (1972)

Other	Japan	France	Italy	W. Germany	Benelux
158,700	57,000	107,000	112,800	178,600	364,200

KYANITE and Related Material

Reserves (in thousand metric tons) — World Total 90,700,000 m.t. (1973)

Other North America	Africa	Asia/Oceania	Europe	U.S.A.
9,070	9,070	22,675	22,675	27,210

Production (in metric tons) — World Total 278,463 m.t. (1973)

Other	India	South Africa	U.S.A.
6,583	73,921	81,630	116,300

Imports (in metric tons) — World Total 107,791 m.t. (1972)

Other	Australia	W. Germany	Benelux	Japan	Isreal
19,328	3,418	16,591	19,665	22,982	25,807

N. B. (1) Difference between total production of contained Boron and total imports of Boron compounds (in the form of crude natural borates, oxide and acid is due to quantity of Boron compounds obtained through refining process.

(2) Totals may not compare to individual listings due to rounding.

(3) Figures for production and imports are approximations only because of incompleteness of data. In isolated cases import figures used in computing totals were those given for 1971.

Data: Department of the Interior, Bureau of Mines, Minerals Yearbook 1973, Volume I, (Metals, Minerals, and Fuels) and Volume III (Area Reports : International)(Washington , D.C., : Government Printing Office, 1976) and, Bureau of Mines, Mineral Facts and Problems, 1975 Edition (Chapter Preprints) (Washington,D.C. : Government Printing Office, 1976. [Reserves data for phosphate rock are based on estimate by Phosphate Rock Export Association, Effective July 1, 1974, and source of world production data for potash is the British Sulphur Corporation, Ltd., Statistical Supplement No.8, November-December 1973, London, 1973.]

Source : Center for Integrative Studies.

Fig. 79 cont.

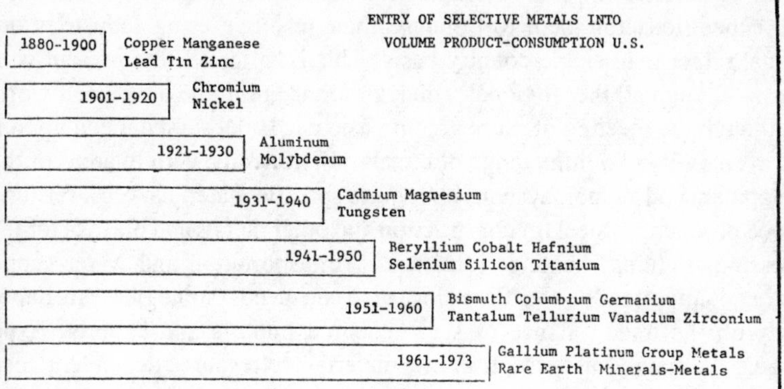

ENTRY OF SELECTIVE METALS INTO VOLUME PRODUCT-CONSUMPTION U.S.

1880-1900	Copper Manganese Lead Tin Zinc
1901-1920	Chromium Nickel
1921-1930	Aluminum Molybdenum
1931-1940	Cadmium Magnesium Tungsten
1941-1950	Beryllium Cobalt Hafnium Selenium Silicon Titanium
1951-1960	Bismuth Columbium Germanium Tantalum Tellurium Vanadium Zirconium
1961-1973	Gallium Platinum Group Metals Rare Earth Minerals-Metals

PERIOD	QUANTITY (TONS)
A. 1880-1900:	
Copper	100,000
Lead	100,000
Manganese	100,000
Zinc	100,000
Tin	10,000
B. 1901-1920:	
Chromium	10,000
Nickel	5,000
C. 1921-1930:	
Aluminum	100,000
Molybdenum	500
D. 1931-1940:	
Cadmium	3,000
Magnesium	1,000
Tungsten	1,000

PERIOD	QUANTITY (TONS)
E. 1941-1950:	
Silicon	500,000
Titanium	250,000
Cobalt	2,500
Beryllium	1,000
Selenium	250
Hafnium	2
F. 1951-1960:	
Zirconium	30,000
Vanadium	1,300
Bismuth	750
Columbium	500
Tantalum	250
Tellurium	100
Germanium	10
G. 1961-1973:	
Rare Earth Minerals	10,000
Platinum Group Metals	50
Gallium	5

Source: Center for Integrative Studies

Fig. 80

The pattern of resource use with changing technologies is illustrated in Fig. 80. It may be seen that the standard minerals such as aluminum, tin, copper, lead, zinc and the steel alloying materials, molybdenum, tungsten, chromium, etc, increase steadily in volume production, however, there comes a point where the lighter metals such as magnesium begin to rise in importance, then the lighter steel alloying constituents, and as the electronics and communications industries gow, the rare earths group come into the menu. Silicon is an interesting example here, it is one of the most plentiful element in the earth's crust, and is central to the key growth areas of electronics and computers.

These changes conform roughly to the pattern of industrial shifts, where, though steel production is still used as a conventional indicator, the most rapid growth in the past twenty years has been in the light metals, plastics, electronics and communications.

For the developing countries there is no real gain to be had in emulating the early stages of growth of the industrial nations, and concentrating on heavy industries. Rather they should explore new and more suitable patterns. In terms of their own collective self-development and resource dispositions, it may be more expeditious for them to organise their resource-using industries on a regional rather than single country basis. This is, after all, the present world pattern—though all the 'regional' concentrations are in the developed world.

Although the meeting of more urgent basic needs does not depend upon the local availability of a large range of metals and minerals, certain areas of their development and support systems do require specific materials, e.g., fertilisers for food production, steel for construction and other metals and plastics for food processing, lighting, heating, furnishings, transportation and water supply. Also, and importantly, the financing of basic needs strategies can depend greatly on the trade balance of such resource imports and exports. Export balances are mainly, at present, in raw materials to resource dependent developed countries.

As we shall discuss more closely in relation to trade, the specific resource-dependencies of the developed world on the developing world's metals and minerals vary greatly. For example, the U.S. imported only about 5 percent of its material requirements in 1973 from developing countries; Europe and Japan were more dependent, generally for about three-fourths of their consumption. But even this balance could change negatively for the developing world as the range of substitute materials expands and the patterns of technologies change.

Material Substitutions

The simple substitution of one material for another enhances the adequacy of supply. Some substitutions are indicated where superior qualities of ductility, hardness, tensile strength of conductivity can be achieved; others are price sensitive where less expensive substitutes are sought, e.g., copper for conductivity is supplemented by other metals and non-metallics giving comparable performance. The possible substitutions of this type are now very large (Fig. 81), and militate against any particular scarcities or abrupt price fluctuations for most common materials.

The other kind of substitution is functional, where a different mode of carrying out a particular task is developed. Nuts and bolts or welding may be replaced by adhesives; and communications substituted for physical transportation.

The range of such possibilities is increasing rapidly as the molecular design of materials to specific functions is enhanced, and more substitutions are made.

Such replacement and substitution of traditional material functions changes demand in the materials range—and is often accompanied by a marked decrease in economic, social and environmental costs. For example, the replacement of copper by glass fibers in communications decreases the impact and cost of metal mining, processing and manufacturing; the replacement of natural fibers

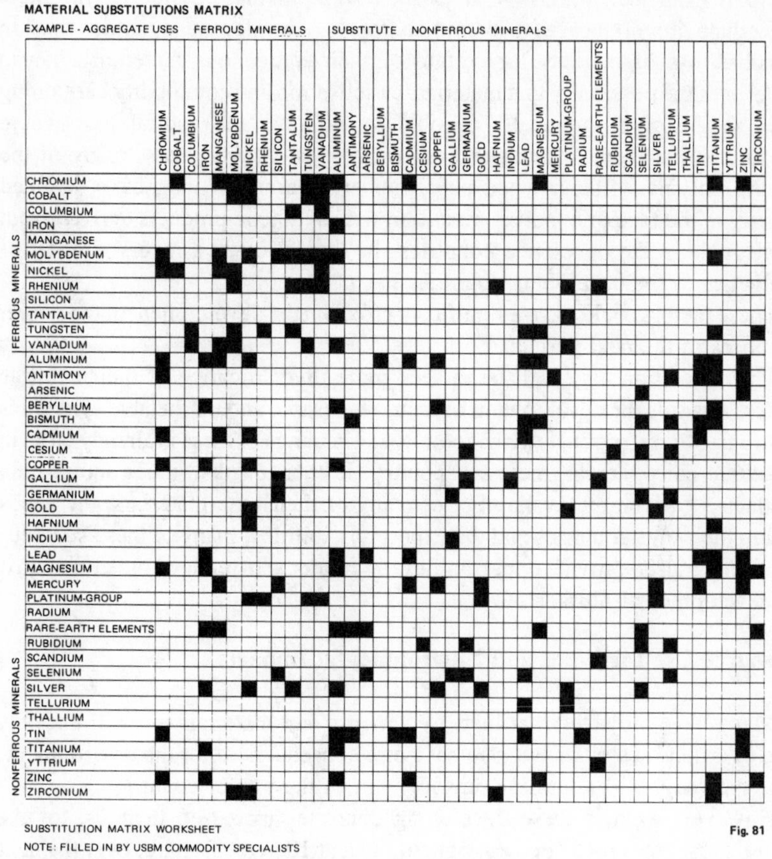

Fig. 81

Source: World Mineral and Energy Resources: Some facts and Assessments by J.N. Hartley with contributions from E.A. Eschbach and O.J. Wick, Battelle, December, 1974.

by synthetic can release cropland for food production—though this gain may not be appreciated by cash crop dependent countries.

The word 'synthetic' might be qualified here as we do not really make wholly new materials but discover new ways to re-arrange the elements of given materials. This synthesising approach has always been prevalent in human materials processing from the earliest uses of fire, foods, fibers, and metal-alloying and fermentation.

The range of potential and new plastics, composites and 'whisker reinforced' materials will considerably change the profile of conventional resource demand in the next thirty years. In terms of plastics alone such as the structural polymers and composites, there has been considerable invasion of the steel, and other metals market.

Apart from indicating new areas for developmental possibility, the more immediate importance of substitution for the developing countries lies in possible loss of markets for certain of their indigenous materials. It also underlines the possibility that materials cartelisation and commodity bargaining may not be as economically feasible as with oil and natural gas, where substitutes are more difficult to find. In the past twenty years, many of the natural polymers fibers, wood pulp, rubber, cotton and jute, have declined heavily in the face of export competition with synthetic products derived from fossil fuels in the developed countries. In several cases a reverse import of synthetics to the developing countries has occurred.

These factors could have a significant effect on the development of the poorer countries in the next period.

Their direction may well be to seek more diversification of their agrarian sectors towards the development of their own usable and marketable synthetics from agricultural products in the food area. The range of these is already large in substitute dairy, cereal, meat and poultry, leather, drinks, juices and protein products.[14] Given the availability of many of their base materials, the needs within their own countries and the export possibilities, many of these substitutions may indeed provide opportunities for greater self-reliance rather than just be developmental obstacles.

Resource Use Increases and Environmental Impacts

Many have projected that increased energy and materials use will not only lead to critical scarcities but also have dire consequences for the environment, this, they say, will retard the development of the poorer countries.

However, even if these developing countries increased their use of the world's resources by 50 percent of their present 10 percent share, over the next twenty years, their share would still be only 15 percent of total world resource use.[15] Also, given the varied state of their economies, any such increased use would be selective, not across the entire resource range, and differentially allocated over time.

Environmental consequences as such materials and energy use increases to meet higher living standards for the poorer countries, is unlikely to have any gross effects on biospheric limits, as has been suggested. Most of the consequences of expansion in extraction, processing and materials use in developing industry, construction and transportation could be locally contained, and so managed as to minimise social and physical impacts. The social and institutional limitations may be much stronger than any physical limits, both in their capacity to adapt and organise such development, and in the commercial and legislative control of environmental side-effects. The 'hard' technologies of development and environmental management are available; the 'soft' technologies of organisational and institutional capacity are more likely to be the real barriers.

Optimization Procedure

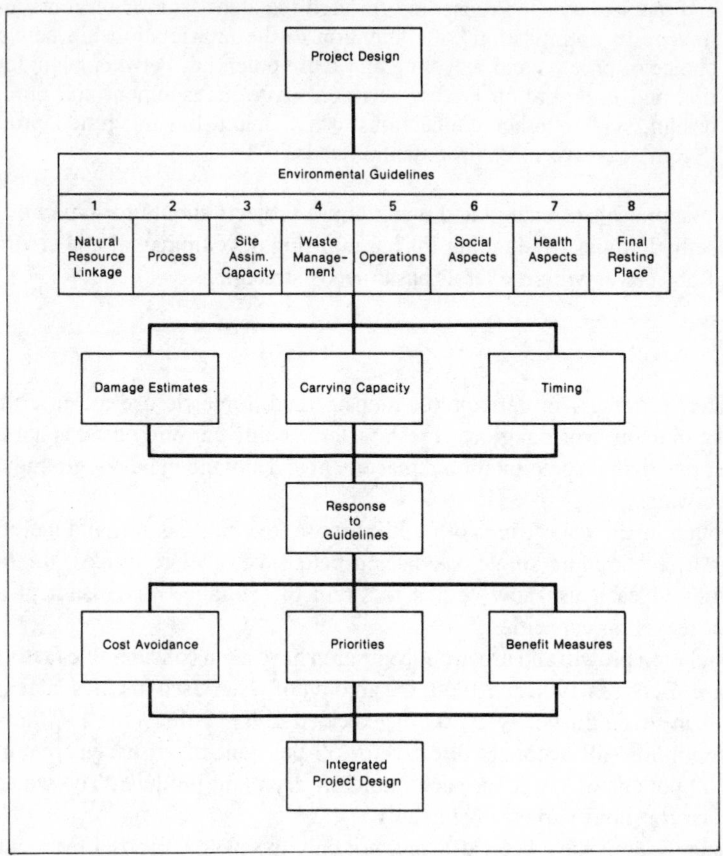

Source : Environmental, Health and Human Ecological Considerations in Economic Development Projects, World Bank/ May, 1974.

Fig. 82

We should especially examine those effects of the expanded uses of resources that are to be designed specifically to implement basic needs strategies and local self-reliance.

In meeting human needs through concerted strategy, some environmental costs may have to be traded against human gains. Local environmental carrying capacities provide a definable space within which an integrated appraisal can certainly be made of costs and benefits of proposed actions in relation to project costs and benefits. Fig. 82 outlines the steps of an optimising procedure for implementing projects from inception through realisation.

> "As indicated . . . the impacts of investments on the human environment requires a systematic and integrated view of projects which links them to

> materials flow within production processes and throughout the economy and the society . . . Proceeding through the steps from natural resource linkage to optimisation calls attention to the interrelationship between choice of process and recycling and reuse potential, between plant location and urbanisation issues, between waste management and process design, and to other connections which make the integrated project design sensitive to environmental needs."[16]

Such appraisals of energy and material use projects should form part of the core methodologies of planning for harmonising developmental and environmental objectives within overall basic needs strategies.

Water

Water resources, in agriculture, industry and domestic use are in critical balance in many world regions. Fresh water is being currently used at a much greater rate than its precipitation replacement and storage in below ground and surface waters.

Though much water use is of multi-purpose 'cycling' nature, and therefore differs from the more single use/discard pattern of other resources, the bulk increases in each use now begins to strain the storage, replenishment and natural recycling capacities.

Population growth and urban concentration have been considerable factors of increase. Between 1900 and 1960, the amount of water used in cities increased more than seven times. By 1980 it is expected to be 12 times the 1900 level.

Agriculture still accounts directly for 50 per cent of all usage, requiring 400-500 pounds of water for each pound of dry plant produce. The water to specific crop-ratio varies considerably.

Water systems have been affected, not only in sewage disposal from cities, and industrial wastes, but from intensified agricultural practices. Large amounts of soil additives are washed off the lands through rainfall, irrigation and drainage into the natural water courses where they disturb the organic balance. The undue growth of algae and plant growths decreases the oxygen supply for aquatic organisms thus attenuating the self-renewal of the water system. Such problems are not localized. In the case of pesticide 'run offs' and other toxic agents in upper river reaches, their effects may only be felt thousands of miles away.

Much requires to be done to replenish and re-use the waters extracted by both agriculture and industry and to ensure that they are 'returned to source' unpolluted by wastes, soil run-offs, and thermal discharges. So far such waters have been treated as a 'free good'; to be drawn upon prodigally as required—but in the next decades this can no longer be tolerated.

Water, a hitherto plentiful resource, may indeed be the most critically impacted areas of resource 'scarcity' in the next period—rather than materials and energy. More comprehensive patterns for its use must be developed, which would, in turn, reduce the pressure on the 'natural' cycling system.

It is unlikely that measures such as direct irrigation by saline waters, desalination, etc.—taken alone will be sufficient in themselves to provide the quantity of water use and re-use which may be required in the next thirty years. The amounts of energy and materials needed to conduct such processing on a large enough scale for irrigation would be an important factor.

Water, like air, seemingly one of our most plentiful common goods in global terms may indeed be one of the bounds of regional criticality in the next few decades. To avoid near catastrophe situations, like that of the South Sahara, we will have to develop more long range outlooks and coordinate action in this area.

Our only overall strategy is to use all such means to the greatest advantage and to recast and revise our present water use practices by redesigning those industrial and agricultural processes which 'over-use' this critical resource.

ADAPTABLE TECHNOLOGIES

Although all human societies are technological by definition, the term, technologies, is generally used to describe the more advanced technical aspects of modern industrial societies.

What we usually refer to as the technological societies are those which have been able to offload human and animal labor onto inanimate machine energies, in which the range and scale of materials and technics is greatly extended, and living standards thereby enhanced.

It is important, here, to separate out the different phases of industrial technological development—both for development purposes and with regard to their impacts upon the environment. It is these impacts which have engaged most critical attention in recent discussion. However, what is being criticised is the older type of industrial practice (Fig. 83) which is highly resource intensive and wasteful, and has gross environmental impacts through its effluents and by-products. Indications are that this type of industrial practice is already partially obsolete as new modes of technology organised around different processes become more dominant. For example,

a) The more recent waves of technology, such as electronics, computers, communications,—the new electro-magnetic spectrum industries—are, by comparison, non-resource depletive, extremely economical in their energy uses and have relatively low impact on the environment.

b) These advanced technological forms trend towards 'ephemeralisation' through their decreasing use of material and energy inputs per function—and in their successive micro-miniaturisation of components. For example, over the past decade, computers have become approxi-

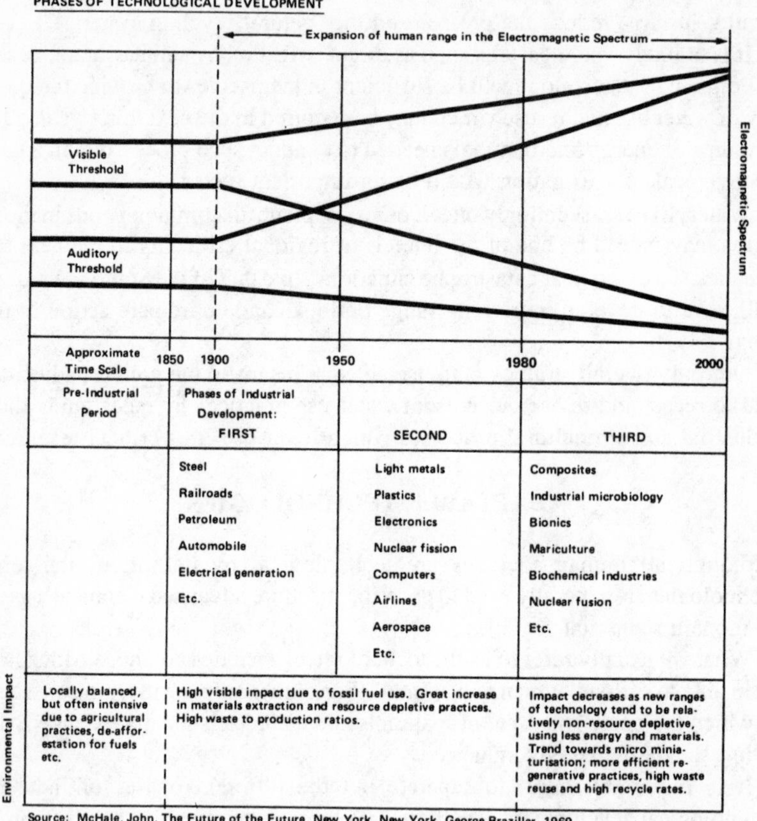

Source: McHale, John, The Future of the Future, New York, New York, George Braziller, 1969.

Fig. 83

mately 10 times smaller, 100 times faster and 1,000 times cheaper to operate.

c) The emerging wave of bio-technological developments will have another range of regenerative capacities, for example, in industrial microbiology, the more efficient use of microbial populations to produce energy, food, and process materials; the extension of mariculture; bionic engineering with its application of biological principles into new technics; the renewed interest in use of insect and other organic populations for various productive tasks.

This would tend to confirm that there is no essential connection between the growth of advanced technologies, better living standards and more pollution and deterioration of the environment.

One key shift in these technological changes, of considerable importance to the developing world, is the emergence of information or organised knowledge as *the* basic resource—now reinforced by the development and fusion of computers and telecommunications. Information as a basic resource ultimately shapes all other resources; in itself, it is not reduced or lessened by wider use, or sharing—rather it gains in the process of distribution and exchange. Where resources such as raw materials and energy are, by comparison, scarce and depletive, information and knowledge are inexhaustible.

The shift in resource base and technologies has therefore changed many aspects of the older zero-sum game condition of society—in which one side had to lose if the other gained, as resources were inadequate to share. Human survival has become more a non-zero sum situation—success or gain are predicated more on the sharing of advantage, on all winning.

Although full access to the use of the new information technologies is still restricted to the affluent countries, many of their applications are at work or in potential development in the poorer regions:

1. earth satellite monitoring and remote surveying of mineral resources, agriculture, forestry and hydrological conditions.
2. computer modelling and control of resource use in agriculture and industry with enhanced capacity, for example, to predict environmental impacts.
3. educational and communications satellite capacities which can give greater opportunities for human resource development.

These are examples of large scale, high cost, 'network' technologies which can be of great benefit to development. In many cases, the local applications need not directly involve very expensive equipment, e.g., in educational satellite transmission and telecommunications, or in the use of LANDSAT or ERTS imagery to aid local farming, in fact, they may in the long run be much less costly than more conventional modes.

In the main, however, the benefits of these technics are restrained by lack of funds, equipment, and particularly by lack of local skilled personnel.

The Choice of Technological Directions

Whichever direction is taken by any specific developing nation, as a whole they have to move towards some appropriate level of industrial development. Even where the primary emphasis is on upgrading the rural sector, more, and better, technology is still needed plus support systems provided by some measure of industrialisation. The choice is not one between 'alternative' technology and Western-style industrialisation but rather the adaptation of elements of both—and the evolution of new modes of technological development to meet particular needs.

Pursuing industrial parity with the already developed nations along the same lines is one direction. However, developing countries, at present, only generate about 7 percent of world industrial production, i.e., "... in 1975, the total value of the world industrial production was something like $2,600 billion. The third world contributed less than $200 billion to this world industrial output."[17] The Lima Declaration approved by UNIDO in 1973, called for an increase in this overall share to at least 25 percent of world production by the year 2000. This is, however, a rhetorical target and does not specify how the goal might be reached. It could not be attempted without considerable expansion of international assistance.

Much has, and can be, done in this direction by adapting current industrial processes to developing situations. Industries based on agricultural products and by-products can be expanded; new mini-steel plants can be more decentralised, need less coking coal and can produce in aggregate as much as large integrated plants; light metals emphasis in conjunction with hydropower may be suitable for many countries; coal and coal by-products can fit others, and so on. More can also be achieved by relocating primary fabrication and manufacture in developing countries closer to their raw materials—aiding both the developing countries' industrial growth and more equitable return on their raw materials extraction.

Reporting on the case of Niger, a recent paper outlines a plan of action for such situations. Based both on industrial directions and rural improvement this covers the important area of multi-country operations. Some summary points are given below:

> 1. mobilising of all material and human potential as yet unemployed to stimulate a 'green revolution'—with concomitant efforts by agronomic research, fertiliser and implement industry. Land to be apportioned within the framework of coherent development plans.
>
> 2. processing industries designed to take full advantage of enhanced agricultural production with more precise planning of what is for export and what is for home consumption.
>
> 3. animal husbandry to be supported and developed to supply national demand and relevant export industries to supply neighboring countries.
>
> 4. Mining industries to be handled so that territorial concessions and entire areas are not left wholly to the judgment of foreign countries; cooperation with other states to carry out mining research and development.
>
> 5. heavy industries, metallurgy, iron, and steel, etc., on a multi-state basis, linked to the mining of local ores.
>
> 6. establish multinational corporations of developing states; with foreign companies having minority holdings if necessary.
>
> 7. trade agreements between neighboring states to unfetter trade, with customs unions as a prelude to economic integration; creation of sales associations to act as pressure groups to promote commodity alliances and trade equity.[18]

The implementation of such plans in combination with basic needs strategies could certainly promote greater individual and collective self-reliance.

Given that sufficient energy and materials are available for such developments there are still some formidable barriers to accelerating industrial development.

> 1. The shortage of scientific and technical personnel which we have already detailed in assessing educational needs. For this and other reasons, only about 2 percent of all R & D in new technologies takes place in the developing world.
> 2. Technical assistance and cooperation have been insufficient. This is the province of a great variety of international agencies and country institutions, efforts have overlapped considerably, information on such efforts and their results have been scattered and there has been insufficient integration and overall planning. The institutional bias has been to use experts from the developed countries, thereby making insufficient use of the many skilled people in the developing countries who may better understand local conditions.
> 3. The role of patenting and licensing agreements has meant restricted access to many new processes and hindered their adoption in the poorer countries.
> "Of the 3.5. million patents currently in existence, only about 6 percent (200,000) have been granted by developing countries. Of these five out of six are hold by nationals of the developing countries . . . the overwhelming majority of these patents are used to secure import monopolies."[19]

This is now being given close attention at the international level particularly with regard to multinational corporate operations in the area.

Implicit in many of these difficulties is the assumption that in order for the developing countries to reach some sort of industrial parity, they must 'catch up' with the developed. The linkage of development with a recapitulation of developed experience in industrialisation may really be the older 'necessary stages' thesis in disguise.

> "It is this equating of 'industrialisation' with 'development' from which stems many of the disillusions, misconceptions and speculations which the Third World witnesses today in its struggle to determine its own economic, social and political fate."[20]

Given the range and flexibility of more advance technologies, there may be better reason to move directly into new areas rather than copy the older patterns.

Counter movements to the spread of industrialisation consider stimulated 'Western' industrialisation as inappropriate to the Third World, because it is: capital-intensive and labor-saving rather than capital-saving and labor-using;

environmentally and socio-culturally destructive; alien to the Third World's ways of life and unmatched to its needs. Although aspects of these arguments are rather specious, the overall direction has been productive of many interesting explorations in alternative technologies. The model and stimulus has been developments in the Chinese People Republic, though others go back to Gandhi's village crafts movement. In both cases, these are ideologies of self-reliance which indicates that there is a political impact to the alternative technologies movement,

> "The problem of adoption of technology is not only a technical problem it is also a political one . . . (which) has a direct bearing on the future of economic, political and cultural relations between the most industrialised countries of the Northern temperate zone and the less industrialised in the tropical and equatorial zones."[21]

We have already touched upon some of the alternative directions, many of which can be categorised under the heading of intermediate rurally oriented technologies.

Some Examples of Low-Cost Technologies in UNDP-Assisted Projects

	Technology	Country	Purpose
1.	Bamboo and fabric windmills and solar crop driers	India	to develop alternative energy sources for agriculture at less than $100 in production/purchase cost.
2.	Production of plows and ox and donkey carts.	Madagascar	to provide farmers with agricultural implements made from old truck parts and rails from abandoned mines.
3.	Biogas generators	India/ Philippines	to supply energy for rural lighting, pumping water and cooking for less than $300.
4.	Small 'walking tractors'	Grenada	to facilitate agricultural production through small-scale equipment.
5.	Ferro-cement fishing boats	Fiji/ Thailand	to provide low-cost small boats for poorer fishing communities

6. Manufacture of farm implements	Tanzania	to manufacture maize shelters, cultivators and wheel barrows, (all about $8), and ox carts ($40), using bush poles, tree trunks and scrap iron.
7. Small village-made grain silos	Pakistan/ Nepal India	to protect grain from pests and rats. Silos cost about $40.
8. Circular or gang saw	Sudan	to improve village lumber forestry projects through more efficient instruments than pitsaws.
9. Mobile pesticide spray units	India	to facilitate plants protection using hand-held motor-operated spray units.
10. Charcoal for fuel	Ghana	to provide more fuel for village households and industries through better charcoal production.

It seems here, that the main emphasis is on the rural sector. Schumacher says that,

> "The rural areas will continue to be bypassed and unemployment, as well as the drift of migration into cities, will continue to grow unless efficient small-scale technologies are made available with assistance in their use."[22]

The appropriateness of alternative technologies to the agricultural sector is partially based on the lack of adaptability of highly mechanised methods available from the developed countries, which are often mismatched to the terrain, skill level, and low land-to-labor relationships in the developing countries.

Direct local participation in the use of these alternative technologies is an important aspect of this emphasis on greater self-reliance and self-development. This participative interest has been widened to include the questions of involving peoples, "in the social and technical processes of developing, implementing and regulating a technology."[23]

The rural focus of low level alternative technologies has certain obvious advantages in being needs-oriented and adaptable to local resources but in the larger context of the society it has demerits:

There is some aura of "the second best" being foisted upon people who are not ready for more advanced forms. The technics are not only conserving of energy and materials but could also be conservative in the social and political sense. The 'unreadiness' to use more advanced technical forms rarely extends, for example, to relatively sophisticated military technologies nor does *their* introduction, or Western origins, presumably threaten indigenous life styles and values.

1. The ambience which accompanies the promotion of such technologies often reflects a Rousseauesque fascination with the primitive which may not be at all shared by those people for whom they are designed.

2. The over-emphasis on rural technics may neglect other aspects of rural/urban development including the evident desire people have to leave rural occupations.

3. Small scale technologies may be appropriate to local needs but restrictive when it comes to larger requirements, e.g., for exports. Goods for local consumption can be produced within local standards but,

> "In empirical studies of the choice of technique one continually finds that a more capital-intensive technology has to be adopted so as to maintain standards for export."[24]

This is an important consideration in the choice of technologies for developing countries, and the United Nations has recently suggested the following principles for identifying the most appropriate technology for each objective.

> "a) Certain basic commodities, including export products, can be manufactured to acceptable standards only through the use of the most modern and sophisticated technologies;
>
> b) A large number of products for domestic massconsumption and for export, can employ imported technologies that are adapted to local needs;
>
> c) Another large group of products for domestic consumption and for export can be processed and manufactured in widely dispersed factories and shops, using traditional technologies."[25]

Towards a New Technological Base

A frontier area of technology which ties many of the needs of developing countries together is that of biotechnology—designed specifically to take advantage of their climates, rural concentrations and required emphasis on renewable resources with low environmental impact and high regenerative capacities.

In terms of scientific and technical development, recent advances in biology, biochemistry and biophysics, indicate that biological engineering and technologies will have the core position in techno-industrial change that was previously held by the mechanical, chemical and electronic technologies.

The biotechnologies comprise a wide spectrum of processes from the use of microbial populations that produce energy and process materials, to the biochemical conversion of organic wastes into fuel, to fishfarming, mariculture and the use of insects and other organisms for productive work. There are many such processes which could help provide an alternative type of bio-industrial base for the poorer countries, one which is closely related to their needs and truly capable of increasing their self-reliance. The coordinate development of such a bio-industry has been somewhat obscured by the more immediate visibility of older mechanical forms and by the compartmentalisation of much of the basic research in this area.

Many of the techniques of industrial microbiology, for example, are very old traditional modes which are now capable of sophisticated extension.

> "Until now, applied microbial ecology (wine, beer, cheese, sauerkraut, vinegar and oriental fermented foods) has gone its own empirical way unaffected by the remarkable developments in microbial physiology and genetics. This will certainly change and we will probably devote much attention to symbiotic fermentations."[26]

Some examples of the potential of such applied microbiological technics have already been noted in the production of methane from wastes in anaerobic 'biogas' systems; others lie with the mass production of yeasts for animal feed fortification; the conversion of cellulose wastes to meat via microorganisms; the production of energy by microbial fuel cells; and many areas of relevance to agriculture such as increasing organic nitrogen-fixation and the biological control of insect and animal pests. Many of the approaches could be used in combination so as to constitute the starting point for an integrated biochemical industry.[27]

Fuel production by plants grown for that purpose is an area which is receiving serious attention in the developed countries due to energy supply constraints. Wood is the traditional example in this area but shrubs such as the Euphorbia[28] give the idea a new horizon. Euphorbia, for example, produces significant quantities of latex and emulsion of hydrocarbons in water, separable into a sulfur-free fuel. Many of the tropical and semitropical plants under review for agricultural diversification have similar fuel-productive properties.

The extraction of hydrocarbons from forestry products and sugar cane bagasse has been mentioned earlier in our discussion. This is indicative of many other alternatives product routes, for example:

> "One can transform, by fermentation, carbohydrates, (sugar, starch, cellulose) into chemical compounds containing two, three, or four carbon atoms, and this is equivalent to the fundamental substances, ethylene, propylene, butylene, isobutylene, and butadiene which the petrochemi-

> cal industry produces by cracking and then transforms into its final products."[29]

The generation of hydrogen, on a large scale, through photo-chemical means, employing green plants and sunlight, is also under scrutiny.[30]

Insect populations have long been used in such traditional technologies as the silk industry and in bee-keeping for honey production but their potentially extended uses via current scientific advances has been little explored.

Then these are apart from the possibilities of marine (and freshwater) cultivation of fish and the cultivation of seaweeds and underwater vegetation, all of which could provide valuable sources of food and pharmaceutical materials. Minerals might also be gained from the sea.

> "The ocean is essentially a dilute periodic table; so the problem is to pick an element, find out what organism concentrates it and refine the organism in quantity."[31]

Many marine plants and organisms concentrate metals in considerable proportions, some specialising in one, others containing several. Research into these kinds of marine metal concentrates have been obscured by the promise of much larger nodule deposits on the sea floor, many of which are only accessible with high cost technologies.

The range of examples of promising biotechnical approaches could be extended considerably. Their inclusion here is to underline a relatively neglected area for the development of new forms of indigenous industry which may be as relevant to meeting human needs in the developing countries as more conventional and low-level alternative forms. Their extensive development would provide an exciting set of long range goals and a leadership role for the developing world's scientists and technicians.

They have the additional advantages of being appropriate to both rural and quasi-urban situations so that they can be used for a variety of productive purposes. They depend upon a renewable and self-generative resource base, so that their encouragement would not contradict developmental and environmental objectives.

TRADE AND AID

Although our emphasis so far has been mainly focussed on internal self-reliance in meeting human needs, the capacity to do so in wholly autonomous ways is limited for any one nation. No one is completely isolated, or insulated in today's interdependent world.

Some countries are naturally more dependent than others, and therefore more vulnerable. Economic and commercial advantage is severely skewed in favor of the affluent industrialised countries in which resource price fluctuations can be

WORLD EXPORTS BY ORIGIN AND DESTINATION

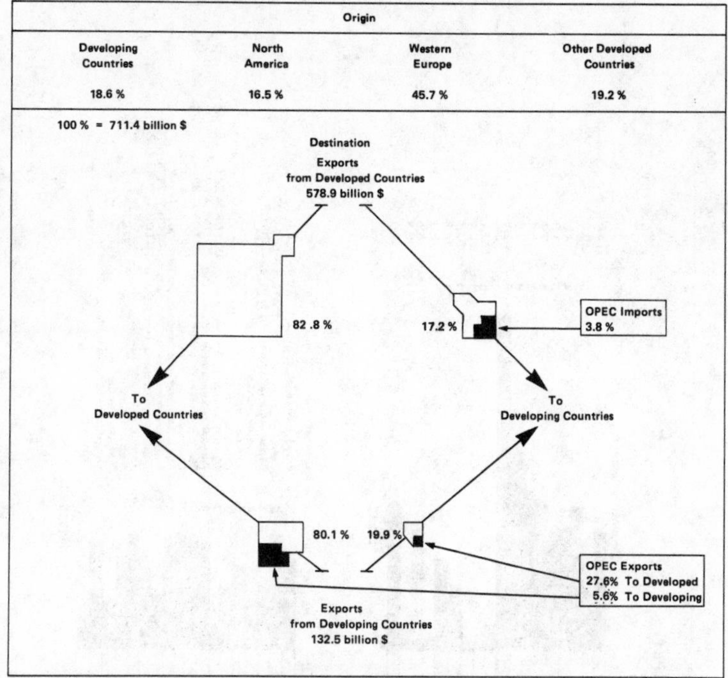

Data : United Nations, Yearbook of International Statistics – 1974, Volume I, Trade by Country. (Statistical Office of the United Nations, New York, 1974). Special Table B, pp 24 – 54, discrepancies exist due to reporting of exports by F.O.B./C.I.F. categories and estimations necessary (source's) for dollar conversions, time periods involved and lack of specific country reports.

Source : Center for Integrative Studies

Fig. 84

absorbed in ways that are not available to those dependent on one or few export commodities. This has been particularly apparent in the past few years and has given rise to the call for a more equitable international economic order.

The comparative trade aspects of this need for change are clear. The balance of trade has increased between the developed nations. Facing inflation themselves they have become more selective in their imports from the developing and, though still dependent on imports of raw materials from these countries their trade in finished products is increasingly amongst themselves.

Fig. 84 and 85 give a compact summary of this position in which the poorer countries mainly figure as raw materials' producers who export cheaply and import dearly. One of the main points at issue in the new international economic order, for example, is the marked imbalance between the basic resource price paid to the producers and that received by the developed processors and manufacturers in the world market. It is particularly noticeable in the case of metals and minerals.

WORLD TRADE 1973 :

Commodity Categories

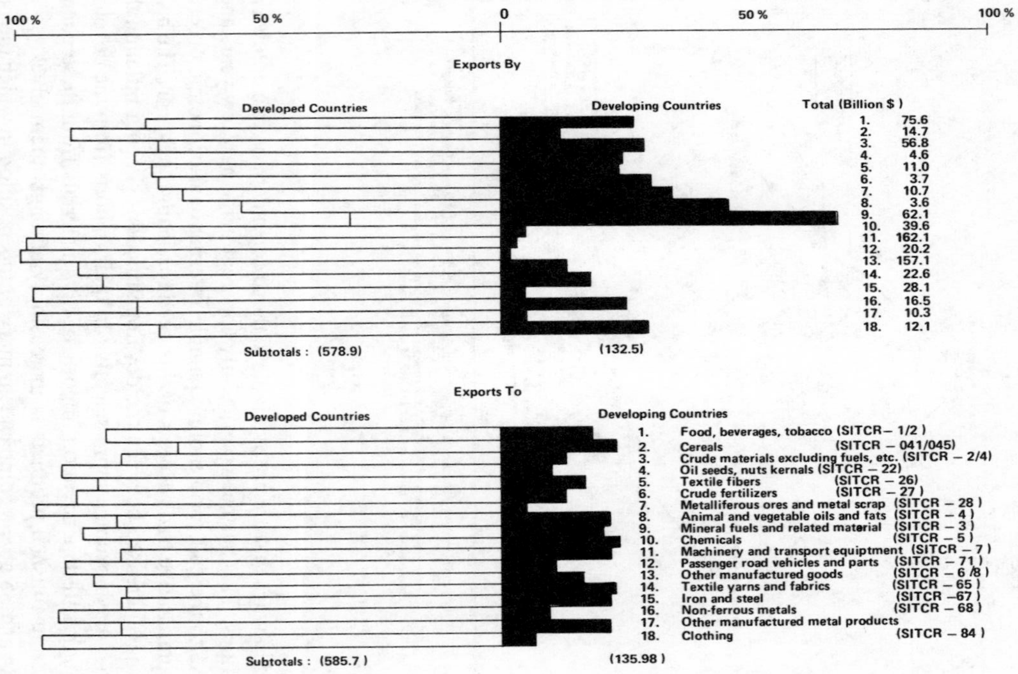

100 % 50 % 0 50 % 100 %

Exports By

Developed Countries | Developing Countries | Total (Billion $)

1. 75.6
2. 14.7
3. 56.8
4. 4.6
5. 11.0
6. 3.7
7. 10.7
8. 3.6
9. 62.1
10. 39.6
11. 162.1
12. 20.2
13. 157.1
14. 22.6
15. 28.1
16. 16.5
17. 10.3
18. 12.1

Subtotals : (578.9) (132.5)

Exports To

Developed Countries | Developing Countries

1. Food, beverages, tobacco (SITCR – 1/2)
2. Cereals (SITCR – 041/045)
3. Crude materials excluding fuels, etc. (SITCR – 2/4)
4. Oil seeds, nuts kernals (SITCR – 22)
5. Textile fibers (SITCR – 26)
6. Crude fertilizers (SITCR – 27)
7. Metalliferous ores and metal scrap (SITCR – 28)
8. Animal and vegetable oils and fats (SITCR – 4)
9. Mineral fuels and related material (SITCR – 3)
10. Chemicals (SITCR – 5)
11. Machinery and transport equiptment (SITCR – 7)
12. Passenger road vehicles and parts (SITCR – 71)
13. Other manufactured goods (SITCR – 6 /8)
14. Textile yarns and fabrics (SITCR – 65)
15. Iron and steel (SITCR –67)
16. Non-ferrous metals (SITCR – 68)
17. Other manufactured metal products
18. Clothing (SITCR – 84)

Subtotals : (585.7) (135.98)

Source : United Nations, Yearbook of International Statistics – 1974, Volume I, Trade by Country (Statistical Office of the United Nations, New York, 1974). Special Table B, pp 24 – 54, (Discrepancies exist / according to source / due to reporting of exports by FOB / CIF categories, time periods involved and lack of specific country reports).

NB – 1) Standard classifications are those used by the United Nations (as revised).
2) Figures may not correspond exactly to percentages due to rounding.

Fig. 85

> "... the value of developing countries' current mineral output is about 30 percent of the market value of the finished products. High profits (and external economics) come from processing, since value is increased by as much as four times through semi-processing and by as much as 20 times through full processing up to the metal bar stage."[32]

One may take this process a step further to the end-product manufacturing stage and the value goes up again so that the raw materials input cost is relatively negligible to the developed processes. In ensuing trade, the continued irony is that the developing country may then buy its exported material back in manufactured form at a relatively enormous finished product cost.

Other developing countries more dependent upon agricultural cashcrop exports have suffered from instabilities in trade prices. For both types of primary exporters, the increasing costs of importing fuel, fertilisers and other products have, in many cases, severely affected their whole development process.

Attempts to achieve more equitable and stable pricing for such developing world resource imports have taken the form of seeking agreements on primary commodity indexing to end-market prices and the formation of commodity organisations based on the OPEC model. This has coincided with the emergence of a broadly shared ideological position on the part of many developing countries that "political independence is not enough; full nationhood requires economic sovereignity."[33] Increased national ownership of internal resources must also be accompanied by increased local processing and more local control over the market pricing of commodities.

These are obvious steps that assist greater individual and collective self-reliance, but the problem with the mini-OPEC's is that, unlike oil, the non-fuel commodities do not lend themselves as well to power bargaining. Chromite, bauxite, tin and manganese are short-term possibles for centralisation but substitutions, the use of other ores and stockpiling could render them less practical in the longer run.

Some of the major difficulties in achieving individual self-reliance through more diversified trade balances is that many of the smaller developing economies are single-product traders hence very sensitive to price fluctuation in one or few commodities.

> "... examples of African countries with virtually monoproduct export trade, are (petroleum apart) ... Burundi (86 percent from coffee), Gambia (91 percent from ground nuts), Mauritius (84 percent from sugar), Zambia (94 percent from copper). Iron ore constitutes 73 percent of total exports of Mauretania and 71 percent of Liberia while Ghana still relies on the export of cocoa (64 percent) and Chad and Sudan on cotton (69 and 59 percent respectively)."[34]

Another problem lies with the economic differences among the developing countries themselves with regard to trade factors influencing self-reliance. In the most recent period of rising inflation, and in the preceding boom, some primary producers benefitted from rising prices, others with export-oriented industrial sectors continued to benefit from developed import demands. The third group were those locked in to product exports such as tea, jute and other agricultural products whose demand has low elasticity.[35] Such developments have made attempts at regional economic integration very hard to sustain and continue to be obstacles to collective self-reliance.

Various tariff and non-tariff barriers to foreign imports are in force, both in the rich and poor countries, which hinder market access and trade diversification by the poorer countries. The simple abolition of tariffs would hardly enhance the latter's position but their rationalisation, and associated measures such as restrictive quotas, are certainly in order.

The role of the multinational, or transnational, corporate entities is also under question at the present time with specific regard to the resource use and trading position of the poorer countries. The negotiating power of such corporations, their effective organisation at the world level, and their capacity to influence governments, eventually affect the lives of millions of people.

> "The value-added of all multinationals was roughly $500 million in 1971 or about one-fifth of world GNP (excluding centrally planned economies). The sales of foreign affiliates of multinational corporations reached approximately $330 billion in 1971, exceeding total exports of all market economies in the same year—and their sales have been growing at a faster rate than the economies of the countries themselves."[36]

The operations of such entities are planned on a world scale, at a level rivalled only by a few sovereign powers. Were they genuinely multinational and representational in their ownership and policies, and more broadly oriented to meeting human needs rather than increasing stockholder profits, they could be considered as a useful and cohesive force in an economically and politically fragmented world. Unfortunately, this is hardly the case.

Their critical role in influencing development lies in their degree of control over the natural resources and local business infrastructure of the developing countries. Although the majority of these entities are corporate business undertakings headquartered in the market economies, many of the international state agencies of the centrally planned economies also function in much the same mode.

Fear of economic colonialism has led to cases of expropriation on the part of host countries and greater surveillance of their operations. Efforts are being made at national and international levels towards the formulation and implementation of operating codes for these multinational entities.

Multinationals are, in some senses, indispensable at the present level of development of many poorer countries, in providing the investment, expertise,

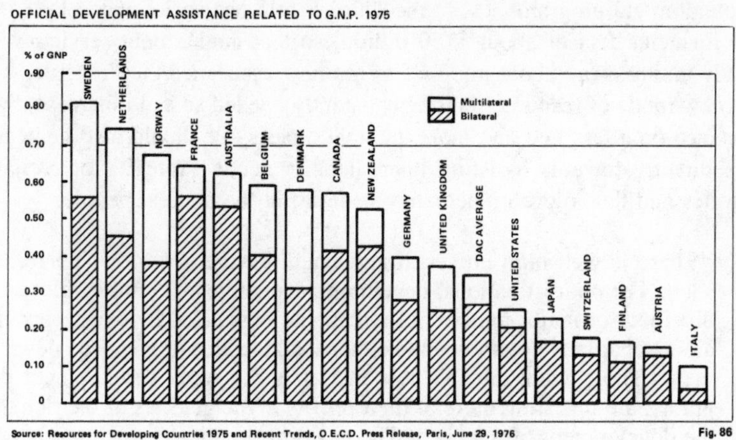

Source: Resources for Developing Countries 1975 and Recent Trends, O.E.C.D. Press Release, Paris, June 29, 1976

Fig. 86

equipment and trained personnel without which the latter would be unable to develop their resources and, paradoxically, become more self-reliant. Given better national and international regulations, and opportunities for local country representation, they can still be effective instruments in aiding this direction. They may also provide a model of economic integration and cooperation which developing countries could follow in setting up their own multinational enterprises for more effective resource utilisation and trading.

Aid flows from the developed to the developing nations have been particularly characterised by their voluntary nature on the part of the donors and their fluctuations in relation to political relationships. The aid position has been better ordered in recent years due to the operations of the World Bank and other international agencies but it is still marked by the low volume of aid in relation to GNP ratios of the donor countries (Fig. 86) and by the atmosphere of 'poor law' administration which accompanies its operation.

Both sides of the aid equation now find it unsatisfactory,

> "... there have been repeated accusations by the developing countries that such assistance has at times been given in such a way as to undermine national resolve, conflict with national planning priorities, transfer irrelevant technologies, education systems and development concepts, promote the interests of a privileged minority in the recipient country rather than the vast majority. The critics of aid in the developed countries allege that aid is largely wasted, that it goes to support repressive governments (or experiments in socialism) and that it discourages indigenous efforts to save and invest."[37]

The present aid and assistance program has also resulted in considerable debt accumulation by recipient nations a fact obscured by the ambience of charity surrounding aid programs, "... the Third World has accumulated by now a total financial debt of about $150 billion, so that annual debt servicing[38] is already taking away about one-half of the new assistance they receive."

A new mode of resource transfer is patently needed so as to increase direct assistance on a less tied and more automatic basis—it should also be geared more directly towards assisting internal basic needs strategies of recipient countries and thus more immediately benefitting the poorest people.

> "There is well-nigh universal agreement on the need for change, and soon. The poorest nations, developing economies without surpluses, of oil, food, or major mineral resources, are persuaded by experience that aid-as-charity is not the road to either social justice or balanced development. Those with valuable raw materials but weak development programs, are investing more of their profits in the markets of the rich than the development of the poor. The developed nations which are poor in resources but rich in industrial and post-industrial skills, find themselves embarrassingly dependent on others for oil, food, foreign exhange, and security. And the really rich, efficient in producing food and energy but wasteful in their use of resources, face inflation, unemployment, social tensions and threats to democracy as the outcomes of industrial success."[39]

More compelling arguments, than merely altruism or greater equity, can also be found for reshaping the world economic order. The instability and imbalance of the present mode of organisation effects developing and developed countries alike. Many of the latter's problems of internal inflation and unemployment are not wholly due to the vicissitudes of the energy problem but are part of the larger structural problems in the world economy.

One of the key aspects of the developed nations' situation, in this regard, is the incapacity of their own domestic markets to continue to absorb such a large and disproportionate share of the world's production and consumption. In economic terms alone, this concentration on a small part of the available market leads inevitably to undue and costly competition, product redundancy, and eventually, as is now the case, to widespread unemployment, where capacities become underutilised and the whole system works below its capacity. Probably the only way to continue positive growth patterns for the developed economies is to begin to extend their trading with the larger underdeveloped market and to increase the international division of labor by sharing their more labor intensive industries with the developing world. This overall process of necessary wealth redistribution is analogous to the earlier history of the developed nations themselves when ways had to be found to increase the equity, credit and market purchasing power of the greater mass of their citizens in order to further their own growth and development. This process is now writ large on the world scale.

Whilst aid is important for the poorest of the developing countries, the more vital longer-term direction is through those modes of direct resource transfer, and redistribution of productive capacities and credit mechanisms which can expand the entire system of world trade. There are parallel needs, also, for reorganisation and redesign of the world's institutional framework not only in the economic sphere but in other areas such as food supply security, environmental and 'global commons' management, arms control, and conflict resolution where no adequate long range safeguards exist.

Some of the major considerations towards reshaping the world economy have coalesced in the various proposals around the new economic order. Others have extended such changes towards the larger requirements of a new global compact or 'planetary bargain'. There is an emerging consensus that the centerpiece for world social, economic and political concerns should be arranged around the proposition that fulfilling the basic needs of the world's poor is one of the most urgent tasks—for which the means exist and only the requisite social and political will is required. Meeting human needs should be the first priority on the global agenda.

NOTES

1. Lambertini, Adrian, "Energy Problems of the non-OPEC Developing Countries 1974-1980," *Finance and Development*, Vol. 13, No. 3, September, 1976, p. 24.
2. Henderson, P.D., "India's Energy Problems," *Finance and Development*, Vol. 12, No. 4, December, 1975, p. 22.
3. Revelle, Roger, "Energy Use in Rural India," *Science* (U.S.), June 4, 1976, p. 974.
4. *Action*, UNDP, May-June, 1976, p. 1.
5. Ridker, Ronald G., Ed. "*Handling Resource Problems of the Fourth World*," Resources for the Future, Washington D.C., 1976, p. 148
6. Makhijani, Arjun, "Solar Energy and Rural Development," *Bulletin of the Atomic Scientists*, June 1976.
7. Tabor, H.S., "Power for Remote Areas," in *International Science and Technology*, May, 1967.
8. Engstrom, Staffon, "Renewable Energy Resources: Wind Energy from a Swedish Viewpoint," *Ambio*, (Sweden), Vol. IV, No. 2, 1975, pp. 66-71.
9. Reddy, Amulya Kumar N., "The Trojan Horse," *Ceres* 50, Vol 9, No. 2, March-April, 1976, p. 43.
10. Frasche, D.F., *Mineral Resources*, Report to the U.S. Committee on Natural Resources, National Academy of Sciences, 1962.
11. Perlman, Robert, "Is the World Running Out of Raw Materials?," *International Affairs*, Vol. 50, 1974, p. 418.
12. Varon, Bension, "Enough of Everything for Everyone Forever," *Finance and Development*, Vol. 12, No. 3, September, 1975, pp. 17-10.
13. Varon, B., and Takenchi, K., "Developing Countries and Non-Fuel Minerals," *Foreign Affairs*, April, 1974, p. 503.

14. *Synthetics and Substitutes for Agricultural Products: A Compendium* Miscellaneous publication No. 1141, Economic Research Service, U.S. Dept. of Agriculture, April, 1969.

15. Malenbaum Wilfred, "World Resources for the Year 2000," *Annals of the American Academy of Political and Social Sciences*, Vol. 408, July, 1973. p. 37

16. *Environmental, Health and Human Ecologic Considerations in Economic Development Projects*, World Bank, May, 1974, pp. 13-14. *N.B.* The outline optimising procedure in Fig. 82 is also accompanied in this manual by more detailed guidelines for specific development projects.

17. Standke, K.H., *The Responsibility of Industrial Research Towards Society Under Global Aspects*, Address to the European Industrial Research Management Association, Paris, May 1976.

18. Ba, Boukabar, "The Problem of Transferring Technology to the Least Industrialised Countries, (the case of Niger)", *Labor and Society*, Vol. 1, No. 3, July/October, 1976, pp. 121-126.

19. *Transfer of Technology to the Developing Countries: Removing the Barriers*, UNDP, Development Issue Paper, No. 10, 1976, p. 3.

20. Standke, Klaus-Heinrich, *Utilisation of New Technologies in Developing Countries*, Address to National Academy of Engineering-National Academy of Sciences, Washington, D.C., April, 1976, p. 3.

21. Henry, Paul-Marc, Preface, *Appropriate Technology: Problems and Promises*, Ed. Jequier, Nicolas, Development Centre, OECD, Paris, 1976, p. 8.

22. Schumacher, Ernst Friedrich, "Patterns of Human Settlement", *Ambio*, Vol. V, No. 3, 1976, p. 95.

23. Carroll, James D., "Participation Technology", *Science* (U.S.) Vol. 171, February, 1971, p. 647.

24. Stewart, Frances, "Technology and Employment in the LDC's" *World Development*, Vol. 2, No. 3, March, 1976, p. 25.

25. *Guidelines for Development of Industrial Technology in Asia and the Pacific*. U.N. Bangkok, 1976, pp. XV-XVI, Summarised in *Op. Cit*, Standke.

26. Heden, Carl-Goran, "Potential of Applied Microbiology", *Environment and Society in Transition*, Joint Conference of the American Geographical Society and the American Division of the World Academy of Art and Science, Annals of the New York Academy of Sciences, Vol. 184, 1971, p. 114.

27. *Op. Cit.*, p. 116.

28. "The Petroleum Plant: Perhaps We can Grow Gasoline", *Science*, (U.S.), Vol. 194, October 1976, p. 46.

29. Bylinsky, Gene, "Green Plants Might Provide the Cheapest Energy of All", *Fortune* (U.S.), December, 1976, pp. 152-157.

30. Bergmane, Ernest D., "Recent Advantages in the Chemical Sciences", *Environment and Society in Transition*, Joint Conference of the American Geographical Society and the American Division of the World Academy of Art and Science, Annals of the New York Academy of Sciences, Vol. 184, 1971, p. 181.

31. Abbott, Walter, "Metallurgical Mariculture", *Ocean Industry*, (U.S.), June, 1971, pp. 43-44.

32. Varon, Bension, "Enough of Everything for Everyone Forever", *Finance and Development*, Vol. 12, No. 3, September, 1975, p. 2.

33. Connelly, Philip, ''Resources: The Choice for Importers'', *International Affairs*, Vol. 50, 1974, p. 600.

34. Cervenka, Adenek, ''Africa and the New International Economic Order'', *Labor and Society*, Vol. 1, Nos. 3/4, July/October, 1976, p. 162.

35. Elliott, Charles, *International Inflation and International Poverty*, Sharing Inflation, ed. Peter Wilmot, Temple Smith, London, 1976, Chapter 9, p. 142.

36. ''Measuring the Impact of the Multinationals'', *Finance and Development*, Vol. 12, No. 1, March, 1975, p. 10.

37. ulHaq, Mahbub, *A New Framework for International Resource Transfers*, June, 1975, p. 2, Prepared in consultation with James Grant for the RIO project, *Reviewing the International Order*, Jan Tinbergen, Coordinator, E.P. Dutton & Co., Inc., New York, 1976.

38. *Ibid*.

39. Cleveland, Harlan, ''The Fairness Revolution'', Introduction to *Human Requirements, Supply Levels and Outer Bounds*, McHale, John and Magda Cordell McHale, Center for Integrative Studies, 1975, p. iii.

Appendix I: Supplementary Data

LIST OF COUNTRIES CLASSIFIED IN ABCDE CATEGORIES

"A" Group	"B" Group	"C" Group	"D" Group	"E" Group
Australia	Argentina	Albania	Algeria	Afghanistan
Austria	Bulgaria	Bahrain	Bolivia	Angola
Belgium	Czechoslovakia	Bahamas	Botswana	Bangladesh
Canada	Finland	Barbados	Burma	Benin
Denmark	Greece	Brazil	Cameroon	Bhutan
France	Hong Kong	Chile	Colombia	Burundi
Germany, West	Hungary	China	Congo	Central African Republic
Germany, East	Israel	Costa Rica	Ecuador	Chad
Iceland	Italy	Cuba	El Salvador	Equatorial Guinea
Ireland	Malta	Cyprus	Ghana	Ethiopia
Japan	Mexico	Dominican Republic	Honduras	Gabon
Luxembourg	Poland	Egypt	Indonesia	Gambia
Netherlands	Portugal	Fiji	Ivory Coast	Guinea
New Zealand	Rumania	Grenada	Kenya	Guinea Bissau
Norway	Singapore	Guadeloupe	Khmer	Haiti
Sweden	Spain	Guatemala	Malagasy	India
Switzerland	Yugoslavia	Guyana	Morocco	Laos
U.S.S.R.		Iran	Nigeria	Lesotho
U.K.		Iraq	Pakistan	Liberia
U.S.A.		Jamaica	Papua New Guinea	Malawi
		Jordan	Philippines	Mali
		Kuwait	Portuguese - Timor	Mauritania
		Korea, North	Sierra Leone	Mozambique
		Korea, South	Swaziland	Nepal
		Lebanon	Tunisia	Niger
		Libya	Zambia	Rwanda
		Malaysia		Senegal
		Mauritius		Somalia
		Mongolia		Sudan
		Martinique		Togo
		Nicaragua		Tanzania
		Netherlands Antilles		Uganda
		Oman		Upper Volta
		Paraguay		Yemen, A.R.
		Peru		Yemen, P. R.
		Panama		Zaire
		Qatar		
		Reunion		
		Rhodesia		
		South Africa		
		Sri Lanka		
		Surinam		
		Syria		
		Thailand		
		Trinidad & Tobago		
		Turkey		
		Taiwan		
		United Arab Emirates		
		Uruguay		
		Venezuela		
		Vietnam		

Fig. i

INDICATOR FOOD AND AGRICULTURE	AVERAGED REFERENCE COUNTRY								
	A	B	C	D	E	USA	USSR	China	India
Arable land : %	19	25	18	11	20	20	10	13	50
Permanent meadows and pastures : %	28	30	12	19	27	26	17	21	4
Forested land : %	29	17	31	40	20	31	41	12	20
Unproductive land : %	24	28	38	30	33	22	32	54	26
Total cereals : metric tons per thosand	252	362	199	177	162	1,011	. . .	503	186
Wheat : metric tons per hectare	3.7	2.2	1.6	0.5	0.9	2.1	1.7	. . .	1.3
Paddy rice : metric tons per hectare	5.7	4.6	2.9	3.1	1.4	4.8	3.8	. . .	1.7
Maize : metric tons per hectare	4.8	2.7	1.9	1.4	1.0	5.7	3.3	. . .	0.9
Millet : mectric tons per hectare	1.0	1.1	1.9	0.5	0.7	. . .	1.5	. . .	0.5
Sorghum : metric tons per hectare	2.9	3.0	. . .	1.3	0.8	3.7	1.1	. . .	0.5
Total cereals : wheat, rice, maize, sorghum, millet : million metric tons	10	8	7	8	4	218	129	. . .	116
Total meat production : beef & buffalo, pig, mutton & goat : million metric tons	1.5	0.8	0.7	0.2	0.2	15.8	11.9	12.1	0.6
Total meat : metric tons per thousand	41	37	19	5	6	74	46	14	1
Fish production : thousand metric tons	545	368	166	366	98	2,669	8,619		1,958
Fish production : metric tons per thousand	14	16	5	9	4	12	34	. . .	3
Tractors in use : per thousand	11.9	5.4	1.8	0.3	0.1	20.3	8.5	0.2	0.1
Nitrogenous, phosphate and potash fertilizers production : kg per hectare of arable land	518	259	34	39	5	85	82	38	9
Nitrogenous, phosphate and potash fertilizers consumption : kg per hectare of arable land	426	205	107	84	14	81	61	50	16

Fig. ii

INDICATOR RESOURCE BASE : INDUSTRIAL PRODUCTION :	AVERAGED REFERENCE COUNTRY								
Metric tons per thousand pop.	A	B	C	D	E	USA	USSR	China	India
Energy Metric Ton Coal Equivalent	1,111	1,000	22	256	6	10,000	5,000	625	161
Iron	27	16	22	32	...	250	476	48	39
Copper	1.0	0.1	0.2	0.1	3	7	4	0.1	0.03
Bauxite	1,111	0.6	8	10	14	11	17	0.7	2
Manganese	0.3	0.2	0.1	0.1	5	0.1	11.4	0.4	0.9
Zinc	1.0	2.2	0.4	0.05	...	2.1	2.7	...	0.02
Steel	556	61	19	12	1.0	667	526	31	12
Plastics	43	3	0.5	3	...	56	9	...	0.2
Cement	476	333	89	16	2	370	434	28	26
Cotton yarn	2.4	4.5	0.4	0.3	0.1	6.6	6.1	1.9	1.7
Wool yarn	1.2	1.5	0.1	0.1	...	0.4	1.6	...	0.03
Rayon / acetate	2.0	0.9	0.2	0.4	...	2.9	2.2	0.1	0.2
Non-cellulose fibers	1.0	1.2	0.8	1.0	...	13.6	1.1	0.02	0.02
Sawnwood	49	43	16	12	6	435	476	20	5
Wood pulp, mechanical	10	2	2	...	...	34	7	0.7	0.1
Wood pulp, chemical	8	10	5	...	...	175	21	1	...

Fig. ii cont.

SUPPORT SYSTEMS TRANSPORTATION AND COMMUNICATIONS	AVERAGED REFERENCE COUNTRY A	B	C	D	E	USA	USSR	China	India
Transportation									
Passenger motor vehicles in use : population per car	4	17	129	328	571	2	...	...	764
Commercial vehicles in use : population per vehicle	25	104	280	440	1,520	9	...	...	1,215
Railway traffic : billion passenger / km.	62	9	4	1	1	15	296	...	131
Freight railway traffic : billion net ton / km.	31	18	4	1	1	1,243	2,958	301	120
Air traffic : billion passenger km.	14	4	2	1	0.4	261	98	...	5
Freight air traffic : million net ton km.	465	83	52	23	14	7,062	1,950	...	184
Km. of roads per thousand sq. km.	318	95	122	44	42	655	61	68	317
Km. of paved roads per thousand sq. km.	47	35	11	7	2	291	22	...	59
Communications									
Radio receivers : per thousand	354	216	104	91	12	1,752	442	16	23
Television receivers : per thousand	262	113	26	11	1	523	197	0.4	0.1
Telephones : per hundred	35	12	2	1	0.2	66	6	...	0.3
Items sent and received in mail : domestic : per caput	190	49	13	5	2	404	35	...	12.2
Items received in mail, foreign per caput	12	9	2	2	0.6	7	1	...	0.3
Items sent in mail, foreign : per caput	12	10	1	1	0.4	2	7	...	0.4
Number of computers, excluding mini - : per million	123	22	8	...	...	...	...	...	...

INDICATOR EMPLOYMENT	AVERAGED REFERENCE COUNTRY A	B	C	D	E	USA	USSR	China	India
Percentage of population economically active									
Total	44	37	33	29	41	41	48	41	33
Male	57	53	51	45	53	53	52	...	53
Female	31	22	15	14	27	30	45	...	12
Percentage of employed working by sectors									
Agriculture, forestry, hunting and fishing	11	27	49	44	91	4	26	...	72
Mining, quarrying, manufacturing, electricity, gas, water	30	22	13	10	2	26	...	...	10
Construction	8	7	4	4	0.5	7	...	...	1
Commerce / service	38	34	24	16	5	55	...	...	13
Transport, storage, and communications	6	6	4	3	1	5	...	...	2

Data Sources : See Figure 9 in text.

Fig. ii cont.

SATISFACTION OF DAILY CALORIE REQUIREMENTS PER CAPUT BY COUNTRY

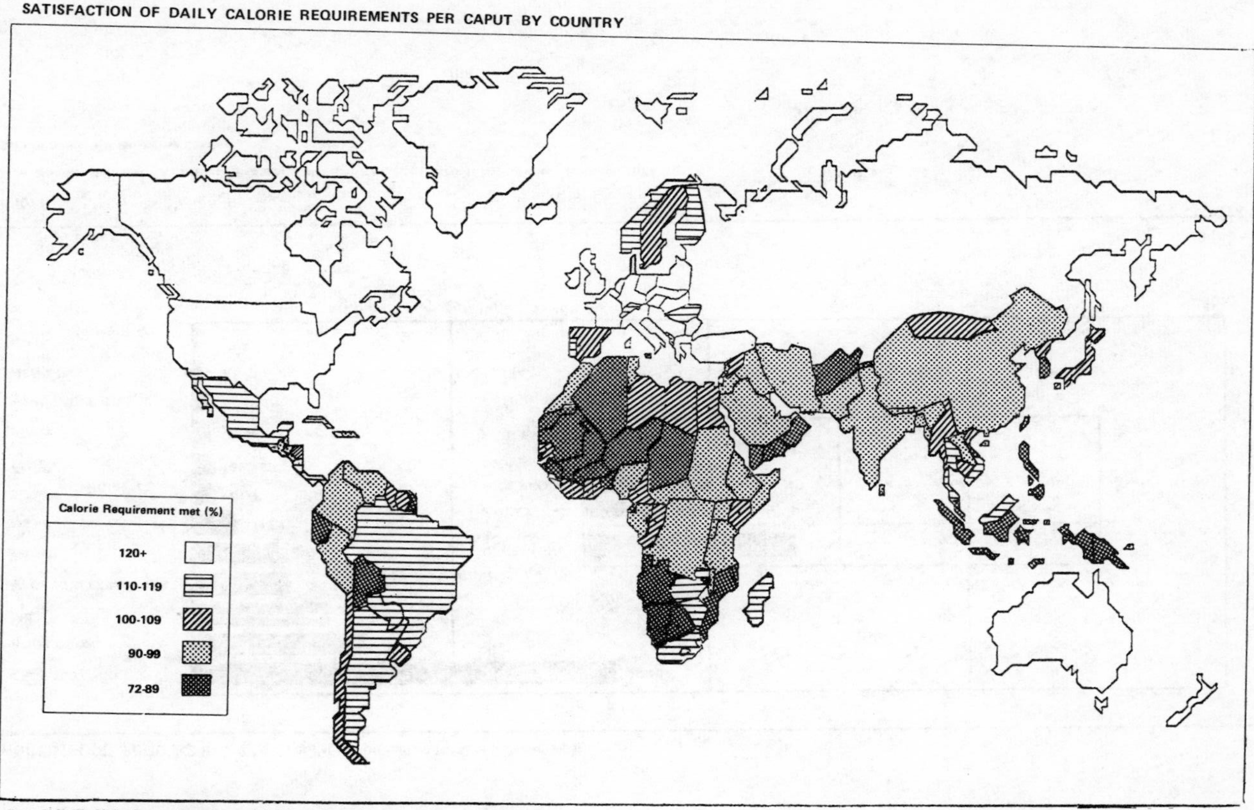

Data: U.N. World Conference Assessment of the World Food Situation, Present and Future

Source: Center for Integrative Studies

Fig. iii

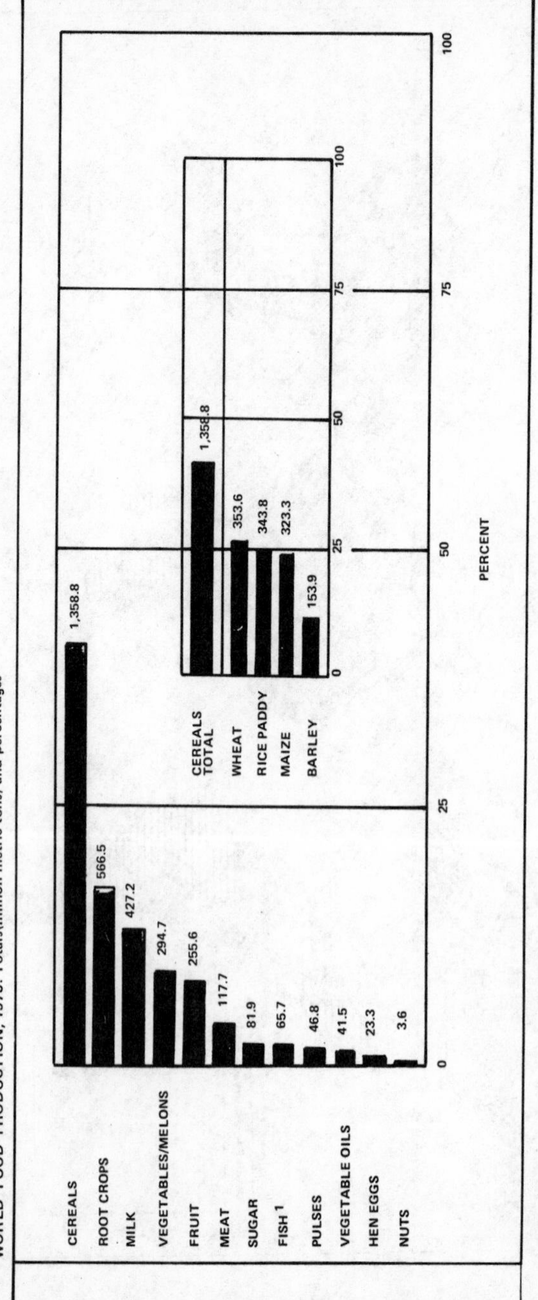

1. 1973

Data: Monthly Bulletin of Agricultural Economics and Statistics, April 1976; U.N. Statistical Yearbook 1974

Source: Center for Integrative Studies

Fig. iv

WORLD PRODUCTION OF CEREALS 1974

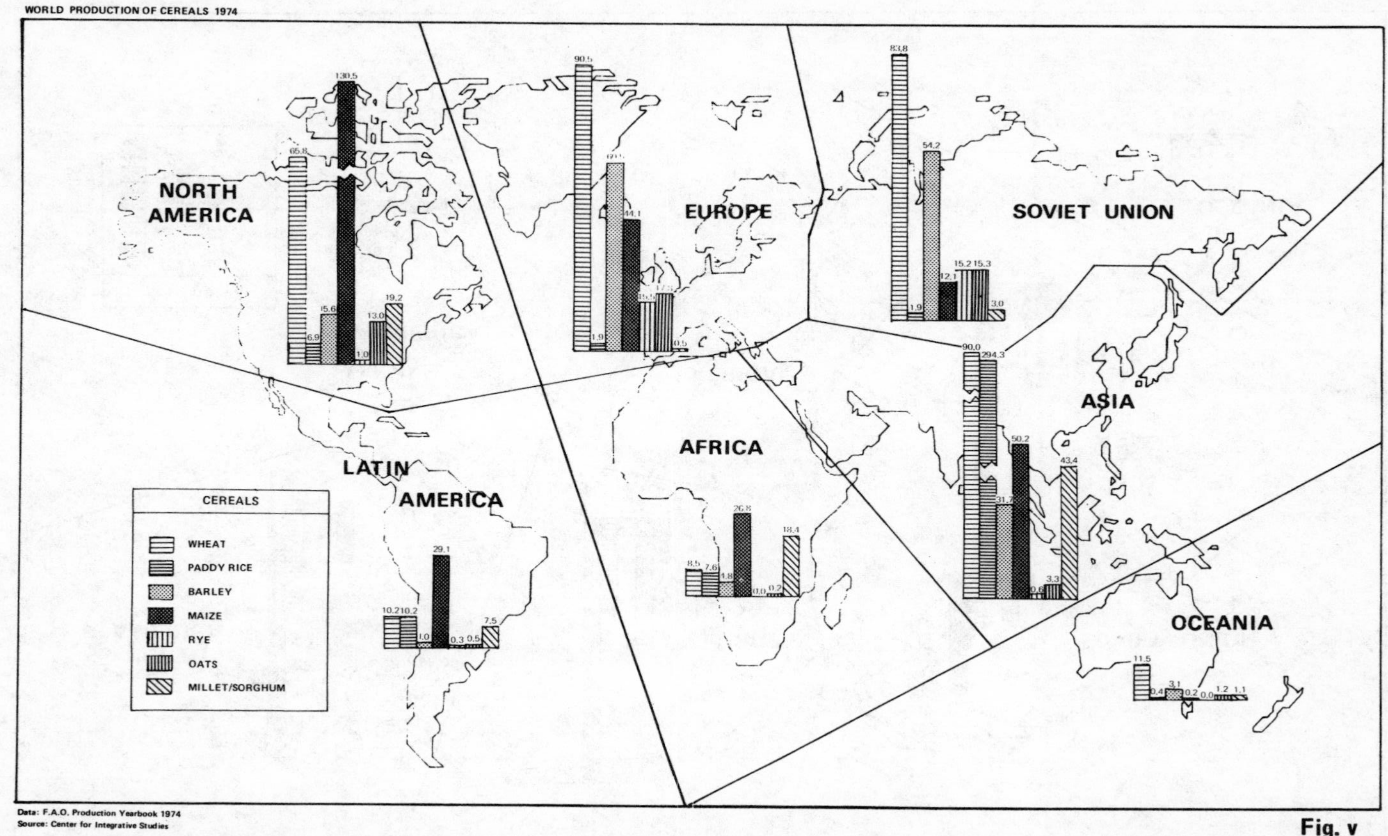

Data: F.A.O. Production Yearbook 1974
Source: Center for Integrative Studies

Fig. v

WORLD PRODUCTION 1974: Meats, Eggs, Milk, Fish

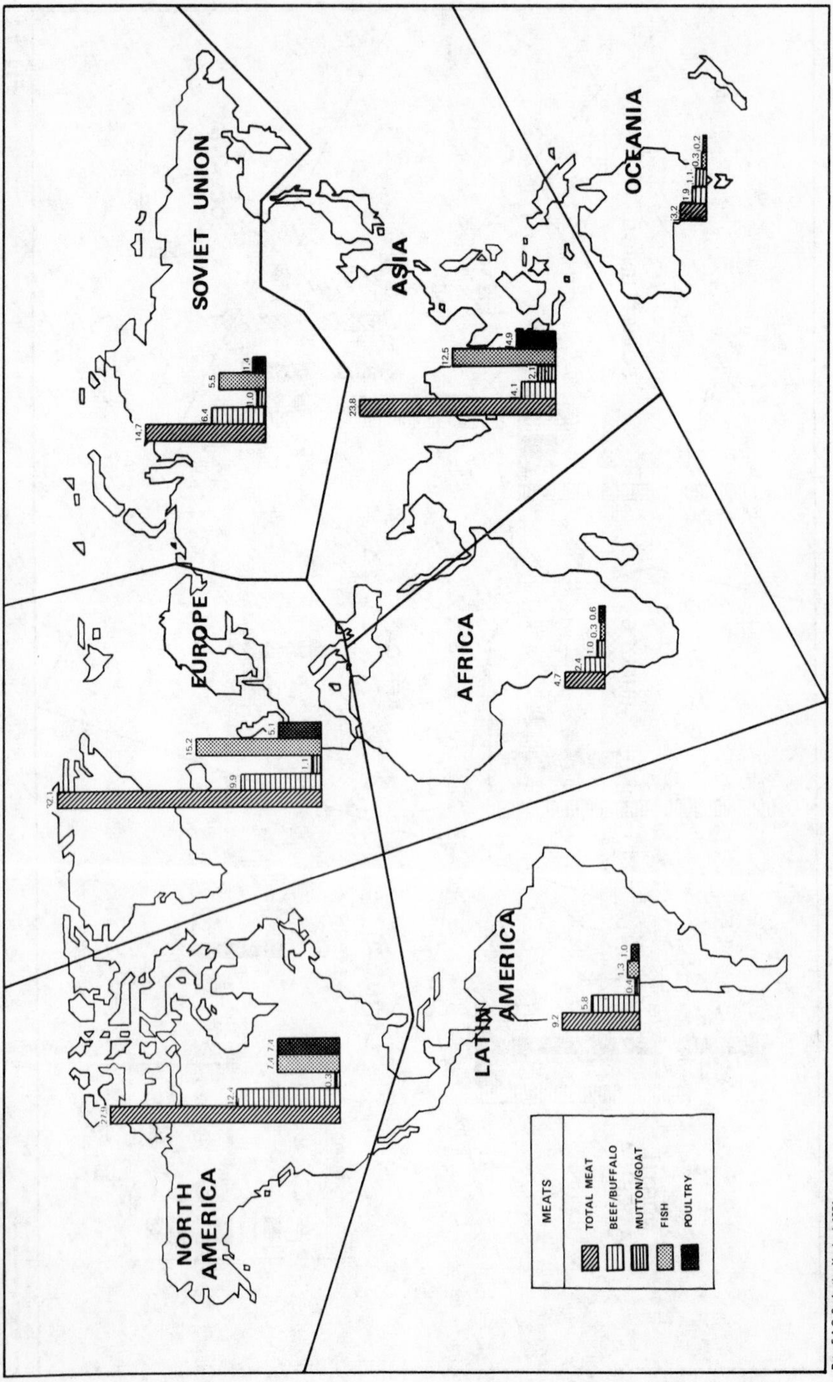

Data: F.A.O. Production Yearbook 1974
Source: Center for Integrative Studies

Fig. vi

PROPORTION OF LAND USE : WORLD AND REGIONAL

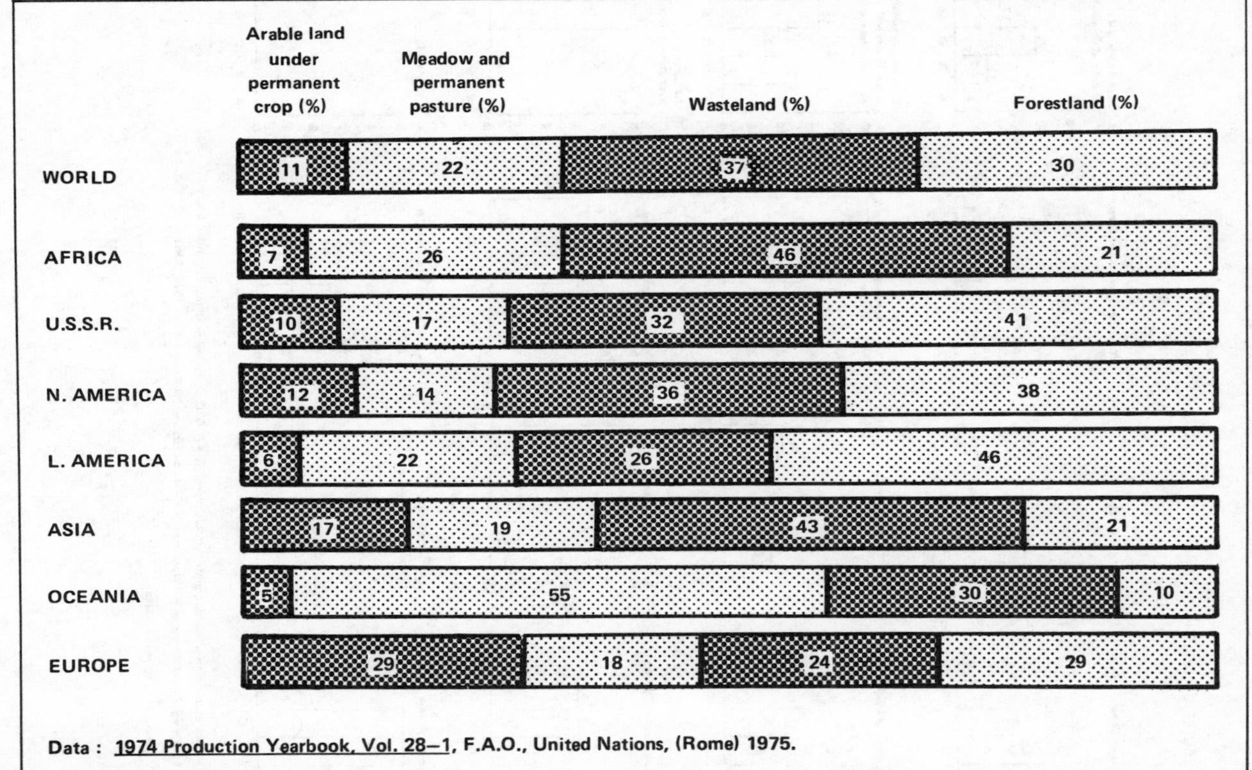

Source: Center for Integrative Studies

Fig. vii

MAIN CAUSES OF DEATH*

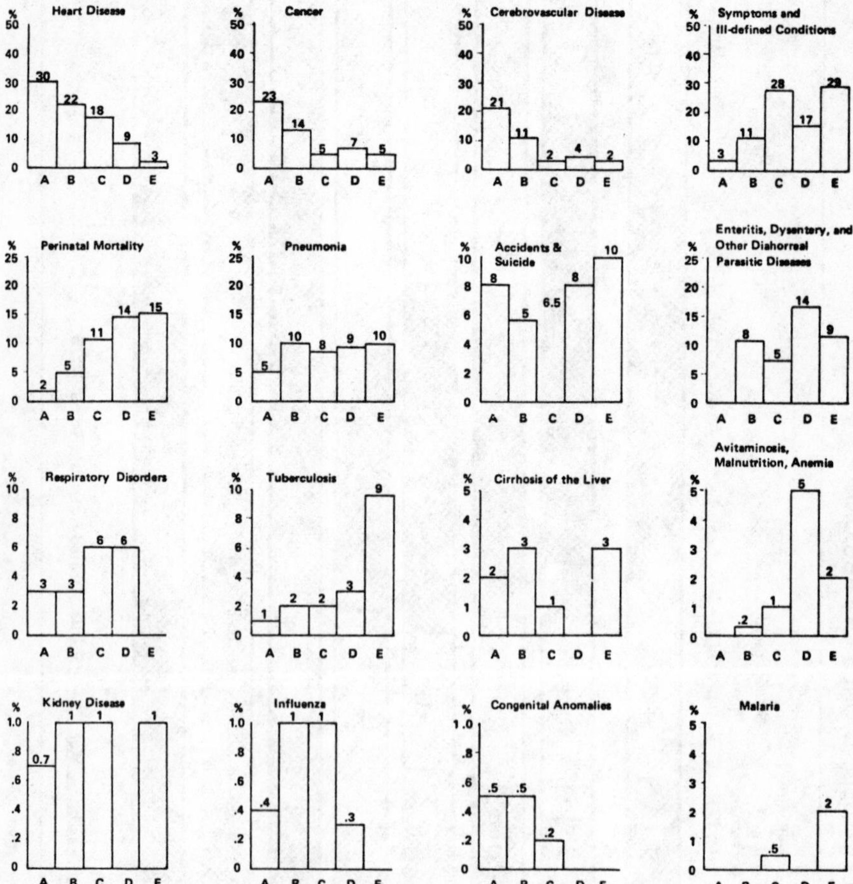

* The average of the seven reference countries in the appropriate A, B, C, D, E classifications. (Reported Deaths)

Data : Fourth and Fifth Reports on the World Health Situation 1965 – 1968 and 1969 – 1972, WHO.

Source : Center for Integrative Studies.

Fig. viii

COMMUNICABLE DISEASES MOST FREQUENTLY NOTIFIED*

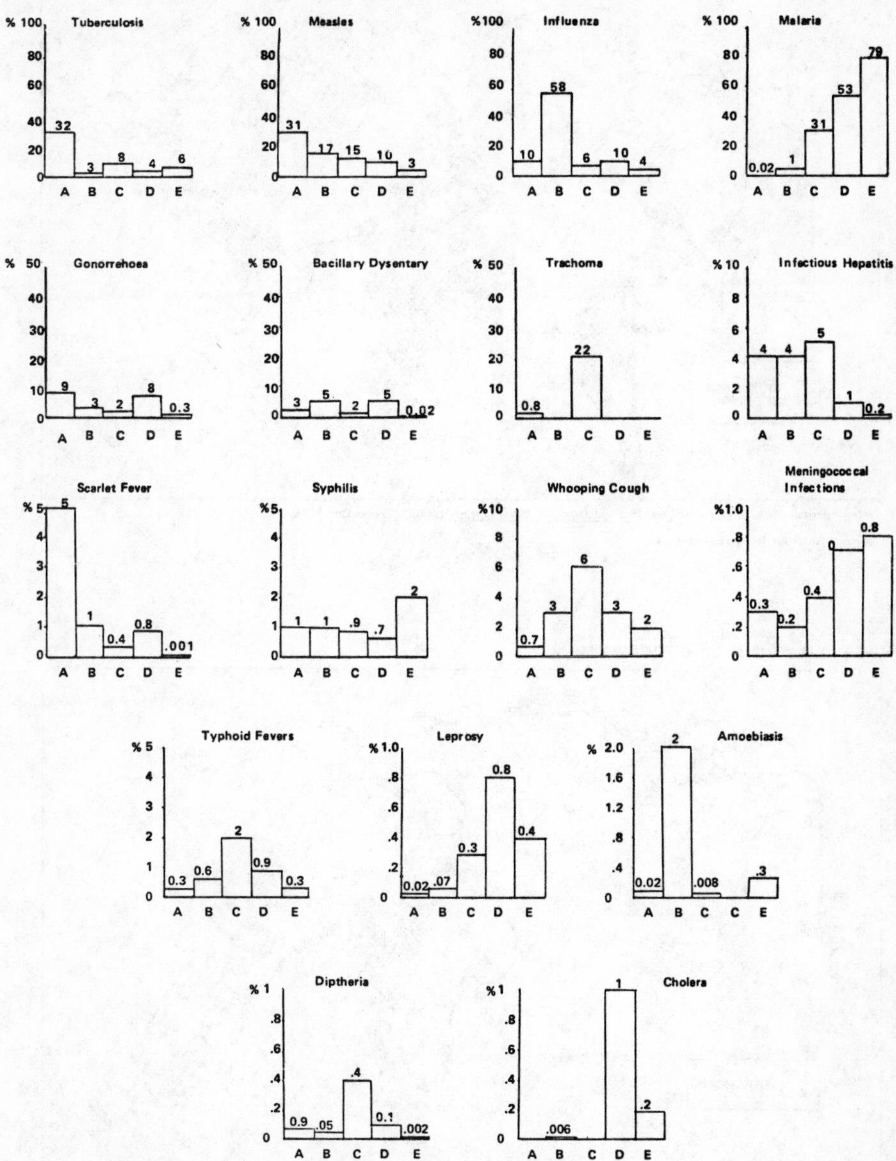

* The average of the seven reference countries in the appropriate A, B, C, D, E classifications.

Data : Fourth and Fifth Reports on the World Health Situation 1965 – 1968 and 1969 – 1972, WHO.

Source : Center for Integrative Studies.

Fig. ix

WORLD DISTRIBUTION OF HUMAN HOOKWORM INFECTION

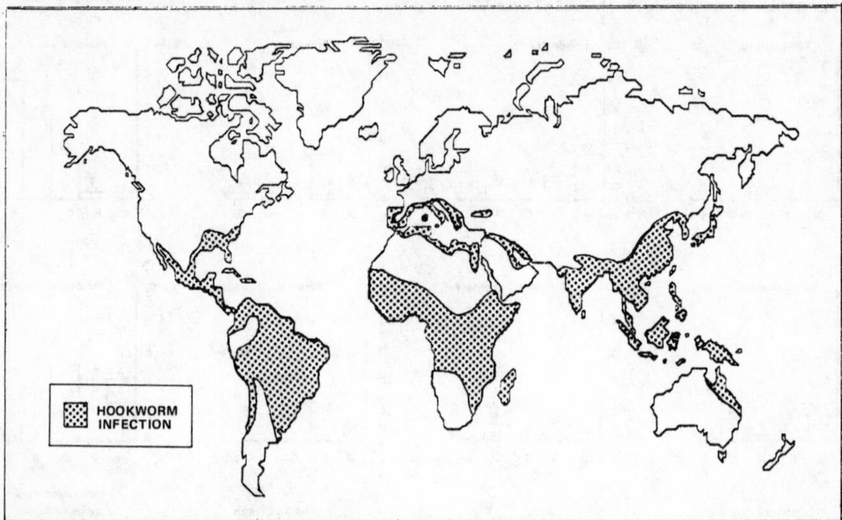

Data: Adapted from G.W. Hunter, ed. Tropical Medicine, Fifth Edition, (W.B. Saunders Co., 1976)

Source: Center for Integrative Studies

Fig. x

WORLD DISTRIBUTION OF TRACHOMA

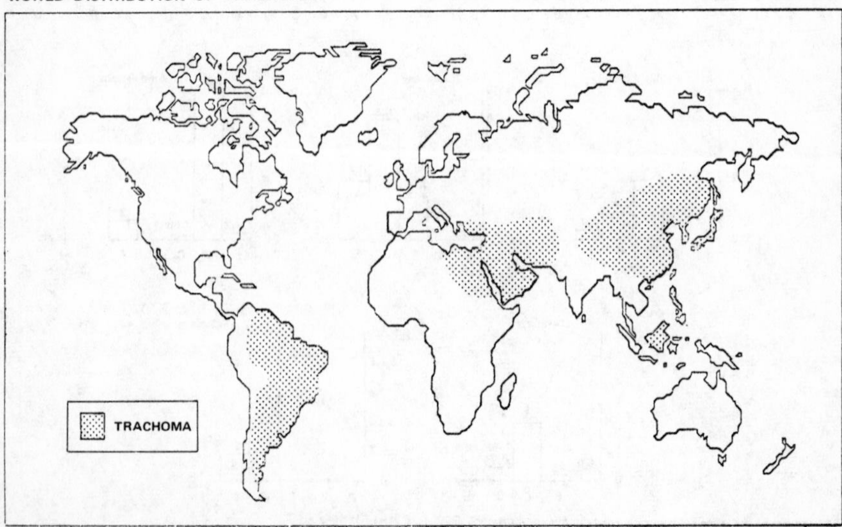

Data: Adapted from G.W. Hunter, ed. Tropical Medicine, Fifth Edition, (W.B. Saunders Co., 1976)

Source: Center for Integrative Studies

Fig. xi

WORLD DISTRIBUTION OF LEPROSY

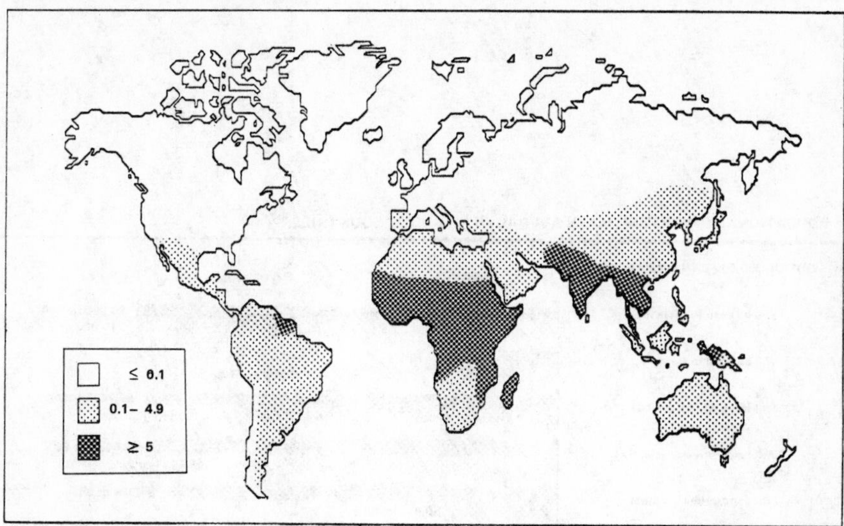

Data: Adapted from P.E. Sartwell, ed. Preventive Medicine and Public Health, Tenth Edition, (Appleton-Century-Crofts, 1973) Fig. xii

Source: Center for Integrative Studies

BACILLARY DYSENTERY DISTRIBUTION

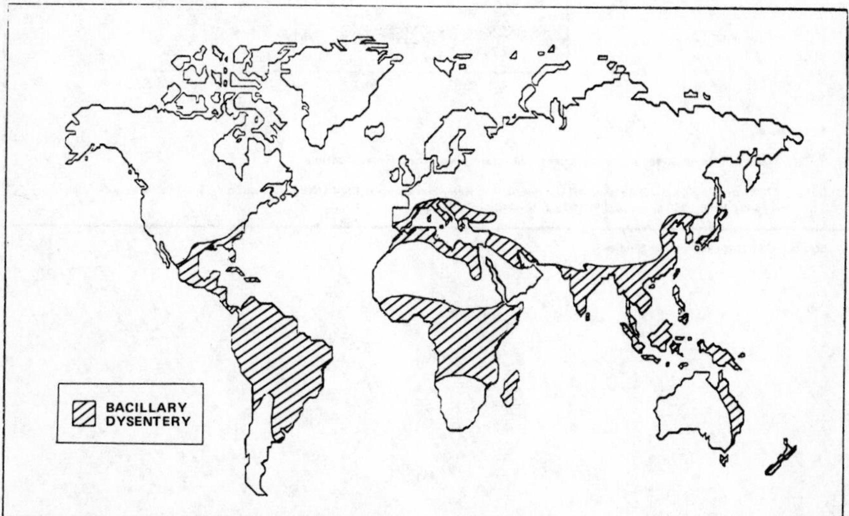

Data: Adapted from G.W. Hunter, ed. Tropical Medicine, Fifth Edition, (W.B. Saunders Co., 1976)

Source: Center for Integrative Studies

Fig. xiii

EDUCATIONAL OPPORTUNITIES IN AVERAGED 'A' AND 'E' COUNTRIES.**

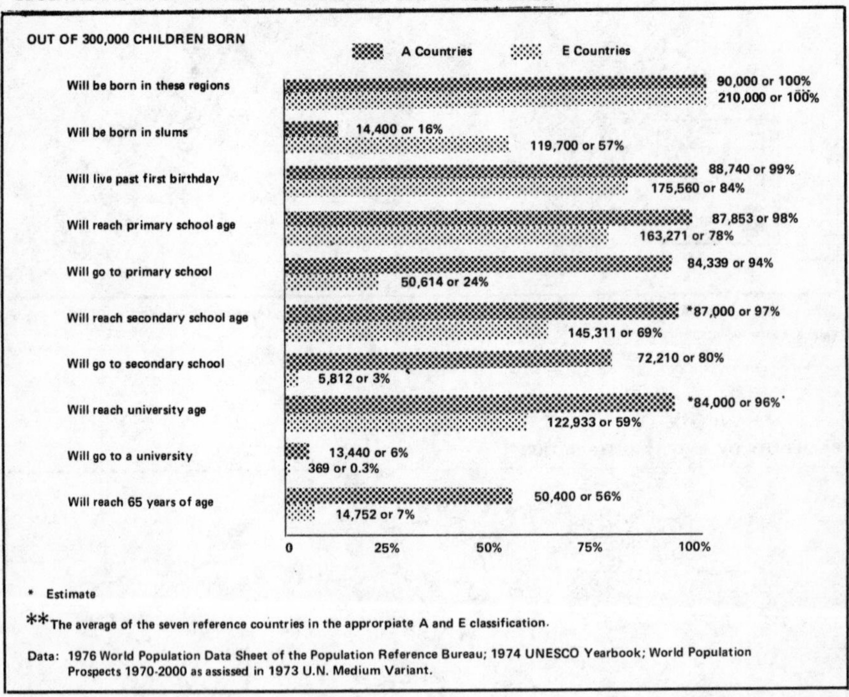

* Estimate

** The average of the seven reference countries in the approrpiate A and E classification.

Data: 1976 World Population Data Sheet of the Population Reference Bureau; 1974 UNESCO Yearbook; World Population Prospects 1970-2000 as assissed in 1973 U.N. Medium Variant.

Source: Center for Integrative Studies.

Fig. xiv

No. and Percentage of Professionals Engaged in Research and Development by Sector, 1972.[1]

Group	Total	Natural Sciences	Engineers and Technicians	Medical Sciences	Agriculture	Social Sciences and Law	Humanities, Education and Art
A	390,484	112,804	125,700	61,014	24,073	33,626	33,268
B	212,034	32,191	117,269	22,025	17,486	12,004	11,059
C	28,996	6,994	6,183	4,178	6,085	4,034	1,525
D	4,653	1,106	620	825	1,583	464	55
E	1,216	143	118	111	309	272	263
Totals	637,383	153,238	249,890	88,153	49,536	50,396	46,170

Group	Total	Natural Sciences	Engineers and Technicians	Medical Sciences	Agriculture	Social Sciences and Law	Humanities, Education and Art
A	61%	74%	50%	69%	49%	67%	72%
B	33%	21%	47%	25%	35%	24%	24%
C	5%	5%	2%	5%	12%	8%	3%
D	0.7%	0.7%	0.2%	1.0%	3.0%	1.0%	0.1%
E	0.2%	0.1%	0.05%	0.1%	0.6%	0.5%	0.6%

1. Available Data. Excluding USA, USSR, India.

Data : 1974 UNESCO Yearbook.

Source : Center for Integrative Studies.

Fig. xv

SHELTER INDICATORS FOR C, D AND E TYPE COUNTRIES

'C' Countries		Population At Year of Statistics (million)	Number Dwellings (thousand)	Average Number Rooms per Dwelling	With 1 With 1 Room (%)	Average Number Persons per Room	Dwellings With Piped Water Inside (%)	Dwellings With Any Type of Toilet (%)	Dwellings With Flush Toilet (%)	Dwellings With Electric Light (%)
Egypt 1960	Urban	9.86	1,639	3.6	7.7	1.6	& outside 39.5			37.8
Costa Rica	Total	1.38		3.8	6.6	1.5	59.0	74.5	29.7	54.6
1963	Urban	0.46		4.2	7.0	1.3	85.1	98.0	63.5	93.5
	Rural	0.92		3.6	6.5	1.7	43.6	60.6	9.8	31.6
Guadeloupe 1967	Total	0.31		3.0	15.3	1.5	18.6	38.5		39.8
Guatemala	Total	4.29		2.0	43.8	2.6	11.3	30.6	9.6	22.0
1964	Urban			2.7	34.8	1.9	29.9	70.6	25.7	56.0
	Rural			1.7	48.4	3.1	1.5	9.5	1.1	4.1
Jamaica	Total	1.81		2.4	34.7		21.6	96.7	31.3	
1970	Urban			2.3	45.2		40.2	99.2	63.0	
	Rural			2.5	26.3		6.4	94.7	5.5	
Nicaragua	Total	1.91		2.2	38.3		27.9	53.9	19.3	40.9
1971	Urban	0.92		2.3	36.0		54.1	90.8	38.2	76.7
	Rural	1.0		2.0	40.5		3.1	18.8	1.3	6.9
Panama	Total	1.43	287	2.2	37.4	2.2	26.1	72.0	41.3	52.4
1970	Urban	0.68	138	2.5	34.4	1.8	47.6	98.4	77.4	90.4
	Rural	0.75	149	2.0	40.2	2.5	5.5	46.7	6.8	16.0
Trinidad & Tobago 1966	Total	0.95		2.5			32.3	97.9	23.8	66.0
Brazil	Total	93.14		4.7	2.8	1.1	27.4	60.6	13.2	47.6
1970	Urban	52.09		4.8	3.6	1.0	45.8	85.6	22.3	75.6
	Rural	41.05		4.5	1.8	1.2	1.6	25.6	0.4	8.4
Guiana	Total	0.56		2.5	22.1	2.1				
1960	Urban	0.09		2.5	31.2	1.7				
	Rural	0.47		2.4	20.6	2.1				
Paraguay	Total	Excluding Indian jungle Population 1.82	327	2.0	47.5	2.6	5.9	88.3	5.0	13.2
1962	Urban	0.65	122				15.3	95.0	13.1	33.2
	Rural	1.17	204				0.3	84.3	0.2	1.2
Peru	Total	Excluding Indian jungle population 9.91	1,975	2.3	37.2	2.3	14.6	44.3	25.4	26.0
1961	Urban	4.70	933	2.7	30.4	2.0	30.2	63.3	50.1	50.7
	Rural	5.21	1,042	2.0	43.0	2.7	0.8	27.5	3.5	4.2

Fig. xvi

'C' Countries		Population At Year of Statistics (million)	Number Dwellings (thousand)	Average Number Rooms per Dwelling	Dwellings With 1 Room (%)	Average Number Persons per Room	Dwellings With Piped Water Inside (%)	Dwellings With Any Type of Tiolet (%)	Dwelings With Flush Toilet (%)	Dwellings With Electric Light (%)
Uruguay	Total	2.60	751	2.5	27.7	1.5	59.4	94.3	58.7	78.4
1963	Urban	2.10	555	2.4	29.3		67.6	97.7	67.4	87.8
	Rural	0.50	107	3.2	19.5		15.9	76.3	13.1	29.1
Venezuela 1971	Total	10.72	2,127	3.9	9.2	1.5	or outside 72.4	53.5	23.9	
Iran	Total	25.08	3,899	3.0	23.3	2.3	13.1			25.4
1966	Urban	9.79	1,301	3.5	9.8	2.2	37.8			68.6
	Rural	15.29	2,598	2.7	30.1	2.4	0.7			3.7
Jordan	Total	1.71					21.3	55.4		17.0
1961	Urban	0.75	111				48.6	90.4		39.2
	Rural	0.96					2.1	30.8		1.4
Korea, Republic	Total	31.5	4,408	3.0	7.3	2.3	19.6	94.9	1.8	49.7
1970	Urban	12.95	1,404	3.3	8.9	2.7	54.6	92.3	4.9	92.3
	Rural	18.51	3,004	2.8	6.6	2.2	3.2	96.1	0.3	29.9
West Malaysa	Total	8.80	1,455	2.3	36.5	2.6	34.6	79.1	18.1	43.4
1970	Urban	2.53	349	3.1	16.5	2.3	73.2	94.4	43.1	84.7
	Rural	6.26	1,106	2.0	42.9	2.8	22.2	74.1	10.0	30.1
Srilanka	Total	12.71	2,382	2.2	35.3	2.5	4.4	64.6	6.7	9.0
1971	Urban	2.84	440	2.4	34.6	2.7	16.3	79.6	22.8	34.5
	Rural	9.87	1,942	2.2	35.5	2.5	1.6	61.0	3.0	3.0
Syria	Total	6.31		2.5	24.6	2.3	or outside 41.9	58.4		38.0
1961 – 62	Urban	2.74		2.9	17.2	2.1	or outside 76.7	97.6		87.7
	Rural	3.56		2.4	28.7	2.5	or outside 22.6	36.6		10.5
Thailand	Total	34.40					8.6	97.9	1.1	
1970	Urban	4.55					54.7	98.8	5.6	
	Rural	29.84					1.8	97.8	0.5	
Turkey	Total	31.39		2.4	24.1	2.4				
	Urban	10.81		2.5	19.6	2.0	or outside 50.9		89.2	68.7
	Rural	20.59		2.3	26.8	2,7				

Fig. xvi cont.

'D' Countries		Population At Year of Statistics (million)	Number Dwellings (thousand)	Average Number Rooms per Dwelling	Dwellings With 1 Room (%)	Average Number Persons per Room	Dwellings With Piped Water Inside (%)	Dwellings With Any Type of Toilet (%)	Dwellings With Flush Toilet (%)	Dwellings With Electric Light (%)
Algeria	Total	12.10	1,795	2.2	34.6	2.8	22.7	49.1		33.7
1966	Urban	4.69	634	2.4	28.3		53.5	93.1		74.0
	Rural	7.41	1,161	2.1	38.1		5.9	25.1		11.8
Congo(Excluding 2 major cities) 1960 – 61	Total			1.6	62.8	2.7				
Ivory Coast (4 Urban areas) 1956 – 57				3.0	29.9	2.5				0.7
Kenya 1962	Urban	671		1.9	58.3	2.5				
Morrocco	Total	15.38		2.1	35.5	2.4				
1971	Urban			2.1	33.2	2.1	64.8	92.6		81.5
	Rural			2.0	36.9	2.6				
Nigeria (Lagos) 1961			93	1.4	76.9	3.0		95.0	7.0	81.3
Tunisia	Total	4.53		1.6	59.7	3.2	or outside 14.8			23.9
1966	Urban	1.82		1.9	46.0	2.7	or outside 35.1			
	Rural	2.71		1.4	68.0	3.6	or outside 1.8			
Zambia	Total	3.88	879	1.9	50.9	2.6	12.4	50.1	15.6	
1969	Urban	0.78	188	2.4	23.7		48.6	92.5	57.3	
	Rural	3.10	691	1.7	58.8		2.5	38.0	3.6	
El Salvador	Total	3.55		1.7	60.8	3.1	26.0	41.3	22.5	34.1
1971	Urban	1.40		2.1	52.5	2.4	59.5	82.4	52.1	73.0
	Rural	2.15		1.5	66.6	3.8	2.5	12.3	1.6	6.7
Honduras	Total	1.89	270	2.3	24.0	2.4	12.1	19.8	14.2	14.6
1961	Urban	0.44	74	3.0	13.3	1.8	42.9	67.3	51.0	56.7
	Rural	1.45	196	2.1	27.2	2.7	2.7	5.4	3.1	1.9
Bolivia	Total	4.12					or outside 10.5			21.9
1963	Urban						or outside 33.8			76.4
	Rural						or outside 4.4			7.6
Colombia	Total	17.49		3.4	13.0	1.9	26.0	32.4	21.0	25.5
1964	Urban	9.24		4.6						63.5
	Rural	8.25							3.3	4.2
Ecuador	Total	Excluding Indian jungle population 4.65	861	2.1	44.5	2.5	12.3	32.9	21.7	32.3
	Urban	1.61	292	2.5	35.4	2.1	32.5	79.4	60.5	78.5
	Rural	3.04	569	1.8	49.2	2.8	1.9	9.0	1.8	8.5

Fig. xvi cont.

'D' Countries		Population At Year of Statistics (million)	Number Dwellings (thousand)	Average Number Rooms per Dwelling	Dwellings With 1 Room (%)	Average Number Persons per Room	Dwellings With Piped Water Inside (%)	Dwellings With Any Type of Toilet (%)	Dwellings With Flush Toilet (%)	Dwellings With Electric Light (%)
Indonesia	Total	118.46	24,574	3.3	19.9	1.7	56.1	78.6	60.0	63.5
1971	Urban	20.77	3,961	3.3	22.0	1.6	60.5	91.3	75.3	75.5
	Rural	97.60	20,613	3.2	15.6	1.9	47.2	53.0	29.1	39.1
Pakistan & Bangladesh (excluding 6 regions)	Total	93.72	16,469	1.7	56.5	3.1				
1960	Urban	12.30	1,957	1.7	56.5	3.1				
	Rural	81.43	14,512	1.8	56.3	3.1				
Philippines	Total	36.68			20.3		34.4	66.4	19.9	22.9
1967	Urban	25.01			23.1		22.1	59.1	7.8	5.8
	Rural	11.68			23.1		22	83.9	48.2	62.8

Fig. xvi cont.

'E' Countries		Population At Year of Statistics (millions)	Number Dwellings (thousand)	Average Number Rooms per Dwelling	Dwellings With 1 Room (%)	Average Number Persons per Room	Dwellings With Piped Water Inside (%)	Dwellings With Any Type of Toilet (%)	Dwellings With Flush Toilet (%)	Dwellings With Electric Light (%)
Central African Republic 1959 – 60	Total	1.2		1.1	89.6	3.4				
Ethiopa (Addis Ababa) 1961	Urban		(1967) 148			2.7	or outside 74.3			58.2
Liberia (Monrovia) 1956				2.3						
Malawi (4 towns) 1967	Urban	0.20	45	1.9	46.6	1.9	21.6	67.7	33.0	15.7
Senegal (Dakar) European type Dwellings 1955			13	2.3	30.3	1.5	87.7			95.9
Sudan (14 areas) 1964 – 66	Urban	1.85		2.2		2.5	or outside 63.9	70.3	2.6	26.4
Tanzania 1967	Urban						or outside 69.8	96.9	17.7	
Zaire (Kinshasa) 1967			168							
India	Total	547.95	100,213	2	47.9	2.8				
1971	Urban	109.09	20,238	2	50.2	2.8				
	Rural	438.86	79,975	2	47.3	2.8				
Nepal (6 areas) 1961	Urban			3.7	9.7	2.0	or outside 47.7	37.2	6.1	30.2

Data : Global Review of Human Settlements Statistical Annex, UN ECOSOC, 1976

Fig. xvi cont.

CUMULATIVE INCREASE IN URBAN/RURAL POPULATION AND HOUSEHOLDS (in millions) Due to Population Growth in E, D, and C Countries

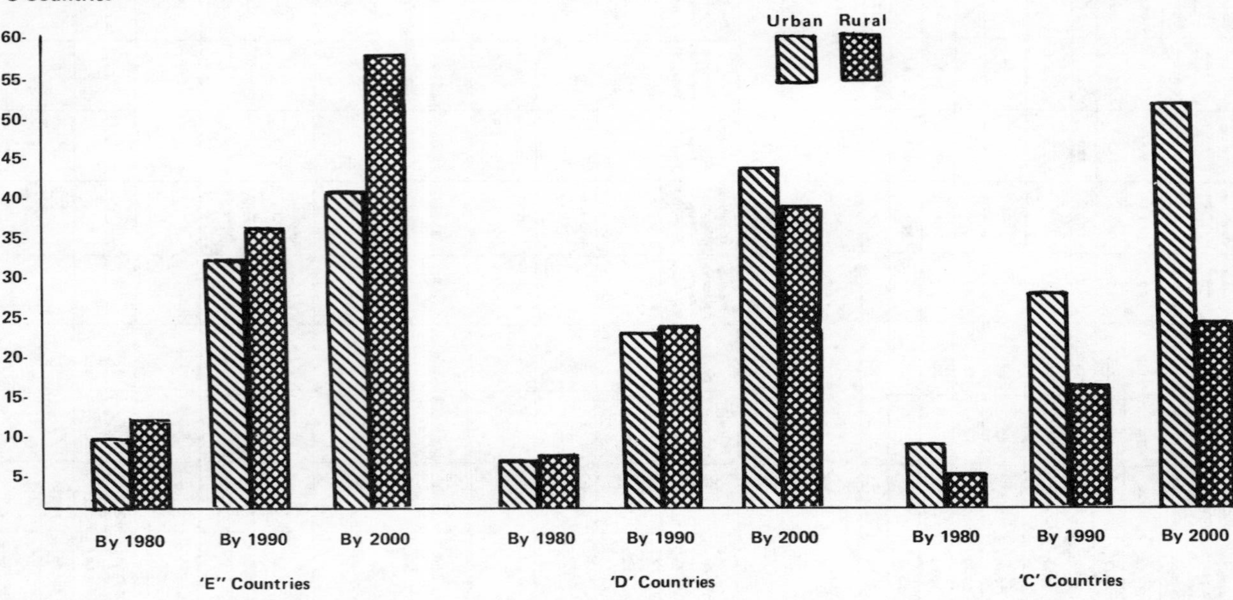

Note : This projection takes account of the different rates of urban growth in the mix of each group of countries, as indicated in Global Review of Human Settlements, Statistical Annex, UN ECOSOC, 1976.

Household size is estimated at an overall average of 6 persons. (Of which 2 are 20 – 44 years, one is 45 + years and 3 are 0 – 19 years Population forecast is that of the UN World Population Prospects 1970 – 2000 as Assessed in 1973, UN ECOSOC, 1975. 1976 population is the estimate of the World Population Data Sheet, Population Reference Bureau, 1976.

Data : Global Review of Human Settlements, Statistical Annex, U.N. ECOSOC, 1976.

Source : Center for Integrative Studies.

Fig. xvii

ENERGY PROJECTIONS : 1974 – 2000
Reference Country Groups *

Reference Group Countries Actual Data – 1974 Projections – 1980, 1990, 2000 [4]		1974	1980	1990	2000		Projections Annual Growth Rates 1974 – 2000 Per Caput Energy Consumption
A	Population [1]	37.2	39.4	42.1	43.2		
	Energy Consumption [2] 1960 – 74 Growth Rate (%)	170.9 (5.5 %)	235.6	402.5	687.5		A
	Per Caput Energy Consumption [3] 1960 – 74 Growth Rate (%)	5,074 (4.8 %)	5,980	9,560	15,914		4.7 %
B	Population [1]	22.0	24.5	29.9	36.3		
	Energy Consumption [2] 1960 – 74 Growth Rate (%)	42.9 (9.4 %)	73.5	180.6	443.5		B
	Per Caput Energy Consumption [3] 1960 – 74 Growth Rate (%)	2,251 (9.0 %)	3,000	6,040	12,218		7.0 %
C	Population [1]	30.8	37.2	48.03	60.4		
	Energy Consumption [2] 1960 – 74 Growth Rate (%)	18.1 (6.1 %)	25.8	46.7	84.4		C
	Per Caput Energy Consumption [3] 1960 – 74 Growth Rate (%)	583 (3.4 %)	694	972	1,397		3.6 %
D	Population [1]	38.7	46.4	60.5	76.8		
	Energy Consumption [2] 1960 – 74 Growth Rate (%)	7.9 (5.9 %)	11.1	19.8	35.1		D
	Per Caput Energy Consumption [3] 1960 – 74 Growth Rate (%)	327.9 (3.2 %)	239	327	457		1.3 %
E	Population [1]	24.2	28.01	36.9	48.1		
	Energy Consumption [2] 1960 – 74 Growth Rate (%)	1.1 (8.8 %)	2.8	4.2	9.9		E
	Per Caput Energy Consumption [3] 1960 – 74 Growth Rate (%)	53.4 (2.7 %)	100	114	206		5.6 %

Data : United Nations Statistical Yearbook 1975 (United Nations Publishing Service, New York, 1976), Tables 18 and 193; World Bank Atlas, Population, Per Capita Product, and Growth Rates (World Bank, Washington, DC; 1975), World Energy Supplies, 1950 – 1974 (Statistical Papers, Series J, No. 19, United Nations, New York, 1976), and World Population Prospects, 1970 – 2000, As Assessed in 1973 (United Nations, New York, 1975).

* The average of the seven reference countries in the appropriate A, B, C, D, E classifications.

1. Millions.
2. Million Metric Tons Coal equivalent.
3. Kilograms Coal equivalent.
4. (a) Population projections are based on United Nations median variant projection rates.
   (b) Energy consumption projections are based on historic average annual growth rates for 1960 – 1974.

NB. Population/Energy/GDP Chart reflects same data.

Source : Center for Integrative Studies.

Fig. xviii

Appendix II:

DEFINITION OF BASIC HUMAN REQUIREMENTS*

One approach towards defining basic human requirements might be to assess minimal physiological needs for the amounts of food, water, clothing and shelter which enable a person to stay alive regardless of social and cultural diversity. We assume that our objective lies beyond this level even though many human beings are living on such minimal need thresholds.

Need or requirement might be initially defined within three categories:

a) *Deficiency Needs* required to augment standards to some defined levels, e.g. physiological adequacy.

b) *Sufficiency Needs* to maintain standards at a desired level.

c) *Growth Needs*, those which go beyond sufficiency to allow for individual development above material sufficiency to the satisfaction of non-material requirements.

We can also distinguish between needs, wants and desires. Beyond deficiency needs, a person may have 'wants' which relate to individually oriented standards of what is sufficient. Aspirations and expectations form a pattern which, though never wholly attained, are part of qualitative growth and development.

Our overall concern, whatever the approach, would be the evaluation of that set of basic human requirements which allow for both sufficiency and growth at the individual level.

The reiteration of individual is necessary at this stage because, as we shall discuss, many individual needs are social. They are both socially defined and culturally conditioned and depend for their satisfaction on social contiguity and communications. For example, above the starvation level, we do not hunger for food but for the specific kinds of food to which we have been culturally

---

**Extracted from Human Requirements, Supply Levels and Outer Bounds*, John McHale and Magda Cordell McHale, A Policy Paper/Aspen Institute for Humanistic Studies, Program in International Affairs, 1975.

accustomed; the need for contact and communication with other persons is almost as basic as water and air.

VARIABILITY

Beyond the level of augmenting deficiency, there is a considerable range of variability in human requirements. The amounts of food adequacy vary according to body weight, level of activity and so on. In addition to such physiological variation, there are individual and cultural preferences for different kinds and amounts of food.

Cultural variance introduces the role of values both in the attempt to assess basic human requirements and in the ways in which the range assessed would fit value systems in different societies.

We may summarise some aspects of variability in requirements as follows:

physiological—age, sex, body weight, level of general activity and work.

climatic—closely associated with the above and affecting many of our quantitative assessments of clothing, shelter, activity levels. Geographical area may also introduce other variables. For example, the base need for transportation may be relatively low in areas where most facilities are within walking distance.

social—ways in which requirements are both defined socially and satisfied through social means. The accepted level of adequacy in one society may be the poverty level in another.

cultural—the range of factors which influence individual and collective needs and wants, modifying the physiological and interacting with the climatic.

individual—the degrees of personal choice, taste and life style preferences within which the individual may satisfy his or her basic requirements.

DIFFERENTIATION

Given this variation we may make a provisional distinction between biophysical and psychosocial requirements:

Biophysical requirements might include food, water, shelter, health, heating (and cooling), light, clothing.

Psychosocial requirements more obviously encompass communications, education, transportation, security of various kinds, recreation and social mobility.

We may note, however, that the differentiation is weak and becomes blurred at various levels of satisfaction. Shelter may be defined very crudely in biophysical terms as some minimal protection from the elements as a cave, a lean-to or a simple hut. But even at this base level it takes on various psychosocial dimensions, as a setting for interpersonal relations, as a ritual 'place', a social locus for various activities. Similarly, health has a biophysical basis but both its more complete definition and its maintenance belong in the psychosocial domain.

Maslow in his various works proposed a 'needs hierarchy'[2] which goes from basic physiological needs such as hunger, thirst and sex followed, in ascending order, by higher level needs for security and belonging, towards self actualisation and aesthetic experience at the top level. This type of classification still has a number of inherent problems due to its vertical implication of 'basic' and 'transcendental' qualities. Even basic needs, such as sex, are at the lowest level of satisfaction inextricably interwoven with learnt social behaviors and 'transcendental' elements of aesthetic experience.

In practice, we leave wholly physical requirements behind very quickly in exploration of the range of human requirements. Certain physical and material sufficiencies are essential—then the more determinant factors become social and cultural.

This should not deter us from attempting to appraise those levels of material and non-material requirements which are necessary for adequate participation in the social and cultural life of the society. The definition of 'adequacy' may vary, as we have noted, but rough agreement may be sought on those standards of living below which individual social and cultural growth is attenuated. Malnutrition stunts both physical and intellectual growth; poor housing, lack of sanitation, inadequate educational and communications hinder social and cultural development in most societies. That such developments may have flourished historically, under similar conditions, is no guide to present needs in the contemporary world.

MEASURES

Various measurements of minimal standards of living have been carried out over the years. Meier[3] refers to several early studies of nutritional standards by Rowntree[4] and others in the United Kingdom in the years 1900, 1936, and 1950 and of more general living standards in the U.S.A., during the 1930's by the Heller Committee.[5]

A comprehensive report on "International Definition and Measurement of Standards and Levels of Living" was prepared by the United Nations in 1954. In its synthesis of various contributions by the ILO, UNESCO and FAO, the report gives a list which,

> "...could be considered as an acceptable international catalogue of the components of the level of living, although the precise connotations of each would to some extent be determined by national attitudes and

standards resulting from peculiarities of environmental conditions, cultures, values and economic, political and social organisation:

1. Health, including demographic conditions
2. Food and nutrition
3. Education, including literacy and skills
4. Conditions of work
5. Employment situation
6. Aggregate consumption and savings
7. Transportation
8. Housing, including household facilities
9. Clothing
10. Recreation and entertainment
11. Social security
12. Human freedoms"[6]

Noting the "immense difference in range and quality of the statistical material now available", this report does not go beyond discussing definition and measurement. In the decade or so since that time, the statistical situation has improved greatly, due in part to the excellent work of the United Nations itself. It is, however, still far from being satisfactory in terms of our ability to estimate the material quantities required to sustain a specific living standard.

Both the statistical indicators and the categories under which they are measured vary greatly from country to country. Almost all the measures are given in terms of money or fiscal indices. These are subject to considerable internal variation and afford a somewhat elastic base for working back to actual physical quantities which constitute a set of material requirements.

Hence many studies in this general area, even where they use sophisticated modelling techniques of various kinds tend to stay with the given fiscal measures. Unfortunately the successive levels of abstraction may somewhat attenuate the value of their end results when they are translated into policies and actions. With reference to our particular task, it is difficult to gauge the impact of a number of dollars, guilders or pesos against the carrying capacity of the biosphere.

Other deficiencies in indicator measures may be noted as follows.

1. *Gross National Product* is a much favored index of development and material standards, but even as a measure of national productivity it is lacking in internal consistency and comparability. Many centrally planned economies do not include government and other services in the GNP and in the developing countries several important components of local market and home produce transactions are not registered. Activities outside of the reported 'market' in the advanced countries are not accounted for,

> "it is estimated that American housewives added last year an uncounted value of $260 billion to our GNP of $1,289 billion, i.e. as much as the GNP's of China, India, and Indonesia combined."[7]

Though GNP may be somewhat unreliable as a yardstick of actual productivity it is even more so when used as an index for standard of living. It may have its place in an array of such indicators but by itself it has low reliability as a focal or leverage point for policies addressed towards the improvement of living standards.

2. *National Income and Income Per Capita* figures, when aggregated, give no true indication of actual wealth distribution.

Even where personal income is disaggregated and used as a measure of purchasing power to gauge living standards, it may still be unreliable in comparative world terms.

a) Unless compensated for, inflationary changes can render such comparisons meaningless. Purchasing power is also constrained if the range of material commodities and services are limited.

b) In many countries, health, public transport, security and other services are provided at low cost, hence a low income/high service society may have a comparable living standard to a high income/low service society.

c) Differential access to services may also be relatively independent of income. In the case of various professionals, for example, personal disposable income may be somewhat small but their access to, and use of, 'public' goods and services may be correspondingly high. Many use computers, air transportation, telecommunications and other complex socio-technical systems far in excess of measure by income.

d) 'Psychic' income in the realm of non-material rewards and status differences is another area which wholly monetary indices may miss. Many occupations and professions have such invisible incomes built in which are not reflected in take home pay.

Wealth and money, as such, are not very reliable indicators in themselves either towards measuring the satisfaction of human requirements, or in gauging our capacity to meet these requirements for more persons. When 'lack of capital' is advanced as the block to greater material improvement for more people it is instructive to recall that in the past fifty years we have simultaneously developed several major world-wide industries—airlines, telecommunications, automobile transportation. In each case, the total amount of capital for their inauguration and amortization was not 'available' at the time but accrued in the course of a developmental sequence in which they themselves contributed a major portion. Capital and wealth accumulation is a complex feedback system in which money is only an indicator, the generating mechanisms are human resources and knowledge.

3. *Energy Consumption Per Capita* as a measurement has the same variability as income per capita. Whether aggregated or disaggregated, it rarely indicates the efficiency of energy use per product or service, or the 'disutilities'

and 'disamenities' which may accompany it in various types of generation and use.

Equivalent or better standards of living may be available at various levels of energy consumption and efficiency of use per capita. West Germany, for example uses half the amount of energy per capita as does the U.S.A. and Switzerland uses less than a third, and all three achieve roughly comparable standards.

4. Many recent studies have used *Consumption of Materials* as an index to suggest bounds due to scarcity, biospheric capacity and environmental deterioration.

a) Materials, other than items such as food, are not 'consumed' in the general sense of the term. They are used in various products which have different 'lifetimes' and are then scrapped, recovered or recycled. Some materials remain in buildings or machinery for many years; others in consumer products may have a shorter lifetime before re-use. Consumption figures should therefore more accurately be termed 'use' figures.

b) Consumption figures given for many materials are not 'internal' use data for countries. Even where input/output may be disentangled in the relation between primary materials and manufactured products, it is still difficult to estimate 'real' internal use as distinct from export, stockpiling and other aspects of the use cycle.

Therefore, when we aggregate materials consumption for various countries to world figures, and reach exponential levels over time, we are often counting the same quantities several times over.

c) Per capita materials consumption attached to some index of basic requirements is a difficult problem in estimation. Most per capita figures given are disaggregated from national consumption data, as discussed above, and therefore have little real meaning. Even if we were to calculate the amounts of metals and minerals used at the individual level in relation to some specified living standard there would still be unspecified extrinsic amounts which feature in the extraction, processing, manufacture, transportation and maintenance of various products over time.

5. The amounts and sorts of *Food* an individual needs are relative to age, body weight, sex, type of work, climate, and are therefore approximations. They are also revised from time to time as more knowledge accrues.

Basic requirements consist of fuel (or calories) and suitable protein intake with adequate levels of trace minerals and vitamins to ensure balance in the diet. An average standard for a 50-60 kg. adult seems to lie between 1,800 to 4,400 calories a day depending on the level of physical work; between 60 to 100 grams of protein and 100 grams of fat. Carbohydrates, fats and proteins can all be used as caloric content.

The nutritional values of various foodstuffs vary considerably. Animal products, including fish, have a better content of essential amino acids (or

DAILY HUMAN METABOLIC TURNOVER

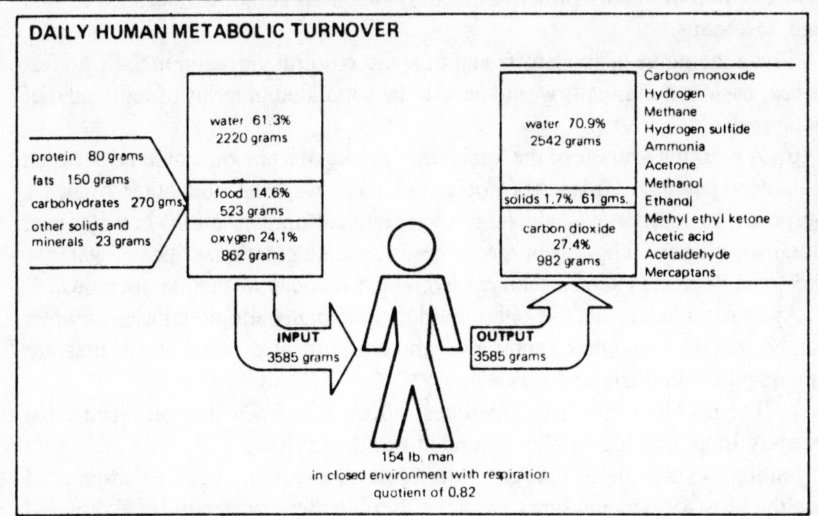

The basic biophysical functions which we share with many other organisms only furnish some of the parameters of our ecosystem requirements. Our distinctive human needs are complicated by the high degree of social development of the human species. Social patterns are more determinant of biophysical events than we generally concede.

There are few specific biological and physical requirements which give human beings any uniqueness as a life form. As with most other organisms, the biophysical requirements for the optimal maintenance of human life fall within a relatively narrow and specific range. The basic energy process is that of consuming food energies in combination with the oxidation process in respiration.

Air, water, and food, within various degrees of temperature and pressure, are the key requirements. Individuals daily needs vary with age, weight, health, activity, etc. (figures given below are for an average male adult):

Air -- Oxygen intake need per day is approximately 1.35 pounds under normal conditions, and about 2.2 pounds of carbon dioxide are exhaled -- i.e., taken up largely by plants and reconverted into oxygen and food in the photosynthesis cycle.

Water -- The need for water is more stringent than for food. The daily water need is approximately 5 pounds per day.

Depending on cultural context, much larger quantities are used for various other physiological functions, e.g. as in washing, general hygiene, etc.

Basic food requirements may be summarized briefly:

(1) Carbohydrates are the main energy fuel sources which compensate for the oxidation and heat energy losses in metabolism. Requirements depend on activity, average about 3,000 calories per day -- to balance daily energy output of approximately the same amount.

(2) Protein is required for the repair maintenance of organic structure and tissue. Though less in volume-demand than carbohydrate, an average of 100 grams per day (or 1.5 grams per kilo of body weight) is estimated as the minimal need.

(3) Minerals, vitamins, and a number of 'trace elements are required for adequate human function. Much attention has been given in recent years to question of trace elements in human diet; the part played by mineral and other deficiencies in growth, retardation, etc.

We may also note how such basic needs are subject to psycho-social adjustment. Though we 'hunger' biologically, we are generally hungry at socially conditioned intervals, and for a given range of culturally defined foods prepared in quite specific ways.

This socio-cultural modification of biophysical function also overlaps, for example, into the technological system -- as various biophysical modifications through sophisticated technical means, become relatively routine.

The most striking 'extension' through such scientific and technological means has been the general increase in human life expectancy and improved physiological function throughout the life span.

Fig. 1

Source: McHale, John, World Facts and Trends, New York, New York, Collier Books, 1972.

protein units) than plant proteins. Cereal grains provide carbohydrates but are also a source of quality protein especially in varied combinations such as rice and soy beans.

Given the range of foodstuffs and of socio-cultural variation in their preferences, basic requirements would need to be stipulated in terms of regional diet balances.

6. A working average of the total *Water* intake of a person would be between 2-3 liters per day. This does not account for washing and other hygienic purposes. In addition we have large social and cultural variations in water use; ritual washing for religious purposes may consume great quantities of water to the same degree as semi-ritualised hygienic practices in secular societies.

Apart from individual use one should include many additional uses of water for household and other functions—and the extrinsic water costs that are embodied in products and services.

7. The problem of what constitutes 'adequate' *Health* has surfaced most recently in attempting to plan extended health services.

Failing positive definition one falls back on the negative, i.e. absence of health. Most of our measures are actually indicators of health breakdown—hospital beds per unit of population, numbers of doctors, indices of morbidity and mortality, effectiveness of drugs, ranges of therapeutic and public health facilities.

In lieu of better measures of health itself these are, at any rate, some index of health maintenance services. Without such services we presume that there is a greater chance of minor ailments becoming chronic, injuries being fatal, higher mortality from treatable diseases and low preventive medical services.

In terms of basic health requirements we need to keep in mind the varying needs of such maintenance through different periods in the life cycle. The health needs of the very young differ from adulthood and, again, from those of old age.

Additional variance factors would be those between rural and urban populations. In the former, at lesser developed levels, main problems would be endemic disease patterns, parasitic infections and nutritional imbalances. Urbanised more developed societies have less endemic infections but more cardiovascular conditions and malignancies, 'overnutrition' and weight problems.

8. However defined *Shelter* is an extremely variable socio-cultural requirement in size of 'floor' area, numbers of rooms, types of construction and in the kinds of furnishings and facilities it contains.

Within the definition and assessment of shelter one would include adequate indoor sanitation, cooking, heating, lighting and cooling facilities plus certain communications and other services either on an individual household or shared basis.

Regional variations also need to be considered. In some areas, traditional building practices and materials are well adapted to climatic and other needs though primitive by other standards; they might only require additional 'plug ins' of energy, water and facilities to enhance their need satisfaction. In other areas, more massive rehousing would be required on a mass production basis.

9. There are no standards against which we might measure *Clothing*, footwear and other articles of personal wear. To arrive at some quantitative assessment of materials one might assign some estimate of amounts of natural and artificial fibers and other commodities within which socio-cultural differences, climatic variation and personal taste could be accommodated.

10. For *Transportation* physically measured units could possibly be assigned to indicate satisfaction of requirements to an adequate level. A generalised ratio of access to individual modes, mass highway transit, and air and rail transportation could be allocated. Satisfaction of requirements such as these go from individual levels of relatively autonomous means such as a bicycle to systemic service dependencies on larger networks which operate at the societal level or in some cases such as airlines at the global level.

11. Though standards and measures of *Education* differ around the world, all agree on minimal literacy. In most of our societies, lack of literacy is a form of disenfranchise. The illiterate individual is hindered in his or her personal development and constrained from full participation in society.

In setting targets for education as requirements, therefore, one may use the conventional indicators of numbers of teachers and schools, those at primary, secondary and third levels and so on, whilst recognising that such means may be greatly augmented by larger 'systemic' facilities. Satellite beaming of self-help educational programs can reach millions via relatively inexpensive receivers thus helping to cut down the time lags of training teachers and building schools. Minimal training for essential skills may also be achieved without literacy through audio-visual means.

Apart from such general education and skill training, meeting of adequate standards in any country now requires a large number of scientific and technical personnel and the requisite range of educational and scientific facilities.

As in many other areas, the invocation of a standard to meet individual needs leads outwardly to a larger systems requirement. This is particularly the case in education where it is directly linked to communications.

12. *Communications* can be measured in terms of newspapers, libraries, telephones, mail, radio and television receivers per capita, but these are somewhat inadequate in describing the full range of information processing and communications capabilities which may subtend requirements even at relatively low levels.

These are very large systems whose individual use level may be represented by some relatively small 'contact' unit such as transistor radio or a telephone. But the provision of the contact instrument presupposes the existence of the larger network system.

13. *Recreation and Entertainment* as an area of requirement is encompassed by several others above, each of which may have its recreative aspect.

Available measurement indicators of 'adequacy' range from cinemas, televisions and theaters to sports facilities and national parks. All are socially and culturally variable in any definition of adequacy. They are related also to the individual and social time budgets of different societies, to work and leisure patterns in those societies and to how they value particular forms of recreative pursuits.

14. Closely allied to the above, even if apparently its opposite, *Work* is both necessary for material survival in economic terms and a psychosocial need. In the latter respect, it satisfies a range of individual requirements relating to the development of social competence, as affording an arena for interpersonal relations and as providing pleasure, satisfaction and recreation activity.

Past and present conditions have laid most stress on its economic dimension, but any serious attempt to assess human requirements would now question the strength of economic necessity as sole motivation and central reward structure for work itself.

Many of our current dilemmas in more developed societies in relation to unemployment may derive from the reduced volume of direct productive work necessary to maintain the material standards of such societies. In the developing societies the reverse may be the case where they still require more labor intensive production patterns but do not have the capacity to absorb workers outside of the agricultural sector.

Apart from the provision of meaningful work, humanising the work situation itself may rank high in setting standards for social requirements.

15. Various forms of social and civic *Security* can be associated with indicators of need satisfaction. For example, the availability of health, social and economic security, as indices of social development, can be quantifiably measured against material needs and roughly translated in qualitative terms.

Civic security as protective of individual liberties and freedoms is somewhat more difficult to define except through the kinds of systems of social justice developed, the level and operation of policing and other services. The latter often become 'overdefined' as more protective of the 'internal security' of the society as constraining upon the individual liberty and security of its citizens.

This is an area where extensive attention has been given to reviewing the standards and practice of national legal systems towards the framing of international standards.

Security and freedom, in this wider sense, is an axial concern which interpenetrates many of the other areas discussed. At is simplest, freedom to choose alternative modes of satisfying one's basic needs is, in itself, an indicator of a level of sufficiency which allows for ranges of personal choice. At deficiency levels such alternatives do not exist, survival security is minimal and individual freedom much constrained.

AGRICULTURAL UNDERDEVELOPMENT AS A CLOSED SYSTEM

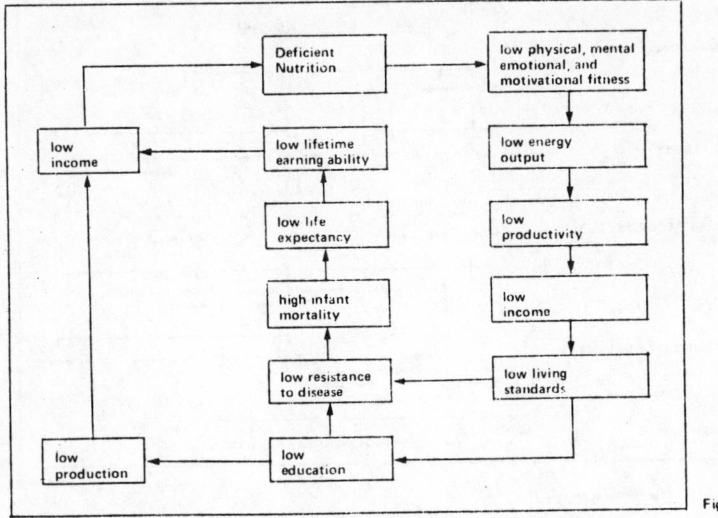

Fig. 2

Source: Ozbekhan, Hasan, The Role of Goals and Planning in the Solution of the World Food Problem in R. Jungk and J. Galtung, ed., Mankind 2000, London, Allen and Unwin, 1969.

THE INTERDEPENDENCE OF REQUIREMENTS

Basic human requirements interrelate in at least three ways. Firstly, the satisfaction of one need may depend on a more pressing need being initially satisfied; i.e., satisfaction of requirements involves a functional interdependence. Secondly, a single person or unit is rarely able to cope with needs in isolation, but depends on the supports and services of society as a whole; i.e., satisfaction of requirements also involves systemic interdependence. Thirdly, the 'quality of life' requirement depends on the availability of alternatives, options and choices accessible to the individual, and the ends/means relationships beyond sufficiency levels.

Functional Interdependence

When we consider positive linkages between requirements in the area of health, we may take life expectancy as an example. A long life is not determined by health factors alone, but by the interactive combination of, "medical services, food, clothing, housing and fuel, (and also by) such other factors as education, security, moral and spiritual values and the desire for living."[8]

The interdependence of dysfunctional linkages at the deficiency level are best illustrated by Fig. 2.

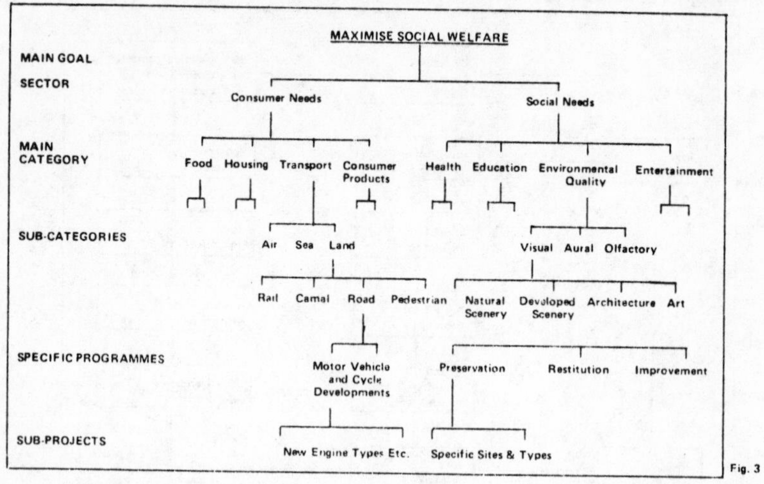

Fig. 3

Relevance Tree for Social Welfare

Source: Jones, P.M.S., Lessons from the Objective Appraisal of Programmes at the National Level Implications of Criteria and Policy, in Research Policy, Vol. 1, No. 1, November, 1971.

> "Agricultural underdevelopment and continuous undernourishment are circular phenomena which make it impossible, in the absence of massive outside intervention to increase food production in areas where population pressure is greatest."[9]

So in practical terms, though we may set priorities in the area of specific deficiency needs such as food, the satisfaction of human requirements in general calls for their development towards sufficiency and growth in all categories of need. Differential quantitative allocations can be made to determine the time scale for policies and actions but the full range of requirement objectives is essential.

Methods for balancing functionally interdependent allocations across a broad range of objectives are relatively well advanced in the planning process. Fig. 3 illustrates a simplified relevance tree approach towards maximising social welfare.

Systemic Interdependence

Meeting requirements at the individual level presupposes various sets of external social and technical organisation.

> "The production of a consumer product . . . requires inputs from all the production processes in the country, and through international trade,

from all the production processes in the world. For example, a loaf of bread requires wheat which has to be milled, cooked and transported. Transport requires fuel and vehicles, for which steel, rubber, copper and energy for fabrication are necessary. Shops and bakeries need bricks, steel, cement, wood and glass; wheat production must have tractors, fertilizers, etc. It is clearly impossible to determine the proportion of all the production processes in the world needed to produce a loaf of bread, or any other single product."[10]

By defining some parts of the subsystem process we can, however, attach estimates of such extrinsic costs to products. For example, by working back from the total energy costs for primary agricultural production, processing, transportation and preparation of food in any one country, down through the industrial sectors involved we could produce an energy budget for the 'loaf of bread' or some other commodity.

In terms of our overall question the exact extrinsic material/energy costs are important but for many immediate practical purposes they can be estimated.

We may re-conceptualise this process of linkage of individual level requirements to external systemic processes by returning to our earlier differentiation between biophysical and psychosocial needs.

It is part of the larger pattern of human development. The species 'sidesteps' the conventional evolutionary paths by externalising functions rather than adapting them. For example, instead of evolving more specialised eyes, we invented microscopes and telescopes; longer leg adaptation was substituted by the wheel and its progressive elaborations. Mining, extracting and processing systems are part of our 'externalised' digestive system. Where the hand tools and machine tools extend physical capacities, our communications networks of radio, telephone, television and linked computer systems are extensions of our senses and nervous system. All of our socio-technical systems constitute external augmentation of the individual processes of the organism.

The interdependence of individual requirements might also be illustrated by taking one need area—transportation—and gauging its systemic interdependence.

We may go from a horse to an automobile to an aeroplane.

The first (horse) requires only locally available resources, grazing space, water and individual care. When we change to automobile there is a change of system magnitude—from the manufacture and distribution aspect to the fuelling and maintenance requirements, spare parts inventories, roads, service stations and so on. The automobile, however, can still be considered as operable at the national society level. Moving to a Boeing 747 as part of a world airline is another system jump. Apart from drawing upon a wider range of resources for its production, the airliner also requires a standardised world network of airports, maintenance and regulatory procedures, etc., and is only functional in these terms.

Many individual level requirements have much larger systemic interdependencies. The telephone hand set is a plug-in instrument to a vastly extended network and is meaningless without this. The individual urban dweller is dependent upon the intricate metabolism of the whole city.

We have extended discussion of this point because it enables us to avoid the error of defining human requirements in terms of piecemeal parts when solutions to critical needs may only be sought via some higher level of systemic organisation.

Hence, basic material requirements extended outwardly to services and systems beyond the level of individual definition. This makes it both more difficult to measure and more complex in terms of quantifying and aggregating such measures as we have.

One further aspect of variability and interdependence is the changing profile of services required during the life cycle.

Their consideration is particularly important in meeting the differential requirements of (a) developing countries with high population growth and with most increase in the younger ages, and (b) the developed countries with more stable populations tending to have a higher ratio of persons at the older range of the age scale.

QUALITY OF LIFE ASPECTS

Various attempts have been made to define quality of life ranging from individual subjective evaluations to large scale cross-national surveys of profiles of concern.[11]

Though an extremely important question, even approximately definitive answers remain elusive. Ways of asking the question are important. One upsurge of interest emerged in the ecology movement, concentrating on environment quality. This approach tended to treat the natural environment as if it had inherently qualitative 'pristine' features which the human intruded upon and sullied. A hypothetical physical absolute was created out of a social judgment.

This does not mean that we should not strive for better environmental quality standards. An oil-stained and sewage contaminated beach is obviously undesirable both in terms of human amenity and ecological habitat.

The more directly social approach to life quality deals with our generalised sense of being satisfied over some felt need; for example, "A sense of welfare . . . A sense of achievement . . . A sense of participation."[12]

It is important to note that for the first time in history we may be entering a period in which we could have sufficient resources and facilities to begin to talk about the quality of life for more people. Such concerns only began to be articulated when we acquired some edge over marginal survival. Previously they were only found in the cultural expression of privileged elites.

In terms of human values and life quality, one key shift takes place.

The value of objects and human relationships to material goods is subtly altered. Where, in previous societies, survival value resided in goods and property as enduring beyond the individual life span, things were unique and the person expendable. With our developed capacities to produce material goods beyond sufficiency, things are expendable and the person is unique. For the first time in history we look at people as lasting longer than things. Value resides only in the human.

Intrinsic value or quality becomes, then, a function of the human use-cycle of an object or process. Use value is now largely replacing ownership value in the developed countries. We note this, for example, in the growth of rental and service—not only in automobiles and houses, but in a range from skis to bridal gowns—to 'heirloom' silver, castles and works of art. Many of our personal and household objects may, also, when worn out, lost or destroyed, be replaced by others exactly similar. Also, and importantly, when worn out symbolically, i.e., no longer fashionable, they may be replaced by another item of identical function but more topical form.

Material levels of need apart, we now need to ask what our quantitative indicators may mean in terms of some 'qualitative' change in human life, in life style and degrees of freedom.

Access to societal services may be an important dimension. We have already noted that as income (or living standards) becomes detached from direct productivity in more advanced societies, access to services becomes a more critical indicator of social equity and participation.

The development of welfare and social security infrastructures is one example of the ways in which need satisfactions and expectations are detached from 'earnings' as base measure. At present, much is still income and status dependent. The more privileged by income or education use more of the public goods in the way of transportation, telecommunications and information utilities in the society. They not only have more physical and social mobility and freedom but more psychic mobility. They literally live in a larger society in both material and conceptual terms.

Alternative choices and constraints are also important considerations. The 'sense of freedom' can be too narrowly construed in terms of political freedoms or in terms of freedoms from want, fear and so on. Freedom is not always 'from' something, but freedom to choose different modes and styles of living. In developing broader conceptual approaches to the quality of human requirements we need to think, therefore, more in terms of the freedom to choose amongst various alternative modes of satisfying both material and non-material wants.

Freedom to choose and to exercise social and cultural preferences may, indeed, be one key measure of the quality of life both for societies and individuals.

It would be impossible to set standards of quality for human beings in absolute terms. But one can suggest that people should have access to a range of options and alternatives which would allow them to select those particular qualities they desire.

Perceived qualities of life depend on culture and internalised values and vary like other human requirements. For one society, collective religious practices or communal life patterns may be primary, in others individually oriented work or recreative pursuits may rank higher. Some societies prize tradition and continuity as important aspects of social quality whilst others may place a high premium on innovation and modernity. Societies such as Japan may seek a balance of both tradition and modernity, in which the tone or quality of life may reside in the creative tension between these modes. Iran may opt for a renaissance of its national culture whilst Sweden and Switzerland seek their qualitative directions in different ways. The emerging nations may need strong assertion and acceptance of their cultural and political identity as a prerequisite for their qualitative development.

It is worth re-emphasising that some level of material standard above deficiency is essential to the quality of life. At lower standards of living most choices are framed in either/or survival terms. It is only when we have material sufficiency that more individuals can exercise their qualitative preferences in more inclusive ways.

The accommodation of these qualitative preferences depends upon a whole range of social settings which would include not just public squares and streets for the large political, ceremonial or religious gatherings, but smaller loci such as houses and private rooms for personal social interactions of the individual. In terms of public goods—national parks, gardens, theaters, sports stadia and museums need not all be enjoyed by all individuals. Their availability of common access is, however, an important qualitative dimension in the life of all persons in the society.

Though income distribution is an important consideration here, the balance of income and services is critical.

Access to various goods and services in society less tied to income, occupation and status would widen qualitative choices for the individual. Such indices of choice might well be related to similar indices of constraints—of the limiting contingencies on social innovation, on discrimination, on self expression and the like.

We have few models which begin to accommodate these more intangible aspects of requirement.

MINIMAL AND MAXIMAL LEVELS

Such conceptual models as we may possess do give insights into the problem of minimal and supposedly maximal levels of need satisfaction.

Recent discussions suggest that in order to achieve minimal levels for all we

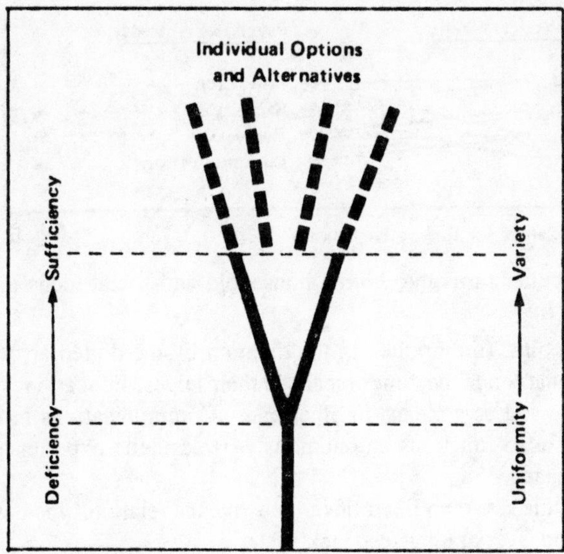

Fig. 4

Source: Center for Integrative Studies.

should also set maximal standards beyond which individuals would not be allowed to use or consume.

The idea of limiting maxima ignores several fundamental principles in need of satisfaction.

(i) Beyond sufficiency we get various satiation levels of demand. Wants may be artificially stimulated beyond this point but it is, as advertising revenues show, a rather costly process.

(ii) Moving from deficiency needs towards sufficiency, the tendency is not towards maximal satiation but towards widened ranges of alternative choices. (Fig. 4)

Even with material products in high consumption societies, in the absence of severe norm and income constraints, most persons begin to choose amongst a variety of alternative products according to desire and preference. Beyond some number of suits, dresses, appliances, cars, etc., the addition of more items of the same kind merely becomes burdensome, so demand is evened out as personal choices become more selective and diverse.

(iii) In thinking about need satisfaction the question is how much of some need (or means) is required to satisfy a specific end?

The first point of interest is that above the minimum, all means turn into ends in themselves. Food becomes 'cuisine', both recreation and communication in

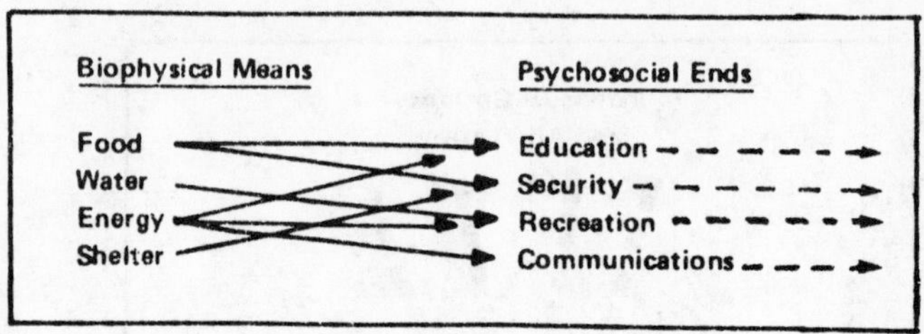

Source: Center for Integrative Studies. Fig. 5

social terms. Shelter turns into home, household and social locus in its own right.

The second point, (represented in the diagram by the dotted arrows to the right Fig. 5) is that 'ends' becomes means in themselves. Education is pursued for its own sake and as a means to other ends. Communications in its many symbolic forms also functions autonomously as aesthetic experience and as interpersonal means.

There are in this sense no fixed linear ends/means relationships but a set of interweaving and overlapping feedback systems.

The third point refers back to the satiation of demand question. If we draw a curve of rising material demand going toward the sufficiency level we may note that it approaches maximal satiation and then declines.

Material satisfaction peaks out below the maximum and then finds expression through progressively dematerialised and, evenutally, symbolic means. (Fig. 6)

At a low income level, a large, heavy, resource hungry automobile may be the material goal. As such goals are reached they tend to transform into an interest in light, high performance sports cars, thence to a recreative and 'aesthetic' interest in sports driving generally. In earlier periods of marginal food survival being plump or even fat had high social status. In the richer countries today, it is the reverse. Many foods are specifically consumed for their low caloric value and have become merely symbols of consumption.

This may be generalised into the proposition that in going from material deprivation and scarcity to abundance and choice, there is an initial trajectory towards tangible material ends. When 'satisfied' the trajectory turns towards more intangible and immaterial means and eventually finds satisfaction less in the object than in its symbolic function and aesthetic enjoyment.

As trend this has other interesting conjectural associations. In wealth transactions we have gone successively from gold as a portable standard of exchange towards coins of various metals, then to paper notes, initially backed by gold or silver, thence to credit cards in which the identifying abstract number satisfies the transaction. In effect the shift is similar to that in the trajectory curve—from material substance to electronic pulse as exchange medium. As technologies

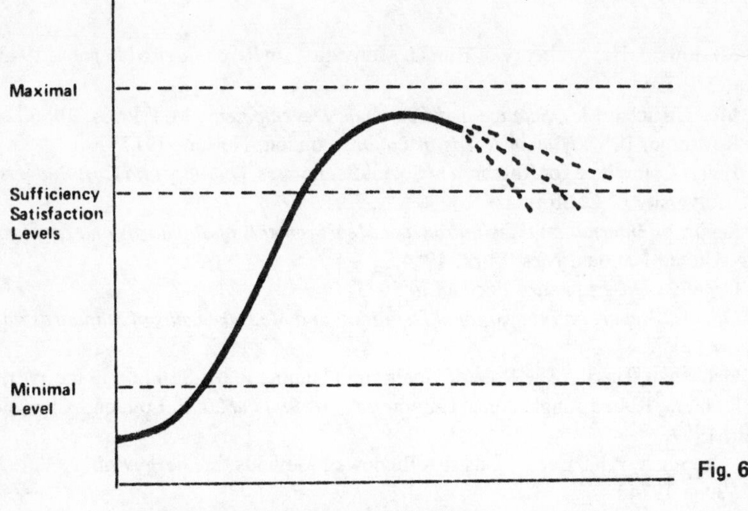

Fig. 6

TRAJECTORY OF NEED SATISFACTION

As needs and aspirations rise and are met on the ascendancy phase they tend to go beyond sufficiency/satisfaction levels to 'conspicuous material consumption' -- then to descend towards more symbolic modes of satisfaction which become less material.

Source: Center for Integrative Studies.

develop we may note similar trends, from large bulky materials/energy costly installations to microminiaturised components operating subvisibly.

Though seemingly far from our central questions regarding 'basic human requirements' these internal transformations of material means to symbolic ends are of cardinal importance.

Many of our current conceptual models extrapolate from historical examples drawn from periods of marginal scarcities and assume continuing and rising demands beyond sufficiency and satiation levels. There is no need to assume that all societies will pursue the rising trajectory towards satiation of material demand. They may take more direct paths towards less material ranges of satisfaction. As we approach more stable population levels and higher material standards of living in the richer countries we may note that the demands are no longer for greater quantitative consumption but for preferred 'qualities' of living which are less materially oriented both as to standards and life objectives.

The possibility is that, if we can begin to satisfy the basic material requirements of the poorer two thirds of the world within the next twenty-five years, rather than facing a continuing need for more resources, more energy and more physical production, we would have a stabilisation of material demands well within our estimated bounds of global capacity.

NOTES

2. Maslow, A.H., A Theory of Human Motivation, in *Psychological Review*, 1943, 50, pp. 370-398.

3. Meier, Richard L., *Science and Economic Development*, MIT Press, 1966.

4. Rowntree, B.S., *Human Needs of Labor*, London, Nelson, 1917.

5. Heller Committee for Research in Social Economies, *Quantity and Cost Budgets*, 1936, University of California.

6. *Report on International Definition and Measurements of Standards and Levels of Living*, United Nations, New York, 1954.

7. Op. cit., *The Planetary Product in 1973*.

8. Op. cit., *Report on International Definition and Measurements of Standards and Levels of Living*.

9. Ozbekhan, Hasan, The Role of Goals and Planning in the Solution to the World Food Problem, Robert Jungk, Johan Galtung ed., in *Mankind 2000*, London, Allen and Unwin, 1969.

10. Chapman, P.F., Energy Costs: A Review of Methods, in *Energy Policy*, Vol. 2, No. 2, June 1974.

11. Bohn, Lewis C., *GNP and Quality of Life in the Third World*, Hudson Insitute, 1968.

12. Cleveland, Harlan, *The Future Executive*, New York, Harper & Row, 1972.

Appendix III

LIST OF PARTICIPANTS AT THE EXPERT REVIEW MEETING ON THIS REPORT BARBADOS 1st TO 6th APRIL, 1977

The meeting was opened with an address by the Honourable Henry de B. Forde, S.C., M.A., L1.B., Minister of External Affairs and Attorney General, Government of Barbados.

Arthur B. Archer
Environmental Engineering Division
Ministry of Health and National Insurance
Jemmotts Lane
Bridgetown, Barbados

Noel J. Brown (Co-chairperson)
Director, New York Liaison Office
United Nations Environment Programme
United Nations
New York, N.Y. 10017

Luther A. Bourne (Co-chairperson)
Chief Town Planner
Government Headquarters
St. Michael
Barbados

William Boyd, II
President
"A Better Chance"
334 Boylston Street
Boston, Mass. 02116

Harlan Cleveland (Chairperson)
Director
Program in International Affairs
Aspen Institute for Humanistic Studies
Rosedale Road
P.O. Box 2820
Princeton, New Jersey 08540

Uttam Dabholkar
United Nations Environment Programme
Nairobi, Kenya

Mahdi Elmandjra
Rector of University of Rabat
or
Boite Postale 53
Rabat, Morocco

Manusour Farfad
Advisor to the Minister of Economic Affairs and Finance
Teheran, Iran

Carl-Goran Heden
Karolinska Institutet and the Medical Research Council
S-104 pl Stockholm 60
Sweden

Marie Jahoda (Chairperson)
Science Policy Research Unit
Nuffield Building
University of Sussex
Falmer, Brighton
Sussex BNI 9RF, England

Stanislaus Kuzmin
International Labour Office
4, route des Moriallons
11211, Geneva 22
Switzerland

Aklilu Lemma
Chief of Science Application Section
for Science and Technology
United Nations
New York, N.Y. 10017

Robert B. Mabele
Director
Economic Research Bureau
University of Dar Es Salaam
P.O. Box 35096
Dar Es Salaam, Tanzania

Carlos A. Mallman
Executive President
Casilla de Correo 138
San Carlos de Bariloche
Peov de Rio Negro
Argentina

John McHale
Director
Center for Integrative Studies
Library Building
University of Houston
Houston, Texas 77004

Magda Cordell McHale
Senior Research Associate
Center for Integrative Studies
Library Building
University of Houston
Houston, Texas 77004

Amir Muhammed
Vice Chancellor
University of Lyallpur
Pakistan

Archie Singham
23 Parkside Road
Silver Springs, Maryland 20091

Chandra Soysa
Director
Marga Institute
61, Isipathana Mawatha
P.O. Box 601
Colombo5
Sri Lanka

Klaus-Heinich Standke
Director for Science and Technology
United Nations
United Nations Plaza
New York, N.Y. 10017

Nicolae Steflea
Senior Researcher
Institute Politology
Bucharest
Btud. Armata
P.O. Box Ru Lui 1
Romania

Guy Streatfield (Rapporteur)
Assistant Director
Center for Integrative Studies
Library Building
University of Houston
Houston, Texas 77004

Paul P. Streeten
Policy Planning Review Department
World Bank
1818 H. Street N.W.
Washington, D.C. 20433

El Sammani Abdalla Yagoub
Vice Chancellor
University of Juba
P.O. Box 82
Juba, Sudan

List of Figures

Environment and Development

Meeting Basic Needs

Appendix I: Supplementary Data

Appendix II: Definition of Basic Human Requirements